Kuwait Transformed

Kuwait Transformed

A History of Oil and Urban Life

Farah Al-Nakib

Stanford University Press

Stanford, California

Stanford University Press
Stanford, California

Printed in the United States of America on acid-free, archival-quality paper

Library of Congress Cataloging-in-Publication Data

Names: Al-Nakib, Farah, 1979- author.
Title: Kuwait transformed : a history of oil and urban life / Farah Al-Nakib.
Description: Stanford, California : Stanford University Press, 2016. |
   Includes bibliographical references and index.
Identifiers: LCCN 2015048590| ISBN 9780804796392 (cloth : alk. paper) |
   ISBN 9780804798525 (pbk. : alk. paper) | ISBN 9780804798570 (electronic)
Subjects: LCSH: City and town life--Kuwait--Kuwait--History. |
   Urbanization--Kuwait--Kuwait--History. | Kuwait (Kuwait)--Economic
   conditions. | Kuwait (Kuwait)--Social conditions. | Kuwait
   (Kuwait)--History.
Classification: LCC HT147.K9 A46 2016 | DDC 307.76095367--dc23
LC record available at http://lccn.loc.gov/2015048590

Typeset by Bruce Lundquist in 11/13.5 Adobe Garamond

For my parents,
Nazha Boodai and Basel Al-Nakib

Contents

Preface

"I kept thinking that there was something missing," said Maryam al-Nusif over a morning cup of hand-brewed coffee at a picnic table in the Secret Garden. Maryam was talking to me about the origins of the community gardening project she kick-started in 2014 with some friends, family, and neighbors in a derelict park in Salmiya, Kuwait's main commercial district. The garden, in which we were sitting, is around the corner from her house. "We live in villas with high walls where we can't even see the street. We have no connection to the pavement right outside our front doors. We like to complain about potholes and filth on our streets, but then we get into our private cars and it doesn't really affect us. So we don't do anything about it. There *has* to be something missing." By her own admission, Maryam has not been able to articulate fully what exactly this absence is; it is something she feels intuitively as a Kuwaiti. It is what stimulated her to create the Secret Garden, a seemingly inconsequential yet potentially transformative social space that encourages people in Kuwait, particularly children, to feel more connected to their natural, urban, and social surroundings. As a Kuwaiti, I too feel that "something missing"; it is what stimulated me to write this book.

In his essay "The Return of the Flâneur," Walter Benjamin asserts that most narrative descriptions of cities have been written by outsiders—allured by "the exotic and the picturesque"—rather than by natives of those cities. "To depict a city as a native," he says, "calls for other, deeper motives—the motives of the person who journeys into the past, rather than to foreign parts. The account of a city given by a native will always have something in common with memoirs; it is no accident that the writer has spent his childhood there."[1] From the start of this project in 2005, I have been deeply conscious of my "native" motives in researching and writing about urban space, everyday life, and the social order in Kuwait. As Benjamin suggests, so much of my own life and memory—and the lives and memories of my parents, who are of the generation that came of age in the first decades of the oil era in Kuwait—shaped the ideas that I explore in this book. Most of the arguments I make in the following chapters began as instincts, things I felt intuitively through my own everyday experiences, observations, interactions, and frustrations. As I began to investigate these ideas through academic research, those instincts that could stand up to rigorous scholarly analysis became my main avenues of exploration. But for me this book has always been more than an objective, academic inquiry into Kuwait's urban social history. It has also been a deeply subjective attempt to make sense of the society of which I am a part (what C. Wright Mills labels one's "sociological imagination"),[2] and a recognition of the importance of the spaces and places that have shaped my life and memories in ways that I have always been acutely conscious of (what David Harvey calls the "geographical imagination").[3] And so this *is* something of a memoir. Even though I have not personally lived through most of the eras discussed in this book, my own life—my childhood, adolescence, and adulthood—haunts its pages, just as Michel de Certeau would say it haunts the city itself.[4]

Being Kuwaiti might give me some latitude to be critical—perhaps even somewhat idealistic—in my analyses of Kuwait's city, state, and society, and of the ways they have changed (including within my own lifetime). However, this book is neither an indictment nor an exoneration of Kuwait's socio-spatial development. It is, rather, an attempt at an explanation, a way of understanding the people, spaces, and places that constitute this city. While recognizing that my personal perspective as a Kuwaiti who grew up and currently lives in the city about which I am writing may result in some inherent biases, I believe that my subjectivity is more of an asset than a hindrance to my scholarly work. Kuwait, like the rest of the Arab Gulf states, is not an easy place to know without living here long-term and becoming part of the everyday life and culture. All Gulf states put up rigid barriers between "insiders" and "outsiders" that require much time and effort to penetrate before reaching a comprehensive picture of local realities. Living in Kuwait gives me insider knowledge on the subtle nuances, intricate practices, and everyday experiences of urban life that cannot be accessed solely through archival research or participant observation. At the same time, overlaying my own personal familiarity with the city with extensive archival research, oral histories with people who lived through the pre-oil and early oil periods, and urban social theory has made me think about Kuwait in jarringly new ways. Once I started on this project I began to take long walks and drives through the city and suburbs, constantly alternating the lenses through which I viewed my surrounding landscape: from a pre-oil townswoman to a foreign urban planner to a suburban citizen to a male migrant worker and so on. Experiencing the city from these multiple perspectives forced me to defamiliarize my surroundings, which admittedly made it challenging to simultaneously carry on living my own everyday life in the same city I was scrutinizing. Without a doubt, writing about Kuwait City as a native has been, in Benjamin's words, a "vertiginous experience"![5]

Acknowledgments

I have relied on many different people in many different ways throughout the production of this book. First and foremost, I am infinitely grateful to two lifelong mentors (and dear friends): Nelida Fuccaro, for her endless guidance, patience, and encouragement over the years; and Dina Khoury, for molding me into a historian. I also sincerely thank Kate Wahl at Stanford University Press for her incredible support and direction throughout this process, as well as Nora Spiegel, Mariana Raykov, Alice Rowan, Madeline Dutton-Gillett, Ariane de Pree-Kajfez, and everyone else at SUP.

This project sent me to numerous archives and libraries around the world. I thank everyone at the Asian and African Studies Reading Room at the British Library, the library of the Royal Institute of British Architects, the School of Oriental and African Studies' library, the Middle East Centre Archive at St. Antony's College (University of Oxford), the Churchill Archives Centre (University of Cambridge), the library of the National Maritime Museum in London, the Lilly Library at Indiana University Bloomington, the Center for Research and Studies on Kuwait, the Center for Gulf and Arabian Peninsula Studies at Kuwait University, and the library at the American University of Kuwait. Particular individuals made the task of conducting archival research and securing access to sources in and on Kuwait infinitely easier: Abdullah al-Ghunaim, Yacoub al-Hijji, Amal Berekaa, Amna al-Omare, Asma al-Kanan, Hana Kaouri, Saleh al-Misbah, Sadoon al-Essa, Ahmed Maarouf, Hamad al-Qahtani, Evangelina Simos, Reda al-Matrook, Charles Haddad, Michael Cassidy, Malcolm Buchanan, and everyone else who shared sources and information with me during my fieldwork. I would like to express my sincere gratitude to Aruna and Zahed Sultan (and family) for trusting me to sort through the records and collections of the late Ghazi Sultan, an inspirational man and pivotal figure in the story of Kuwait City's development. I sincerely thank the Sultan family for their generosity and support, and for their permission to use excerpts from Ghazi Sultan's unpublished writings in this book. I also thank Mutlaq al-Qahtani, Yousef al-Kandari, and Mohammed al-Basry at the Kuwait Oil Company for giving me access to, and permission to use, images from their incredible photo archive.

I am extremely thankful to the British Foundation for the Study of Arabia (formerly Society for Arabian Studies) for awarding me a research grant to conduct oral histories in Kuwait in the spring of 2009. I thank everyone in Kuwait (particularly Ziad Rajab) who helped me identify people to interview, and all the men and women who were so generously willing to share their memories, experiences, and life histories with me. I sadly regret that a few individuals I interviewed did not live to see this book come out, but I am thankful I was able to document their memories in time. I am also grateful to the Kuwait Foundation for the Advancement of Sciences' Kuwait Program at Sciences Po for providing me with a three-month research fellowship in Paris in the summer of 2012, during which the theoretical framework of this book was developed. I also thank the Guarini Institute for Public Affairs at John Cabot University in Rome (particularly Federigo Argentieri) for giving me a base at which to write in the summer of 2013.

I feel privileged to have received feedback on my work and to have engaged in countless discussions with an amazing group of scholars in the field over the years: Lawrence Potter (an incredible editor!), Diane Singerman, Reem Alissa, Mona Damluji, Ahmed Kanna, Ala al-Hamarneh, Łukasz Stanek, Roberto Fabbri, Neha Vora, and Attiya Ahmad (with whom I have walked through many cities), to name only a few. My deepest gratitude goes to friends and colleagues who meticulously read and provided feedback on parts or all of the manuscript along the way: Nelida Fuccaro, Helen Meller, Madawi al-Rasheed, Andrew Gardner, Mary Ann Tétreault, Pascal Menoret, Asseel al-Ragam, Mai al-Nakib, and Rania al-Nakib. Thanks also to Reem al-Ali for her incredible translation and research skills, and for making the last few months of this process infinitely easier on me! And a special wink to Adam Gauntlett for his expert advice as a literary agent, and for our fortuitous meeting in Paris that solidified my belief in cities as places of remarkable chance encounters.

I must recognize the many inspirational people in Kuwait who continuously awe me with their individual and collective efforts to counter the very same urban and social conditions I write about here. Their work compelled me to bring my analysis of Kuwait's urban transformation into the present day. I am particularly grateful to those who have shared their thoughts with me: Deema al-Ghunaim, Sarah al-Zouman, Sarah al-Fraih, Abdulatif al-Mishari, Zahra Ali Baba, Besma al-Qassar, Faisal al-Fuhaid, Maryam al-Nusif, Yusra Ahmad, and Brian Collett, as well as all the new small business owners in the city with whom I have had wonderful conversations over the years. Equally motivating are my students at the American University of Kuwait, with whom I have enjoyed sharing, discussing, and rethinking several of the ideas that I examine in this book. They have inspired me in more ways than they may realize; I hope I have reciprocated.

Finally, there are a few people whose unwitting support and willingness to put up with my myriad demands on their patience and unique kindness over the years truly made the completion of the manuscript possible. Christopher Ohan, Amal al-Binali, and B. L. Morgan: without each of you I could never have finished this book. Patrick Semaan, whose life over the past ten years has been intimately intertwined with this project: thank you for your unwavering support, flexibility, and affection, and for always listening and talking out ideas with me—and of course for your expert design skills! My love and deepest gratitude go to my sisters Wijdan, Mai, and Rania for their constant encouragement, friendship, laughter, and intellectual exchange. This book is dedicated to my dear parents, Nazha Boodai and Basel al-Nakib, to whom I owe everything that I am.

Note on Transliteration

This book largely follows the English transliteration system of the *International Journal of Middle East Studies* (*IJMES*) for Arabic words, without diacritical marks (except for *'ayn* and *hamza*). For Kuwaiti names and place names, the conventional local English spelling is used instead of a transliterated version, and the *'ayn* and *hamza* are omitted from the first letter (for example, Salmiya instead of Salmiyya, Abdullah instead of 'Abd Allah). Rulers are referred to by their first and middle names (for example, Abdullah al-Salem) or simply by first name if repeated in succession, without including al-Sabah. Family names are indicated with *Al* when referring to the family in general (such as Al Ghanim) and *al-* when used as an individual's last name (as in Ahmed al-Ghanim). In most cases, Arabic words are given in Kuwaiti dialect (such as *'abat* instead of *'abaya*) and transliterated in Kuwaiti pronunciation (such as *niq'a* instead of *niq'a*); plurals are also kept in Kuwaiti dialect (as in *diwawin* instead of *diwaniyyat*). The only exception is *suq* (because this is the common English spelling), and for consistency its plural is kept as *aswaq* (as opposed to the colloquial *swuga*).

Kuwait Transformed

Introduction

Kuwait, the former sleepy village, has awakened with the coming of oil and is stretching its strong new limbs.

Paul Edward Case, *National Geographic*, 1952

On a busy Friday night in late December 2012, twenty-six-year-old Jaber Youssef argued with four young men[1] over a parking space at The Avenues, Kuwait's largest shopping mall. The men followed Youssef, a Lebanese national with a Kuwaiti mother, from the parking lot into the mall. One of the men purchased a meat cleaver from a store while his friends continued to trail Youssef. The four men then attacked the young dentist, stabbing him multiple times in front of hundreds of people. No witness intervened to stop the attack, nor did anyone follow the killers when they fled. Youssef bled out onto the mall floor as bystanders took photographs that were circulated through social media. His friends called an ambulance, but the paramedics took too long to reach the scene. Most entrances into The Avenues are within the underground parking garage. The mall contains a few street-front entrances but these can be reached only by the same narrow access road that leads into the garage, a road that is always gridlocked on busy weekend nights. Youssef's friends finally took him to the hospital in their own car, and he died in the emergency room at 1:00 A.M.

The public was shocked and outraged by the crime. Blame was thrown in every direction: at the mall for the lack of security, at the parents of the stabbers for raising them as "reckless youth,"[2] at the paramedics for not getting there in time to save the victim, at the Minister of Interior for not condemning the crime quickly enough, and at the "lack of moral values that has become prevalent in Kuwait."[3] The latter statement was seemingly confirmed the following week. Mohammed al-Falah, a college student visiting home from the United States, was running along the paved seafront corniche in Salmiya, Kuwait's main commercial district. He stopped to ask a group of men on motorcycles not to ride on the pavement where people walked and children played. In response, the men stabbed him, though he survived. Less than a year later, in October 2013, a twenty-four-year-old man, Jamal al-Anezi, was fatally stabbed on a busy Friday night after a fight at Marina Mall, which is connected by a pedestrian bridge to the same seaside corniche where al-Falah was stabbed. Once again the crime was watched and photographed by many bystanders. The Ministry of Interior responded to the crime by announcing a new, stringent system for security control and surveillance in shopping malls across the country.[4] These measures did not prevent the occurrence of another fight (allegedly caused by one young man staring at the other) at 360 Mall in August 2015, which resulted in the fatal stabbing of a sixteen-year-old Kuwaiti male and the severe injury of his adversary.[5]

Though public discourse after these incidents focused on the apparent rise of violent crimes among disaffected youth in Kuwait, neither stabbings nor youth violence were new to Kuwait. Rather, what was new about these crimes was their open and public nature, which exposed another sociological phenomenon. All of the incidents occurred on busy weekends in the midst of hundreds of witnesses who chose not to intervene. This passive noninterference was not necessarily due to fear of being drawn into the violence. A few weeks after the Marina Mall murder, a man hemorrhaged to death from natural causes in the middle of a market. Though his wife screamed for help for several minutes, none of the people watching came to his assistance. Rather, a man standing very close by filmed the entire scene, including when the bleeding man began to lose consciousness, and uploaded it to YouTube. (The video has since been removed.)

The sociological explanations behind both public violent crimes and passive responses to them are undoubtedly complex and multifaceted, and neither phenomenon is unique to Kuwait. Indeed, the mall stabbings recall the infamous murder of Kitty Genovese in Queens, New York, in 1964, when thirty-eight neighbors allegedly witnessed her late-night attack from their windows and did nothing. The *New York Times* focused the story on the witnesses more than on the crime itself, prompting questions about urban apathy and giving rise to the "bystander effect" theory: that the more people there are witnessing an emergency situation, the lower are the chances of one of those people intervening. The editor of the *Times,*

A. M. Rosenthal, described the witnesses' alleged apathy and indifference to their neighbor as a "matter of psychological survival" in the big city, the implication being that the high volume of people living in the city fostered impersonal social actions and interactions and in turn encouraged people to "walk away" from "person-to-person responsibility."[6] Decades later the exaggerated accusations that the *Times* hurled at Genovese's witnesses were refuted: only four or five neighbors actually saw anything, at least one did call the police after the first attack, and though more may have heard Genovese's screams, at 3:15 A.M. they did not know exactly what was going on or what they should do to help. These revelations challenged Rosenthal's ideas on a "metropolitan brand of apathy" (as did the largely unpublicized fact that Winston Moseley, the killer, was captured days later in another Queens neighborhood after residents saw him burglarizing a neighbor's house and called the police).[7] The disputed story of the "thirty-eight witnesses" has also led to new social science research that is reconsidering the effects of groups on helping behavior; some scholars in particular have challenged the presentation of Genovese's neighbors as a "group" rather than as a collection of individuals.[8] The case of Youssef's stabbing and the other Kuwaiti episodes described earlier in which groups of hundreds of bystanders did in fact watch without intervening could provide interesting material for such research on bystanders.

However, in these cases, unlike in the Genovese case, it was not the inaction of the witnesses that received the most public attention (indeed, their passive response triggered no community soul-searching in Kuwait as occurred in New York in 1964). Rather, what stunned people most was that three of the crimes—those that received the most coverage in conventional and social media—occurred in shopping malls. According to the local English newspaper the *Arab Times*, the residents of Kuwait consider the country's "various malls to be havens of recreation and relaxation. This unprecedented disruption has upset Kuwait's otherwise relatively peaceful existence, cutting a little too close to the bone, for those who relish the quiet comfort of this small desert land."[9] Malls are paradoxical places in terms of the types of social feelings and behaviors they embody. People are often lulled into a false sense of security inside them. As private, enclosed, guarded, and (in the Arab Gulf) often gilded places, they give "the public good reason for feeling safer there than on downtown streets. Malls have better lighting, a steadier flow of people, and fewer hiding places and escape routes for muggers."[10] In its architectural design and in the names of its shopping areas, The Avenues offers its visitors an artificial experience of shopping in a city without actually having to be in a city. Its multiple sectors include the Grand Avenue (designed to look like a British High Street or American Main Street), the SoKu ("South of Kuwait," which mimics New York's SoHo district), and the Souk (which replicates Kuwait's own city streets). The mall thus sanitizes the idea of the city by reconstructing it as a clean and orderly place protected by roaming security guards.

But despite its idealized representation, if The Avenues really was a city district it would be what Jane Jacobs—urban writer, activist, and critic of "rational" city planning—would label an unsuccessful one. "The bedrock attribute of a successful city district," she argues, "is that a person must feel personally safe and secure on the street" amid a large number of strangers.[11] In well-functioning city districts, throughout the day and night different people are doing different things simultaneously: going to work, running errands, meeting clients, sleeping on park benches, taking the kids to school, loitering, running, walking the dog, shopping, having dinner, and so on. Though this diversity makes city streets seem more dangerous and unpredictable than the seemingly protected and contained mall, it is precisely this diversity, Jacobs argues, that generates safety. The more diverse interactions and public contacts people have on a street (no matter how ostensibly marginal those encounters might be), the more feelings of mutual trust can emerge among the people who use that street. Trust in this context can be defined as "an almost unconscious assumption of general street support when the chips are down—when a citizen has to choose, for instance, whether he will take responsibility, or abdicate it, in combating barbarism or protecting strangers."[12] Though in the city most encounters between strangers are trivial and fleeting, people are silently yet constantly negotiating various public spaces—sidewalks, parks, benches, bus stops—with one another. The sum of these repeated casual contacts "is a feeling for the public identity of people, a web of public respect and trust, and a resource in time of personal or neighborhood need."[13] Unsuccessful city districts are ones where that sense of public trust is lacking and where there is no diversity in activities and encounters. When the need to constantly negotiate difference is removed—as it is in a mall, where everyone is doing the same thing—one's engagement with the public, and inherent concern for the public good, erodes. Malls, like deserted city streets, are therefore prime venues for antisocial behavior, be they acts of violence or acts of passive noninterference.

Since the late 1990s, malls have become the quintessential urban form in Kuwait and across the Arab Gulf states. Malls in the Gulf states, like malls elsewhere in the world, contribute to the privatization of cities as places governed by consumption from which diverse social groups are implicitly (by income level) or explicitly excluded. (In Qatar, for instance, security guards bar south Asian laborers from entering malls.) In her fascinating study on the daily lives of young urban women in Saudi Arabia, Amélie le Renard convincingly argues, however, that malls can also be accessible places for groups excluded from other parts of the city. For her female interlocutors, who have limited access to most public spaces in the highly segregated city of Riyadh, malls provide a sense of freedom and privacy.[14] But the purpose in highlighting the ubiquity of shopping malls in Kuwait and the Gulf today is not to engage in debates about accessibility and exclusion but rather to emphasize a prominent yet problematic feature of Gulf urbanism today: the absence of diversity in urban space and everyday life experiences, and the impact that this absence has on the functioning of society.

The Modernist Project

Kuwait Transformed analyzes the intricate relationship between the urban landscape, the patterns and practices of everyday life, and social behaviors and relations in Kuwait, and traces the historical transformation of these three interrelated realms in the shift from the pre-oil era to the oil era. In the two centuries between its founding in 1716 and the launch of its oil industry in 1946, Kuwait developed into an independent and prosperous port with an ever-growing population engaged primarily in trading, shipping, and pearling, as elsewhere along the Gulf coast (see Chapter 1). The advent of oil and the accession to power of Abdullah al-Salem in 1950 triggered a massive state-led modernization project over the next four decades (see Chapter 4) that transformed Kuwait—city, state, and society alike—in irreversible ways. The first step in this transformation was the state's commissioning of a master plan in 1951, with the aim of making Kuwait City "the best planned and most socially progressive city in the Middle East."[15] By connecting urban planning with social progress, the Kuwaiti ruler echoed the city-planning discourse of the high modernist avant-garde led by Le Corbusier and the Congrès Internationaux d'Architecture Moderne (CIAM). The premise of modernist city planning in the decades after

World War I was social transformation. Rather than seeing transformations in urban form and organization as by-products of changing social
conditions, CIAM's development inversion saw modernist architecture
and planning as "the means to create new forms of collective association,
personal habit, and daily life."[16] That is, urban form and organization were
instruments of social change.[17] Furthermore, as James Scott explains, modernist planning ideology required a powerful state with unrestrained power
to achieve these designs, as well as a prostrate civil society that lacked the
capacity to resist the new plans. Abdullah al-Salem was the ideal modernist ruler "with grandiose and utopian plans" for his society coupled with
unlimited oil revenues, while their sudden affluence made "the populace
more receptive to a new dispensation" (thereby obviating all resistance).[18]

Though the Kuwait City that oil built was not designed on quite the
monumental scale on which CIAM cities such as Brasília and Chandigarh
were designed, from 1950 onward centralized planning became a key state
strategy of social control and served as a bulwark against the substantial economic, political, and social upheavals brought about by oil. Oil disrupted
every aspect of life in Kuwait, and total state-led planning as advocated by
Abdullah al-Salem could help weed out future threats to state stability and
control. Urban planning in particular would make the city and, by extension, the future knowable. The purpose of city planning from the days of
Baron Haussmann's redesign of Paris in the mid-nineteenth century was to
minimize the chances for unpredictable and uncontrollable actions (such
as social insurrections) in the city.[19] Urban plans—with all the maps, statistics, and projected goals that went into their making—made it possible
to think about the city (of today and tomorrow) as a unified, orderly whole
rather than as a collection of disjointed, disorderly parts.

As Kuwait's oil revenues went directly into the hands of the ruler, the
government claimed it was responsible for society's well-being in order "to
make up for years of suffering in the pre-oil phase."[20] More accurately, the
massive state-led modernization project—which included both the transformation of the city as well as the creation of a cradle-to-grave welfare
system—minimized the risk of public protest against the substantial increase in political power and autonomy that oil brought the Al Sabah rulers
and their burgeoning state. With the country's overnight shift from scarcity
to affluence, "a new era, a new life" could be constructed from scratch,[21] one
that made people forget the pre-oil past (a time when the rulers played a
minimal role in public welfare and governance) and look toward a brighter

future—under the patriarchal leadership of Abdullah al-Salem. Like most modernist projects, building this future required total decontextualization, or what James Holston calls a "strategy of defamiliarization."[22] This process began with the systematic demolition of the pre-oil port town—giving the state the "blank piece of paper" that, according to Le Corbusier, was essential to achieve "total efficiency and total rationalization"—and the construction of a brand new cityscape in its place.[23]

Kuwait experienced the shift from a maritime town to a sprawling city with remarkable speed. British anthropologist Peter Lienhardt visited Kuwait in 1953 to study "a society in flux." When he arrived at the city gates, "the commotion of digging and building gave one the feeling that the whole city of Kuwait was a vast construction site."[24] Zahra Freeth grew up in Kuwait in the late 1920s and early 1930s as the daughter of a British political agent. After a visit in 1970 she wrote, "The town of my childhood had gone. . . . it had been destroyed as effectively, if not as brutally, as by an earthquake."[25] In only two decades, Kuwait had seemingly "hurtled out of medieval simplicity into twentieth-century complexity."[26] In 1983, Stephen Gardiner, an architect and a writer for the *Observer*, made a similar observation:

There was no breathing space between ancient and modern, rags and riches; from a tiny place in the sand on the edge of the Gulf . . . Kuwait hurtled like a missile into the high technology of the mid-twentieth century. And over the next thirty years, the new city of Kuwait—optimistic, imaginative, confident and utterly modern—was conceived, planned, built, replanned and rebuilt. The unique creation of oil, the story of this city is astonishing.[27]

Though the city's physical transformation was indeed substantial, this linear rags-to-riches narrative (constantly reiterated by the Kuwaiti state) conceals the tensions, paradoxes, and problems that characterized Kuwait's oil-driven modernization in the shift from scarcity to affluence. The complex social, political, and spatial realities behind this facade form the subject matter of this book.

The Modernist Paradox

The rapid transformation of Kuwait's urban landscape gave rise to a radically different lifestyle (see Chapters 2, 5, and 6). The townspeople moved from crowded, traditional courtyard houses in close-knit neighborhood clusters into large single-family villas in spacious American-style suburbs. Their formerly complex and diverse everyday lives in functionally mixed and integrated urban spaces became fragmented into discrete functional zones and privatized spheres of behavior. The ways in which these spatial and lifestyle changes impacted and transformed Kuwaiti society (see Chapters 3 and 7) are rarely addressed in either popular or scholarly discourse. The idea of using the urban form as an instrument to transform the existing social order was carried out by a complex process riddled with paradoxes and unintended outcomes everywhere that this modernist agenda was deployed. The universal goal of modernist planning was to use architecture to build a more egalitarian society and create a more orderly social life. In Brasília, Brazil (the classic example of this utopian plan), the former was to be achieved through *superquadra* apartment blocks, designed to be uniform in height, facade, and facilities. Residents of all social classes would, it was thought, live harmoniously under equal living conditions in order to eliminate the social stratification common in other Brazilian cities. One way in which urban order would be established was by replacing street corners and intersections (which in other Brazilian cities were always crowded with pedestrians and public activities) with traffic circles to improve circulation and remove people from the street. This elimination of the corridor street—the typical city street edged with continuous facades of shops and residences—killed the hustle and bustle of public street life. Commerce was relocated to designated sectors between the *superquadra*. Many Brasilienses (Brasilia's residents) rejected these new systems. Higher-class residents moved out of the *superquadra* and built more ostentatious houses for themselves elsewhere, inscribing onto Brasília's landscape the stratification of Brazilian society that the modernist plan sought to negate. At the same time, instead of using their commercial unit's planned front garden entrance, shop owners converted their rear service entrance into the unit's storefront, thereby putting their shop back into contact with the street and reproducing the market street life with which they were familiar. As Holston describes in his seminal study on this archetypal modernist city, Brasilienses thus "reasserted social processes and cultural values that the architectural design intended to deny."[28]

In Kuwait, by contrast, Kuwaitis of all stripes embraced the changes they were experiencing and rarely reasserted the social and cultural values of old Kuwait that the new city denied. Perhaps oil wealth made the acceptance of such substantial lifestyle changes more palatable for Kuwaitis than for societies undergoing similar modernist projects elsewhere. People in

Kuwait knew that they were experiencing something remarkable, and they approached this change with pragmatism, openness, and excitement. Only four years after the first barrels of oil were exported, an article published in the March 1950 issue of *al-Bi'tha*, a monthly journal written and published by Kuwaiti students in Egypt, claimed that the Kuwaiti people were "thirsty for reform, capable of development, and adjusting to change."[29] In 1964, Abdullah al-Salem's chief economic advisor, Fakhri Shehab, praised Kuwaitis' willingness to experiment with new ideas and adopt new institutions and practices without being handicapped by rigid traditions or conventions.[30] Even Freeth, one of the fiercest critics of Kuwait's rapid modernization, admitted that "its people had embraced the opportunities of wealth with hard practical sense and an exuberant self-confidence."[31] As one of her Kuwaiti friends told her, "It is the new Kuwait and not the old which is worthy of admiration."[32]

So, in accordance with the ultimate modernist goal, Kuwaiti society was ready and willing to be transformed. Over the next four decades the existing social order, like the city, changed dramatically. It was not just that the Kuwaiti people absorbed new lifestyles, such as American-style suburban consumerism; as a port, Kuwait had a long history of borrowing from the Indian Ocean cultures with which its merchants and mariners were in regular contact before oil (though the sources of influence were now more Arab and Western). The social changes engendered by the new urban landscape were much more subtle and complex than the obvious changes to the patterns and practices of everyday life that the new city embodied, and were not necessarily those that either Abdullah al-Salem (as the symbolic agent of Kuwait's modernization, in state rhetoric) or Kuwait's city planners intended. The ruler's "avowed aim" was "to make Kuwait the happiest state in the Middle East."[33] State-funded welfare (education, health care, housing, employment) coupled with urban development (infrastructure, wide streets, luxurious houses, modern buildings) would relieve Kuwaiti society of the hardships of the past and create a more egalitarian, thriving, and content citizenry. Though Kuwaitis' reactions to change were different from those of Brasilienses, the paradox of Kuwait's two-pronged development, like that of Brasília, "is not that its radical premises failed to produce something new, but rather, that what they did produce contradicted what was intended."[34]

In 1960 the government hired Palestinian-American architect and town planner Saba George Shiber as chief architect in the Ministry of Public Works. When he arrived that May, a decade into the implementation of the master plan, Shiber was shocked by what he saw. He believed that Kuwait was an unfortunate victim of modern planning, and he described the impact of oil on its urban and social landscapes as "meteoric, radical, ruthless."[35] Pre-oil Kuwait Town,[36] he said, was "the expression of a culture": an "organic city" in which every street, space, and form grew over time to respond to specific everyday needs.[37] The planners who designed the new city lacked depth and imagination. Rather than using Kuwait's historic urban pattern as an inspiration for the evolving structure and texture of the new city, they simply satiated their own "almost childish happiness and preoccupation with superhighways, round-abouts and the haphazard, inorganic procedure in the choice of sites for major urban functions."[38] To make matters worse, building in the city center over the decade since the plan was conceived had been "piecemeal and spasmodic," which Shiber attributed to "the meteoric rush into construction which often precluded thorough design" alongside "the rush to make quick-profits irrespective of the consequences bequeathed to the city."[39] The outcome of all this effort was a chaotic, rapidly obsolescing landscape, and a poorly functioning planning apparatus that never quite managed to repair itself (see Chapter 4).

Compounding the unintended consequences to the city was the impact that oil-fueled modernization had on Kuwaiti society and social relations (see Chapter 7). In 1964, Shehab provided one of the first assessments of the fundamental problems of "super-affluence" lying behind Kuwait's "spectacular physical change." Kuwait's modernization introduced sharp distinctions between citizens—who benefited almost exclusively from the country's welfare system—and foreign-born residents. The government's desire to carry out numerous "ambitious projects" immediately and all at once throughout the first decade of oil created a high demand for work that Kuwaitis were either untrained or unwilling (due to their newfound affluence) to do.[40] This situation led to an influx of skilled and unskilled workers, initially from Arab countries and then increasingly from south and southeast Asia. The country's first census in 1957 revealed that the number of foreign-born residents was rapidly growing, almost outnumbering the indigenous population (which in 1965 became a reality). A new nationality law was passed in 1959 that made access to Kuwaiti citizenship extremely restrictive. Naturalization by virtue of birth or long-term residence in Kuwait became very difficult (and normally occurred only in exchange for "great services" to the country as decreed by the Minister of Interior), while the total number of naturalizations was limited to fifty per year.[41] By limiting Kuwaiti nationals to families who had been in the country since 1920, the nationality law served as another means, in addition to urban planning, of making the future more predictable. Keeping the option (as provided in the original 1948 nationality law) for Arabs or Muslims to become citizens if they were born in Kuwait or had lived there for ten years would make it more difficult to know what the future population of the country might look like. The new law was passed just as Kuwait's contentious Arab nationalist movement—which ideologically threatened the existence of Arab monarchies—reached its peak. By 1959, Kuwait's nationalists had become a thorn in Abdullah al-Salem's side. Although many Kuwaitis were influenced by Arab nationalism while studying abroad in Beirut or Cairo, Arabs living in Kuwait—who made up the majority of the country's expatriate population at the time—were also perceived (particularly teachers) to be a source of this new ideology in the country.[42] The 1959 law effectively precluded these potentially troublesome individuals from one day becoming citizens themselves. Restrictive access to Kuwaiti citizenship thus limited the possibility of future conflicts or instability for the state.

Over the ensuing decades, rigid legal distinctions between expatriates and citizens "permanently estranged and embittered" the former and made the latter a more insular and, over time, intolerant society.[43] This outcome contrasted sharply with the cosmopolitan port city culture that characterized Kuwaiti society before oil. Foreign travelers to Kuwait in the eighteenth and nineteenth centuries regularly described the town as a friendly and accommodating place whose residents were "tolerant to others and not overly rigid to themselves."[44] A century later, in 2005, an American expatriate living in Kuwait polemically described "every Kuwaiti" whom he and his foreign coworkers met as "a rude and conceited xenophobe."[45] A 2013 readers' poll in Condé Naste Traveler magazine ranked Kuwait the world's fifth "unfriendliest city," and the following year, in the Expat Insider survey report published by InterNations, Kuwait ranked as the worst place (among sixty-one countries) for an expatriate to live. This apparent shift from an open, friendly, and cosmopolitan society to an insular, hostile, and parochial society is one of the key social transformations that this book unpacks.

The most obvious way in which the new city altered (intentionally or unintentionally) the existing social order was by transforming Kuwaitis from a community described in the mid-eighteenth century as "closely

united, and free from feuds and factions" into a highly segregated and fac-
tional society.[46] The creation of new suburbs and the state-led distribution
of the population within them led to intense levels of social segregation
along class and sectarian lines. The former townspeople were relocated to
lavish suburbs bordering the city center, the sedentarizing Bedouin were
relegated to large housing projects in so-called "outlying" districts, and
non-Kuwaitis were sequestered to crowded commercial areas (including the
city center itself) in rented apartments due to their inability to own land
in Kuwait. In 1982, social geographer Abdulrasool al-Moosa found that
differential housing standards and services within these districts imposed
"severe social barriers inside the Kuwaiti community." He concluded that
such extreme social segregation was "dangerous and ominous for the future
well-being of the state. Steps must be taken immediately to arrest further
deterioration of the value system and social cohesion between groups."[47]

The most worrying division that al-Moosa identified was between
the former townspeople (*hadar* in present-day social discourse, meaning
"sedentary urbanites") and the Bedouin (*badu*) who began settling permanently in Kuwait after the advent of oil. Because no tangible steps were
ever taken to fix the problems that al-Moosa identified in 1982, today tensions between *hadar* and *badu* have indeed become volatile. In the lead-
up to the February 2012 parliamentary elections, members of the Mutair
tribe burned down the campaign tent of notoriously anti-tribal candidate
Mohammed al-Juwaihel because he made insulting remarks about their
tribe and tribal candidates in his campaign speeches.[48] Al-Juwaihel had
been beaten unconscious at a political rally the previous year for similar
reasons.[49] The day after they burned down the campaign tent, members
of the same tribe stormed the headquarters of al-Watan television station
for airing an interview with candidate Nabil al-Fadl, a close ally of al-
Juwaihel who similarly spoke publicly against Kuwait's Bedouin population. Twenty people were injured as protestors clashed with riot police and
caused some damage to the station's furniture and equipment.[50] A month
later, members of the Awazem tribe stormed Scope TV headquarters in
protest against an interview with Shi'i parliamentarian Hussein al-Qallaf,
whom they accused of defaming the tribe's leader.[51] Such episodes of violence led to stringent efforts on the part of the state—such as screening
social media sites and threatening legal action against individuals "who
incite divisions in the society"—to protect "national cohesion," which al-
Moosa had warned three decades previously was rapidly deteriorating.[52]

Kuwait's Urban Crisis

In 1964 Shehab described Kuwait as a "land of superlatives." It was then the largest oil producer in the Middle East, and the fourth largest in the world. It boasted the world's largest oil port, and the largest oil reserves.[53] Its new seawater distillation plant, which was able to turn out millions of gallons of desalinated water a day, was also one of the largest in the world.[54] Today the "superlative" attribute is more commonly ascribed to Dubai, a city whose image over the past two decades has overshadowed that of its regional predecessor.[55] Nonetheless, Kuwait today remains a land of superlatives of a different nature: it ranks first in the world in number of deaths and injuries from traffic accidents, highest in number of obese people (42.8 percent of the population in 2014),[56] and highest in level of water consumption (500 liters per capita, more than double the international average),[57] and it has one of the world's highest per capita rates of waste generation. These negative side effects of affluence reveal a growing self-indulgence and privatization among many members of Kuwaiti society, for whom concern for the public good (be it the safety of the city's streets or the protection of the country's environment) is subordinated to individual prerogatives. Shehab first warned about this emerging trend in 1964. He believed that the "most serious social danger" resulting from oil wealth was that the lavish welfare state was forcing competition out of national life and producing an idle and unproductive citizenry.

Young people have lost their perspective, their urge to acquire knowledge, their acceptance of discipline. As a result, the drive, diligence and risk-taking that characterized the old Kuwaiti are no more. At both ends of the social scale the new citizen is content to enjoy a life of leisure and inertia, and is unwilling that this happy state of affairs should be disturbed. Protected, pampered, lavishly provided for and accountable to no one, he lives in a world of make-believe.[58]

This sentiment very closely echoes those of Saudi author Abdullah al-Ghadhami (as discussed by Pascal Menoret in his seminal study on joyriding, youth culture, and urban development in Riyadh), who believes that his country's oil boom also "transformed independent and proud hard-workers into lazy and arrogant retainers."[59] Because the accumulation of Kuwait's national wealth required no public effort or participation, Shehab believed that most Kuwaitis had lost their sense of duty to serve the common good.[60] This was a major change from the pre-oil period, when

economic scarcity had necessitated a significant level of communal cooperation, sharing, and support between members of society to ensure their
individual and collective survival (see Chapter 3). With oil-driven modernization, Kuwaitis became more insulated and privatized (see Chapters 5
and 6). This rapidly eroding concern for the public good, already observ-
able a decade into oil, may partially explain the passive response to the mall
stabbings described early in this chapter. It may also, of course, explain the
violence. In Menoret's ethnographic narrative of Riyadh's oil urbanization
(similar to Kuwait's in many ways), a young Saudi man rants that one of
the consequences of the oil boom was the transformation of Saudis "into
aggressive troublemakers."[61]

The super-welfare system certainly fostered an atmosphere in which
personal privilege superseded public well-being. However, this book links
Kuwait's present-day social malaise—the growing intolerance toward outsiders, the volatile tensions between social groups, the inertia of the average
citizen, the lack of concern for the public good—to the country's rapid oil
urbanization that began in 1950. I argue that the transformation of urban
space and everyday life brought about by oil-fueled modernization had a
de-urbanizing effect on Kuwaiti society. Kuwait today is 99 percent urbanized, meaning that it no longer contains a pastoral population (in truth,
the vast majority of the population is suburban). But in the context of this
book, *urban* does not entail simply living in a city's metropolitan area.
Urbanity here is defined as a particular kind of lifestyle and social quality.
Henri Lefebvre describes urban life as a lived opportunity for "meetings,
the confrontation of differences, reciprocal knowledge and acknowledgement (including ideological and political confrontation), ways of living,
'patterns' which coexist in the city."[62] Modernist planning approaches
that focus on functional zoning, suburbanization, and the reordering of
cityscapes to eliminate unexpected confrontations and encounters are
therefore "violently anti-urban. . . . One could call it a de-urbanizing and
de-urbanized urbanization to emphasize the paradox."[63]

Early in this chapter I referred to Jane Jacobs's (perhaps idealistic)
ideas on a well-functioning city. She admits that many of the urban policies she advocates in her seminal book *The Death and Life of Great American Cities* are mainly applicable to big cities, which Kuwait is not.[64] Kuwait
before oil was a port town of modest size, though its social and cultural
complexity made it more "urban" than "village."[65] After oil the town was
remade into the new "city center" while the desert beyond the old town's

wall was built up into a sprawling suburbia. Kuwait City is therefore now a small city with a relatively large suburban metropolitan area. Nonetheless, one element that Jacobs emphasizes is necessary for cities everywhere to "sustain their own civilization" is "diversity" (of functions, people, buildings, lifestyles). Diversity makes cities safer and people more accepting of strangers; it generates economic growth and vitality; and it makes for a more dynamic and interesting everyday experience. City planners tend to focus on a city's various uses one by one, and then put these different parts together into a broad picture: the master plan. By nature, however, cities consist of multiple combinations of uses, and it is this diversity that distinguishes urban life from other forms of social organization or experience.[66]

In Kuwait's case, diversity was a key aspect of what Greek architect Georges Candilis, who worked in Kuwait in the late 1960s, called the city's "primordial quality of urbanity" before oil. This urbanity entailed a close association of the different "functions of city life"—habitation, commerce, worship, and administration—which corresponded to the spatial integration of houses, markets, mosques, streets, and squares. The functional and spatial diversity of pre-oil Kuwait Town created its particular "quality of urbanity." The mix of domestic, economic, social, and political activities within the town's main morphological sectors—the residential areas (*firjan*), market (*suq*), and seafront (*sahel*)—stimulated a vibrant everyday life in which the townspeople were constantly surrounded by diverse people and activities, and engaged in a steady "exchange of ideas and goods."[67] In this port and market town, Kuwaitis were accustomed to coming into regular contact with different cultures and lifestyles. The realities of economic scarcity, coupled with the absence of a bureaucratic state, contributed to the complexity of urban life by necessitating the creation of formal and informal networks of cooperation and mutual support among the townspeople.

After 1950, affluence, suburbanization, functional zoning, the privatization of public space, and the lack of people's participation in the making of their spatial surroundings all contributed to the erosion of Kuwait's historic diversity. The country's demographic diversity remained and in fact increased, but interactions between people of different backgrounds became restricted under new conditions of social exclusion and spatial segregation. In 1968, Candilis lamented that Kuwait had "lost the qualities of the traditional urbanism of the past" due to the "brutal dislocations in the conditions of life" that were provoked by the oil boom.[68] It is this loss, I argue, that ultimately led to the social crises the country faces today. However, the damage is not irreparable. Kuwait's eroded urbanity may be salvaged through a restoration of what Lefebvre calls a "right to the city," which entails not only spatial centrality (de-suburbanization) but also the right to participate in a vibrant urban life. Kuwait today is witnessing a demand for just such a restored right to the city by various social forces—political protestors, entrepreneurs, civil society actors, and regular residents—who are seeking (largely unconsciously) the kind of urban life that oil-era modernization began to erase sixty-five years ago (see Chapter 8). Collectively, these groups point to a possible urban alternative for Kuwait that could potentially solve some of the social problems described in this chapter.

The call—both in these present-day movements and in this book— for a return to, and restoration of, the city that modern planning eliminated is not a simple case of nostalgia for a lost city, lifestyle, or urban community that no longer exists.[69] Nostalgia for Kuwait's lost past has certainly been part and parcel of its development all along. As early as the 1950s, Kuwaitis began to look back nostalgically at the pre-oil period as an easier time; in 1956 Freeth's friends complained that new activities such as commuting to work by car from the suburbs had "complicated a once simple way of life."[70] As Ash Amin and Nigel Thrift claim, all too often critiques of modern urban life "tell a story of an authentic city held together by face-to-face interaction whose coherence is now gone. . . . In the great accounts of history, the modern city is more loss than gain."[71] However, though on the surface pre-oil Kuwait Town (perhaps because it was more spatially compact) may have seemed much simpler and more coherent than it became after 1950, this book reveals that oil-era modernization in fact purified what was, before 1950, a more complex, dynamic, and multifaceted urban life. But though the pre-oil city may emerge in better light than the city that oil produced, this book is not a lament for a bygone era. Although the underlying premise here is indeed that something has been lost in Kuwait over the past sixty years since the launch of oil urbanization, this book is not a nostalgic call to go back to the pre-oil city (the simplified approach that heritage industries across the Gulf see as the antidote to the dislocating newness of the present-day city). Rather than serving as a guide for how cities should be built today, the conditions of city life before the era of affluence and modern city planning provide a more critical perspective on what is missing today. This absence might in turn provide a new perspective on the problems with which the country is currently grappling.[72]

Rehistoricizing the City

Retracing the history of Kuwait City is not just about resurrecting the "primordial quality of urbanity" that modernist planning negated. It is also a matter of rehistoricizing the city, and the process of city formation, that modernist planning dehistoricized. In every city in which it was embraced, modernism in architecture and planning proposed a radically different future, and provided a means to get there. The past was a hindrance to this goal, and served only to endorse the state's projection of that future; in Kuwait the pre-oil era was depicted as a period of suffering in order to justify the state's total intervention in transforming the city and the social order. Once it had served this purpose, the past was swiftly swept away, because reaching the imagined future required the removal of all historical context.[73] Thus "the modernist view of history is paradoxically dehistoricizing."[74] The idea that the future could be planned and known denied the "dissonance and unexpected conflicts" that could make a society different from what it was expected to become. That is, modernist planning put a halt to the very idea of history: "the unforeseen movements in the real time of human lives."[75] Furthermore, as Holston explains, the only historical agency that modernism acknowledges is the agency of the "prince" or state head and of the "genius" architect-planner.[76]

In Kuwait's case, more often than not the modernist story has been told as a linear, successful rags-to-riches narrative in which Abdullah al-Salem, a coterie of international architects and planners, and the state's planning machinery heroically transformed Kuwait from a simple, sleepy, medieval town into a complex, dazzling, hypermodern city. In 1986 the Information and Research Department of the state-run Kuwait News Agency prepared a booklet entitled *A Twenty-Five Year Era of Kuwait's Modern Advancement* to commemorate the silver jubilee of the country's independence from Britain in 1961. The purpose was to assess Kuwait's national achievements and contributions to humanity in its "great strides on the path of development, prosperity, and progress" over the previous quarter century.[77] After a brief overview of Kuwait's prehistoric and pre-oil eras, the booklet states that with Abdullah al-Salem's assumption of power on February 25, 1950, "Kuwait went into a distinguished stage in its developing history . . . which represented a great political, economic and social leap, conferring upon Kuwait a distinct position alongside the civilized and developed world states."[78] This focus on Kuwait's quantitative growth distills the turbulent decades of oil urbanization into a more simplified narrative of effortless advancement. As Nelida Fuccaro puts it, such accounts of oil-driven modernization tell "the story of an economic miracle which created a more uniform landscape, and a 'rational,' disciplined and affluent society."[79] The social problems that Shehab and al-Moosa identified in the 1960s and 1980s (respectively)—and associated directly with the country's rapid modernization—disappear. So do the many problems of the city itself—chaotic buildup, traffic congestion, shoddy construction, rapidly obsolescing buildings—which Shiber noticed and documented only a decade into the modernist project, and many of which still exist today.

To avoid interpreting Kuwait's "modern advancement" through the lens of modernism's own heroic assumptions, a more critical analysis of the material and social effects of oil modernization has to consider the historical agency of diverse social actors beyond just government officials and architects, and has to examine the interplay of other structural forces alongside plans and modern technologies in this transformative process.[80] This book therefore combines the realm of state-led urban planning with the everyday experiences of people who lived through these changes in order to complicate the linear narrative of Kuwait's oil urbanization. But just as the excavation of Kuwait's pre-oil past is not a nostalgic search for a bygone era, this reinterpretation of the "modern era" is not meant to be an indictment of the country's oil urbanization, nor is it meant to be a denial of the many positive outcomes of modernization. As the British Political Resident pointed out as early as 1954,

it cannot be denied that almost every Kuwaiti is now better off than he was before the exploitation of oil and that the proportion of revenue which has gone towards projects of public benefit and towards the raising of the standard of living is much greater than the similar proportion in any of the other Middle Eastern oil producing countries.[81]

Rather, the main objective here is to provide a more nuanced and critical understanding not only of Kuwait's past but also, and perhaps more importantly, of the state of Kuwait City and Kuwait's urban society today.

The current social realities described in this chapter give us a different perspective on the early oil decades than the one expressed by the state, by Kuwaitis who lived through the change, and by foreign observers such as Lienhardt or Gardiner. The early oil decades were certainly full of hope and potential, and it was the future they anticipated that Gardiner captured in 1983 when he described Kuwait as "optimistic, imaginative, confident and utterly modern," and its story of oil as unique and astonishing.[82] None-theless, today's realities expose the failure of oil-driven modernization to achieve the utopian vision of the future in which everyone at the time, citizens included, believed: that oil would make Kuwait the best planned, most socially progressive, and happiest state in the Middle East. By ignoring the essential features of the functioning social order in favor of grand (foreign) plans to create a new life, Kuwait's oil-era modernization became another one of the many "well-intentioned schemes to improve the human condition" that tragically failed in the twentieth century.[83] The disjuncture between the optimistic intentions of the early oil era and the present-day reality that Kuwait is *not* the best planned or most socially progressive state it thought it would become (and that state rhetoric even four decades into oil continued to claim it was becoming) necessitates putting to rest the long-held myth of Kuwait's heroic "leap" into the future, and rehistoricizing the real-time processes by which the past became the present.

In so doing, this book borrows Lefebvre's "regressive-progressive approach" to historical research on the production of space.[84] This process takes as its starting point the realities of the present, which then "[act] retroactively upon the past, disclosing aspects and moments of it hitherto uncomprehended."[85] Moments from the past (such as the discovery of oil) make a certain number of events or outcomes possible in the present or future. Each time one of these possibilities is realized—that is, every time something occurs in the present that can be traced to be an outcome of some event or moment in the past—we are forced to think about that initial event differently. The past is cast in a new light, and therefore the process by which that past became the present must also be reinterpreted. This book argues that Kuwait's current social crisis is a realized possibility of oil urbanization, and therefore seeks to cast new light on the country's modernization between the 1950s and 1980s. The advent of oil certainly unearthed an unlimited number of possibilities for Kuwait. However, the realities of the present are not quite the possibilities that were envisioned for the future at that time. The early oil era can therefore no longer be viewed simply through its own optimistic lens, and it must be reinterpreted. The following chapters work their way back from the current realities presented here into Kuwait's pre-oil past and retrace its steps to the present, in an attempt to build a more comprehensive understanding of the origins of the country's present-day problems, "along with the preconditions and processes involved."[86]

As an urban historical study, *Kuwait Transformed* builds on Fuccaro's pioneering work on Manama, Bahrain, in its attempt to dispel the myth of "exceptionalism" that is so prevalent in popular and academic discourse on the Gulf's oil urbanization.[87] Gulf cities are often described in the scholarly literature as newly "emerging" metropolises that are "unburdened by history" and therefore "free to create a new identity."[88] This rhetoric echoes not only the "blank sheet" aspirations of midcentury modernist planners, but also the assumptions of present-day "starchitects" such as Frank Gehry (under the patronage of the region's "visionary" rulers) who view cities like Dubai as "clean slates[s]" giving them the unfettered freedom to experiment in ways that no other city is willing to risk (or pay for).[89] Thankfully, the field of Gulf studies is currently experiencing an "urban turn,"[90] with newly published works by Mandana Limbert, Ahmed Kanna, Andrew Gardner, Neha Vora, Pascal Menoret, and Amélie le Renard providing a more complex, dynamic, and nuanced view of Gulf cities that challenges both the "rags-to-riches" and "blank slate" narratives. Nonetheless, though most of these studies take historical factors into account, their primary ethnographic focus and vantage point is the present-day Gulf. The largely ahistorical nature of this urban literature inadvertently reinforces the de-historicizing view of modernist planning; as Fuccaro puts it, it is "as if oil modernization had swept away urban history along with the traditional urban landscapes."[91] Although some historical studies of Gulf cities are slowly emerging, they focus, with the exception of Fuccaro's extensive work on Bahrain, almost entirely on the pre-oil period.[92] This temporal bifurcation of the literature is not entirely surprising. Across the Gulf the pace of change between the pre-oil and oil eras was undoubtedly meteoric, and it is hard to think of the cities that emerged after the discovery of oil as having any connections to the pre-oil towns they so rapidly (and deliberately) obliterated. However, as Richard Dennis argues, when we shake off the "shock of the new," we see that there is "an ongoing dialogue between past and present" in the making of modern cities.[93] This book opens up that dialogue between the pre-oil and oil periods in order to investigate how the intervention of oil affected the ongoing process of city formation and the continuous practice of urban life in Kuwait.

1

Pre-Oil Urbanism

The Settlement of Kuwait

Kuwait was established in 1716 as a predominantly urban society. During the "tribal outbreak" of the eighteenth century, tribes from central and southern Arabia migrated toward the northeast coast of the peninsula to escape severe drought and famine.[1] One group of families who migrated together, known collectively as the Bani 'Utub,[2] came from the Najd-based Anizah tribal confederation and had been settled cultivators prior to their migration to the coast.[3] When they reached the head of the Persian Gulf around 1716, they found a spacious bay with a nearby freshwater supply. There was no existing town or significant community settled in the area; aside from a few fishermen's huts, the only physical structure of significance was a fort (*kut*) of the Bani Khalid tribe, which had seized control of eastern Arabia from the Ottomans in the 1660s. The 'Utub set up their new settlement on a small hill known as Tell Bhaiteh, which faced the Bani Khalid's *kut* (for which *Kuwait* is a diminutive meaning "small fort").

Within less than a hundred years this cluster of families grew into "a thriving commercial settlement" whose residents engaged in fishing, pearling, shipping, shipbuilding, and trade.[4] Kuwait's auspicious location in the northwest corner of the Gulf and its enviable natural properties fostered its growth into a vibrant port and regional entrepôt. The area around the town was "of the most barren and inhospitable description, without a tree or shrub visible as far as the eye can reach, except a few bushes which mark the wells, of which the water is particularly salty and bad."[5] The place would have been uninhabitable without its large natural harbor, "capable of containing the navy of Great Britain,"[6] which allowed the townspeople to import everything they needed. Kuwaiti merchants imported grain and wheat from Basra, Iraq; piece goods, rice, sugar, spices, and teak for shipbuilding from India; mangrove poles for house-building from east Africa; coffee from the Red Sea region; tobacco and dried fruits from Iran; and fresh water from the Shatt al-Arab river in southern Iraq.[7] Because of the importance of trade, Kuwait Town was established as a free port and no customs duties were levied on sea imports until the beginning of the twentieth century. Its strategic position between the Gulf and the deserts of northeastern Arabia made it an important gateway between the sea and the hinterland. The town grew into a chief center of the transit trade linking the transnational Indian Ocean maritime network with the caravan trade extending inland as far as Damascus.[8] The town's proximity to the Shatt al-Arab also gave Kuwaitis access to the fertile river channels of Iraq, and dates from this region became the principal export cargo of Kuwait's long-distance traders.

According to local tradition, for the first forty years the settlers had no leader but paid tribute to the shaykh, or chief, of the Bani Khalid. When their population increased due to the town's economic prosperity, the heads of the main families decided that a leader must be chosen to settle all problems and disputes and to protect the town from external attack.[9] Many leading 'Utbi families turned down the job because governing the town would interfere with their maritime trades. The Al Sabah, however—"the poorest of the important families"—agreed to provide a ruler for the town "both for the honor of it and because the opportunity costs for them were very low."[10] Therefore, in 1752 Sabah I was selected for this position.

In 1760 Sabah I built a wall around his small settlement, signaling the moment when Kuwait became an independent, viable, and self-sufficient town. Over the next two centuries Kuwait developed from a small coastal settlement enclosed within a dilapidated boundary wall into a city-state with territorial boundaries that, when finally locked in place in 1922, extended well beyond the town's limits to incorporate expanses of desert. The coastline enclosed within the 1760 wall was approximately six hundred meters long, with an inland depth of around three hundred meters. This small area was unable to accommodate the substantial demographic growth that occurred at the turn of the century, so a second wall was built in 1811 that reflected the extent of the town's achieved and anticipated spatial expansion. The new wall had a semi-circular shape similar to the first wall, but the length of the town's shoreline from one end of the new wall to the other was now approximately sixteen hundred meters, and the town had expanded an additional four hundred meters inland. Kuwait experienced a period of unprecedented economic and demographic growth from the 1890s until around 1920 due to a pearling and trading boom throughout the region. This growth may explain why sometime after 1887, when J. R. Povah made the last recorded reference to its existence, the second wall was removed and urban expansion became unbounded.[11] Kuwait Town's population grew substantially during this period. The demand for buildings to accommodate new immigrants increased, leading to a peak in the house-building industry.[12] The British Political Agent reported in 1916 that "building operations are in evidence in all quarters of the town, which is rapidly extending."[13] By the time the third wall went up in 1920, it was much longer than the earlier walls and encompassed a significantly larger area. The urban coastline within the new wall had reached 5,600 meters. The total area inside the second wall before it was demolished, after nearly 170 years of settlement, was .724 square kilometers; the area incorporated within the third wall was 7.5 square kilometers—a spatial increase of more than 900 percent within only thirty to forty additional years of settlement (Figure 1).[14]

In 1899 Mubarak I signed a protection agreement with Great Britain, although Kuwait still had tenuous ties with the Ottoman Empire. Mubarak pledged not to receive the representative of any other power, nor to cede any portion of his territory to any foreign government or subject without the previous consent of the British government.[15] This treaty and those signed with other Gulf rulers "protected the position of local dynasties" because they were signed directly in the names of individual rulers and their successors.[16] Unlike in other parts of the Gulf, the British rarely interfered in Kuwait's internal affairs. But they did largely take control over Kuwait's external affairs, including establishing its boundaries. In 1913 the British and Ottoman Empires met to settle, among other existing disputes in the region, "the status and limits" of Kuwait.[17] They identified the undisputed territory of the Al Sabah as having Kuwait Town at its center and including all areas inside a radius of forty miles in all directions. The tribes in this area were considered loyal to Mubarak because he was able to extract from them the *zakat* (alms collected from a fixed portion of one's wealth to help those in need), a key factor in determining the extent of a ruler's jurisdiction in the desert. In exchange, the tribes received access to the *suq*, or

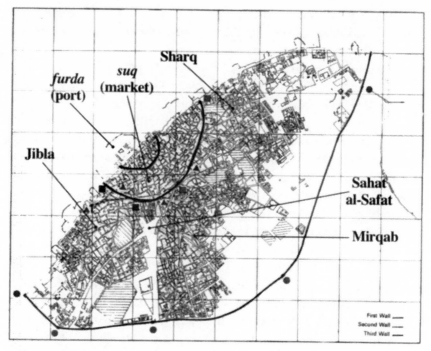

FIGURE 1. Map of Kuwait Town showing the three walls, residential quarters, and different morphological sectors. *Source*: Kuwait Municipality, *Planning and Urban Development* (modified with labels).

town market, and nearby water wells, as well as the ruler's protection along the caravan trade routes.[18] Mubarak was further authorized to collect *zakat* from tribes outside this undisputed territory that were within a radius of 140 miles from the town's center.[19] The agreement was never ratified, however, due to the outbreak of World War I.

Kuwait's borders were formally established in 1922, as a result of a boundary dispute between Mubarak's son Salem (r. 1917–21) and Ibn Sa'ud, the ruler of Najd.[20] The conflict between the rulers led to a bloody battle between Kuwait and Ibn Sa'ud's militant Ikhwan tribes in Jahra—an agricultural village twenty miles west of Kuwait Town under Al Sabah jurisdiction—in October 1920. It was in this context that Salem ordered the building of a new wall, the town's third, to protect against attack.[21] Though the *sur* (boundary wall) was never assailed, it was Kuwait Town's first true fortification. Unlike its predecessors—which had been "more for show than protection" in that they were less than a foot thick, quite low, and dilapidated—the new wall was a real protective barrier.[22] As American missionary doctor Stanley Mylrea put it, "For more than three miles stretched the great wall completely shutting off the city from the landward side. . . . Kuwait was now a 'fenced city.'"[23] The path of the new *sur* forever marked the extent of Kuwait's urban limits, even after the wall was torn down with the advent of oil (Figure 2). The conflicts with Ibn Sa'ud also led to the fixing of Kuwait's permanent boundary with Najd at the 'Uqair Convention of 1922, during which the boundaries between Kuwait, Iraq, and Najd were defined. In this agreement, which was brokered by the British, Kuwait maintained the area within the forty-mile radius that was delineated in the 1913 Anglo-Turkish agreement but lost most of the area beyond that radius to Najd.[24]

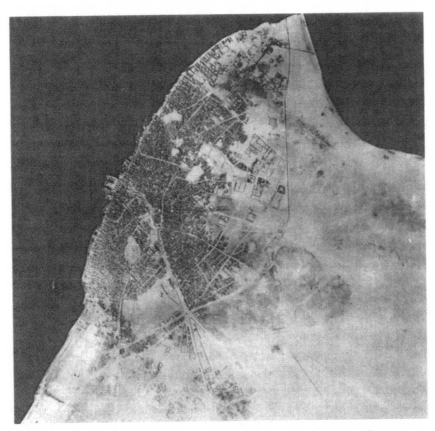

FIGURE 2. Aerial photo (taken in 1951) showing the permanent boundary of Kuwait Town (later Kuwait City) demarcated by the 1920 *sur*. *Source*: Kuwait Municipality, *Planning and Urban Development*.

Occupying the space between Kuwait's new urban and national boundary lines were the Bedouin camel- and sheep-herding tribes of the hinterland, and a few small agricultural and fishing villages under Al Sabah jurisdiction.[25] Though generally self-sufficient, the tribes and villagers were dependent on the town market to sell their produce and buy supplies. The two largest villages (Zor on Failaka Island and Jahra) were governed by a representative on behalf of the Al Sabah. The rest had no recognized head-man, and the Al Sabah ruler dealt with them "through the first inhabitant whose presence he [could] secure."[26] The only revenue the ruler collected from the tribes and villagers was the Islamic *zakat* and a 2 percent tax on goods taken out of Kuwait Town. By 1922 Kuwait's city-state status was well established.

Demographic Growth

Kuwaiti society before oil could thus be divided into three distinct categories: urban-mercantile (the townspeople), sedentary-pastoral (the agricultural and fishing villages), and nomadic- and semi-nomadic pasto-ral (the Bedouin). Members of the latter group continuously settled in the town or villages, thereby adopting new social and economic lifestyles and reflecting the porosity of these social categories.[27] Many of the townspeo-ple and practically all of the villagers (such as the Awazem, who settled in Dimnah, or present-day Salmiya) therefore shared lineage with the desert tribes. As A. R. Lindt observed in 1939, because of their shared origins cou-pled with the close interaction and interdependence of Kuwait's urban and pastoral populations, "there is not that deep cleft between town-dwellers and nomads which is so great an obstacle to a national unity in other Arab countries."[28] In 1904, John G. Lorimer estimated the fixed population of what he called the "Kuwait principality" to be approximately fifty thou-sand people: thirty-five thousand inside the town, two thousand in the villages, and thirteen thousand Bedouin.[29]

The town's population increased between the mid-eighteenth and mid-twentieth centuries as much by immigration as by natural growth, and this increase paralleled the town's steady economic expansion. Kuwait's first period of commercial prosperity came during the Persian occupation of Basra, where the British East India Company's factory was located, begin-ning in 1777. Kuwait's neutral position during the regional conflict kept the town and its desert trade routes safe from molestation. The Company therefore chose Kuwait as a safe and suitable place to divert its desert mail and trade between India, the Middle East, and Europe for the duration of the two-year occupation.[30] The experience revealed the small town's strategic importance as a major caravan trading post, and the shipping potential of its large harbor, which provided satisfactory anchorage for the Company's cruisers. Though the Company's trade was rerouted back through Basra after the cessation of the conflict in 1779, Kuwait's role as an entrepôt grew substantially. In 1790, Company officials Samuel Manesty and Harford Jones wrote that Kuwait was "a sea port of occasional commercial importance," with its degree of importance depending on "the prosperity or distress" of Basra.[31] By 1829 the town had grown into a "port of some importance" in its own right,[32] and by the middle of the nineteenth century Kuwait boasted "a singular instance of commercial prosperity" that rivaled the other coastal settlements of the Gulf littoral.[33] Kuwait's prosperity from the late eighteenth century onward encouraged the immigration of many families from Najd, Zubara, Zubair, and Iran.[34] By the early nineteenth century the town's population had reached ten thousand, and the original 'Utbi settlers, who numbered in the hundreds, were far outnumbered by the thousands of newcomers.[35] By the mid-nineteenth century the population doubled to around twenty thousand.[36] This continuous immigration was key to Kuwait's sustained economic growth and expansion: the more inhabitants there were, the larger was the labor force, and the more Kuwaiti vessels could participate in trading, shipping, and pearling.

The town experienced a period of unprecedented demographic growth from the 1890s until around 1920 due to an economic boom stemming from two factors. One was a general increase in trade stimulated by the arrival of British steamers in the Gulf, the suppression of piracy in the region, and the opening up of Kuwaiti merchant agencies in India and other places around the Indian Ocean. The second factor was the pearling boom of the late nineteenth and early twentieth centuries that was experienced around the Gulf region, largely the result of global demand for the luxury commodity coupled with particularly plentiful harvests in the local pearl fisheries. The peak of prosperity came between 1910 and 1912, when Kuwait saw a remarkable increase both in the standard (and cost) of living and in wages.[37] The rise in pearling had a "trickle-down effect" on all other maritime and commercial sectors. The *dhow*-building industry boomed, providing increased employment opportunities and higher wages for the builders of these Arabian sailing vessels.[38] The increased personal income that pearling brought to merchants and mariners was usually spent purchasing goods in the *suq*, thereby stimulating the trading sector as well as local craft industries. Kuwait Town's population grew substantially during this period as newcomers were attracted by bourgeoning opportunities in construction, commerce, and of course pearl diving, which mainly drew in young Bedouin from the surrounding hinterland. Whereas in 1904 the town's population was thirty-five thousand, by 1913 it had grown to fifty thousand.[39]

Though urban society before oil was not stratified into sharp socioeconomic tiers three broad social strata can be distinguished on the basis of occupation and distribution of wealth. The members of each stratum were of diverse backgrounds, occupations, and, to an extent, income levels. However, as Abraham Marcus identifies in his analysis of similar patterns of social differentiation in the urban society of premodern Aleppo, "the members of each class shared a set of comparable social circumstances and opportunities that distinguished them from others outside their level."[40] The highest social stratum, which was also the smallest, consisted of the notable merchant families. Though most of the town's 'Utub were part of this wealthy class, inclusion in the merchant elite was not restricted to members of any single religious or ethnic group. Very rich and influential Shi'i families, such as the Ma'rafi and the Behbehani, stood as important pillars of the mercantile oligarchy, and the capital of at least two Jewish merchants matched that of the 'Utbi elite.[41] The merchants' elite status stemmed primarily from their control of the town's pearling, shipping, and trading industries. Some local notable families, such as the Al Sager and the Al Naqib, also owned large date plantations along the Shatt al-Arab that supplied the outbound cargo of the Kuwaiti deep-sea fleet heading to India and east Africa.

The majority of the town's population consisted of laborers. Most laborers were sailors and pearl divers who worked on board the merchants' trading and pearling ships and spent most of their lives in poverty and debt due to the profit-sharing and credit-based systems of the maritime industries. Others were port workers, coolies, porters, water carriers, and construction workers. On the whole, this social stratum depended highly on the town's merchant elite—who were their employers, creditors, and benefactors—for their everyday survival (elaborated further in Chapter 3).

Occupying the wide gap between the merchant elite and the laboring poor in the town's socioeconomic hierarchy was a broad middle stratum that mostly lived comfortable but subsistence lifestyles. They were not rich, but they were not in dire need as were the laborers. Some worked as professionals: teachers, religious scholars, and *qadis* (Islamic judges). Others were shopkeepers and petty traders in the town market, skilled shipbuilders, and foremen within the town's construction industry. Also included were self-employed fishermen and craftsmen of more minor industries such as butchers, goldsmiths, lamp makers, tailors, and cloak embroiderers (to name a few).[42]

Rulers and Merchants

The role of the Al Sabah rulers and of the state in the townspeople's everyday lives was never entirely pervasive in Kuwait before oil and was always balanced out by the weighty presence of the influential merchants. When Sabah I came to power in 1752, he and the prominent urban families entered into a social pact. The Al Sabah would ensure the safety and stability of the town so that the rest of its inhabitants could live and work comfortably and peacefully while the merchants provided the ruler with financial backing to manage the town. In the absence of taxes or customs duties, the ruler received voluntary merchant donations that served as the town's revenues rather than as his personal income.[43] Due to this division of labor, the Al Sabah did not have the same freedom of mobility as the rest of the townspeople to participate in lucrative commercial and maritime activities, and were therefore quite poor.[44] In 1841, the ruler Jaber I and his sons were described as "perhaps the worst dressed and most ill-lodged residents in the place."[45] Local tradition claims that the Al Sabah had taken over the Bani Khalid fort when they came to power in 1752. In 1860, the residence of ruler Sabah al-Jaber was described as a "ruin," which may have been the Bani Khalid fort in disrepair.[46] By the 1890s, the rulers' residence was located next to the port in the center of the town's coastline. Whether this structure was the old fort or a newer building is unknown, but it displayed no ornamentation or outwardly superior characteristics as a palace.

Though the Al Sabah played an important role in fostering Kuwait's territorial expansion and autonomy, they played a minor role in governing the internal affairs of the town itself until Mubarak's reign in the early twentieth century. In 1792 an English East India Company official described the ruler as "more a father than a governor" to the townspeople.[47] By 1865, British Political Resident Lewis Pelly reported that in Kuwait

Town "there seems indeed to be little Government interference of any kind, and little need for any."[48] The ruler's main responsibilities toward the urban population entailed settling disputes (usually trade-related), administering justice, and protecting the rights of Kuwaiti merchants and mariners abroad.[49] But he played only a minimal role in providing for their everyday welfare aside from the allocation of the *zakat*, which was paid directly to the ruler by the townspeople who could afford it and by the surrounding tribes and villagers. To settle the townspeople's daily affairs, the ruler held a public audience (*majlis*) every morning at the Abdulrazag Gate in the second wall, near the town market, accompanied by the town *qadi*. Here he could collect the small tax on the Bedouin and "hear the news, superintend trade, and administer justice"[50] as he "[looked] on, in patriarchal fashion, at the busy scene" around him.[51] When it came to decisions affecting the internal functioning of the town at large, the Al Sabah sought the consultation (*shura*) and approval of the merchant notables who subsidized their rule, particularly in economic affairs.[52] The ruler therefore held a second *majlis* every evening in his own residence, which gave the urban notables direct access to the decision-making process. This political arrangement and balance of power between the rulers and the merchants maintained a high level of sociopolitical stability in Kuwait that remained relatively undisrupted until the rise of Mubarak I.

Mubarak came to power in 1896 by killing his brothers Jarrah and Mohammed (the legitimate ruler). By eliminating competition within the Al Sabah, Mubarak acquired the majority share of the family's date plantations in southern Iraq, giving him some financial autonomy from the merchants. His alliance with the British in 1899, which guaranteed the ruler protection from external as well as internal threats, also brought him some political freedom. In 1904 Mubarak therefore took the unprecedented step of imposing a 2 percent customs tax on mercantile imports.[53] Though they were unhappy with the changes, the merchants did not resist, because the town's trading and pearling industries were flourishing during this period. Furthermore, though Mubarak had a private income, the new tax on the merchants' trade was his only source of public revenue, which kept him firmly accountable to the commercial elite. Nonetheless, Mubarak used his newfound wealth to transform the rulers' nondescript residence on the seafront, or *al-seif*, into a fortified and luxurious palace complex, perhaps as a symbol of his growing prestige. In 1908 he built a "very fine suite of reception rooms in front of his old house" that were furnished in a "quasi-

European style."[54] Two years later he added more extensions,[55] and by 1912 his palace had become a compound divided into his private residence; quarters for his bodyguards, servants, slaves, and guests; and the *sarai*, or government building. The roof of the palace became the highest point in town, giving the ruler and his guards a clear view of the sea, port, market, and residential areas.[56] Despite its central position on the town's coastline, the building was almost entirely closed off from its surroundings by high, windowless walls with few entrances.[57] As a further reflection of his increasing political power, Mubarak constructed a new double-story building (popularly known as his *kishk* or kiosk) in the town market in which to hold his daily *majlis* with the townspeople. His office was located on the second floor, from which he observed and monitored all activity in the market below in panopticon style.

The rulers' financial dependence on the merchants both before and after Mubarak's imposition of taxes meant that the latter played more of a role in the provision of everyday services in the town than the former. At first this support was conducted primarily through individual philanthropy, largely under the terms of Islamic endowments, or *awqaf* (singular *waqf*). Rich merchants often endowed their properties or shop revenues to less affluent families; in 1920, for example, a woman from the prominent Al Ghanim family made a *waqf* of her house in Farij al-Matabba for the benefit of the sons of Khalifa al-Dabbous and their descendants in perpetuity.[58] Mosques were also built and maintained through *awqaf*, usually in the donor's own neighborhood as a contribution to the community.[59] In 1923, Abdullah al-Sayer (along with two other men) turned eight shops in the water market into *awqaf* for the maintenance of the Al Sayer mosque in Sharq.[60] Prominent individuals also provided the townspeople with access to free fresh water (known as *ma' sabil*) in tanks, some of which were also maintained through *waqf* endowments. Most well known was Abdulaziz Ahmed al-Du'aij, who built a large tank in the *suq* that he kept filled with water bought at his own expense from the water import *dhows* or brought in by camel from one of the freshwater wells outside of town.[61]

Because of this philanthropy, "people preferred the merchants over the rulers because the merchants paid," a sentiment vividly reflected in the pearl merchant secession of 1910.[62] Shortly before the start of the annual diving season that year, Mubarak decreed that the pearling fleet would not be permitted to leave Kuwait because he needed the divers to serve in a standing yet idle army in his conflict against the Montafiq tribe (of southern Iraq). In protest, three powerful pearl merchants (*towawish*) pulled their revenues out of Kuwait and seceded to Bahrain. The vast majority of the townspeople supported the *towawish*, and many other merchants hinted that they might follow.[63] Against the threat of economic collapse, Mubarak disbanded his force and negotiated with the pearl merchants to return to Kuwait. The success of the secession indicated that public loyalty was a valuable source of urban power and leverage, and the merchants had this power because they were the principal providers of public welfare and communal services in the town. Mubarak therefore began experimenting with ways of becoming more involved in public welfare. In 1909, after a particularly dry winter, local merchants decided to import freshwater from the Shatt al-Arab to sell to the townspeople rather than depending on rainwater and the surrounding wells, which were very brackish.[64] Mubarak was quick to follow suit. In 1912 he purchased a three-hundred-ton water-tank steamer to transport water from the Shatt, and he commissioned the Anglo-Persian Oil Company to build a desalination plant. The British praised Mubarak for this sudden display of "so enlightened a public spirit."[65] However, he still needed the merchants to finance nearly 40 percent of the building costs in return for shares in the plant, which opened in 1919 but closed down in 1924 due to continuous technical difficulties.[66]

Though Mubarak was personally unable to take over the provision of public welfare in the town, in 1909 he approved the opening of a hospital by the Reformed Church in America's Arabian Mission, which also opened a small school for boys and girls. The merchants had never been involved in the provision of health care or education before this period, but the presence of the missionaries stimulated their interest in such public services.[67] In 1911, the merchants collectively contributed 77,500 rupees to establish the town's first public school. (Prior to this project, children went to private neighborhood Qur'anic schools.) The Al Khudhair family donated a house near the *suq* for the school,[68] named Mubarakiyya as a "calculated gesture of flattery" to the ruler.[69] In 1913 a group of prominent townsmen under the leadership of the young Farhan al-Khudhair opened a free clinic with a Muslim doctor funded by charitable donations.[70] They secured a "good house on the seafront," bought instruments and medicines using merchant contributions, and brought a Turkish doctor to Kuwait.[71] The venture was short-lived, however, because Mubarak soon deported the doctor and the hospital was forced to close. The missionaries viewed the merchants' clinic and school as opposition to their own work. But rather than being simply a reaction to the Christian missionaries, the establishment of these new enterprises arguably represents the merchants' attempt at institutionalizing their own traditional role in urban governance and community welfare in the face of competition. In truth, neither Mubarak nor the missionaries could ever fully replace merchant patronage in the town; the missionaries themselves relied on philanthropic merchant contributions. Ahmed al-Khorafi, for example, supplied the hospital with a large tank that he kept filled with freshwater, free of charge.[72] During the battle with the Ikhwan in Jahra in October 1920, the leading town notables donated more than six thousand rupees and furnished the hospital with blankets and supplies for caring for the wounded.[73]

Nonetheless, with rising competition from both the ruler and the missionaries, the merchants became more organized in their role as the town's primary benefactors. In 1921 they raised a subscription of ten thousand rupees a year for the opening of a second school, the Ahmadiyya.[74] In 1923, the Ahliyya Library was established through joint donations of cash, property, and books; in the mid-1930s, Shahah Hamad al-Sager donated her large shop in the Suq al-Tujjar (Merchants' Market) for the library.[75]

Early State-Building

In 1934, Ahmed al-Jaber (r. 1920–50) signed an oil concession agreement with the Kuwait Oil Company, an Anglo-American joint venture.[76] Because the agreement was made in Ahmed's name rather than on behalf of Kuwait (as was common in all Gulf oil concessions), royalties went directly into the hands of the ruler, to be utilized in whatever manner he chose. This arrangement completely transformed the role of the ruling family in Kuwait. The concession guaranteed Ahmed a steady and independent income even before oil was found in commercial quantities in 1938, thereby granting the Al Sabah economic autonomy. Ahmed used the oil income for his own personal gain rather than on the town. He bought large estates abroad and spent money on such luxuries as yachts and palaces.[77] For town revenues, the ruler continued to depend on taxes.

The signing of the oil concession and the sudden arrival of Ahmed's newfound wealth occurred during a period of severe economic recession stemming from three factors: a trade embargo between Kuwait and Najd that lasted until 1937; the collapse of pearling in the Gulf due to the invention of the Japanese cultured pearl, coupled with reduced foreign markets for luxury items; and the general decline in trade during the world economic depression. Kuwait Town was not hit as hard by the decline in pearling as other parts of the Gulf because of the strength of its long-distance trading sector.[78] However, many small and mid-level Kuwaiti merchants, both pearling and otherwise, did not survive the recession and went bankrupt.

During this period of economic decline the merchants began experimenting with more formal civic institutions that maintained their role in public welfare but relieved the double financial burden of paying taxes and funding public services out of pocket. It became difficult for the merchants to supply donations for schools and other facilities during the economic crisis, and the Ahmadiyya School closed in 1931 due to lack of funds.[79] The merchants therefore established a municipality in 1930 and an education council in 1936. The Municipality's responsibilities included the supervision and cleaning of the *suq*, the registration of land and housing, the provision of public health and other social services, and some early zoning and street planning. The Education Council took over the opening of new (and the management of existing) public schools. Although technically these state institutions were headed by members of the ruling family, both were run by the merchants. But instead of depending on merchant donations, the institutions received a fixed portion (2 percent each) of the town's customs revenues that were already being levied against the merchants' trade.

Soon after the establishment of the Municipality, Ahmed introduced a series of new "municipal" taxes on boats, shops, slaughterhouses, motorcars, and houses, and even a tax for people selling wares on the ground in the market.[80] Such taxes were not well received by the merchants and townspeople, who were already suffering from the economic recession.[81] The merchants tried "to ease the lot of the many poor who today were finding it very hard to keep themselves alive" by taking on the burden of Ahmed's incessant taxes themselves. They requested a .5 percent increase on their own import tax in 1931 in exchange for the abolition of a house tax that the poorer members of the community were struggling to pay.[82] Ahmed's reliance on taxation did not diminish once the oil royalties started coming in after 1934, because the revenues from oil went straight into his own pocket rather than being spent on the town. Still, in 1936 the merchants again requested another .5 percent rise in the customs duty in order to increase the income for education.[83] The merchants were not averse to paying taxes; they knew that public expenditure would be more organized and consistent if based on taxes rather than relying on individual donations. But they were becoming increasingly aware that Ahmed had no intention of spending his oil income on public welfare. In 1938 the ruler's total income (from customs and taxes, oil royalties, and private sources) was 828,400 rupees, while his total expenditure was 156,440 rupees (or 19 percent). Of the expenditure, only 2,000 rupees went toward education (separate from the Education Council's customs intake) whereas 119,540 rupees went to family allowances. Apart from 10,000 rupees that was spent on "donations to the poor and other contingencies including 'hush money,'" the remainder went to managing the ruler's own household and private expenses, including 671,960 surplus rupees that went into his private savings.[84]

Although it functioned on a relatively small annual budget of 45,000 rupees, the Municipality was very active throughout the 1930s. In addition to improving the town's hygienic conditions, it made many building and road improvements, established a new fish market and slaughterhouse, and set up fire services in the market. The ruler expressed little interest in the municipal administration; for instance, he never visited the new fish market that opened in 1937.[85] So, in January 1938 when Bari Radio Station in Italy broadcast that Kuwait "had attained a high degree of efficiency in education, civilization, financial management, and town improvements at the hands of her present [ruler]," extreme resentment emerged among the townspeople, particularly the merchants, toward Ahmed. The praise he received on the radio was countered by graffiti all over town calling for reforms and criticizing the "crookedness" of the ruler.[86] It was known that Ahmed had been communicating directly with the Italian radio station, and people resented that he took credit for the recent improvements when in fact he had not contributed much funding, nor had he shown any support for, the Municipality and Education Council initiatives.[87]

The demands for reform that emerged after the Bari broadcast led to the *majlis* (meaning, in this context, council or assembly) movement of 1938, the same year in which oil was discovered in commercial quantities. The merchants realized that oil income could "deprive them of their critical role in providing revenue, and with that cost them their power."[88] They therefore petitioned the ruler to form an elected council to grant them more formal access to decision-making, to which Ahmed agreed.[89] In July 1938 an electorate comprising the heads of 150 leading families elected a legislative assembly of fourteen members, all prominent urban notables, under the presidency of Abdullah al-Salem (Ahmed's cousin and nemesis within the ruling family and a strong supporter of the reformists). One of the principal grievances of the *majlis* was that Ahmed was not spending any of his newfound revenues on public services. They wanted better government-funded education for all members of urban society, the establishment of a hospital at the government's expense, and other general improvements.[90] To meet these demands, the *majlis* asked Ahmed to hand over the next oil check.[91] He responded by dissolving the council in December 1938.[92] As the Political Resident put it the following day, the "balance of power between Sheikh and Council has been readjusted in favor of the former."[93]

The failure of the 1938 *majlis* movement sounded the death knell to the historic social pact between the merchants and the rulers in Kuwait. Oil revenues officially made the rulers independent. Ahmed spent his oil income on building up a state apparatus and bolstering the status of his own family. The latter he accomplished by significantly increasing their personal allowances and by delegating power to them. Prior to this period, members of the Al Sabah were "allowed to take no part whatever in administrative affairs, and were kept in the background socially."[94] But by the end of the 1930s, all of Ahmed's new state departments, including public security, the treasury, the police, the arsenal, and the port, were under the headship of a member of his family.[95] The Municipality and the Education Department were also under the presidency of an Al Sabah, although municipal, educational, and health services continued to be funded by customs revenues and merchant donations rather than by oil royalties, which went into Ahmed's own bank accounts abroad.[96]

Throughout the 1940s the British strongly advised the ruler to invest his income in public spending. As the Political Resident put it, "When a ruler gets to the point of enjoying vast royalties, the State has to emerge from its position of being really a private estate, and the only way he will command the public confidence will be by framing some sort of a budget, so that the public, even if they don't see it, will know that they are getting a square deal."[97] Ahmed never heeded this advice, even after the official launch of the oil industry in 1946. It was not until after his death in 1950 that the oil income was utilized for the establishment of a large welfare state in Kuwait.

Unplanned Urbanism

Until the establishment of the Municipality in 1930, urban growth was an entirely unplanned and largely uncontrolled process in Kuwait. In the early years of settlement, land was acquired simply by an individual taking possession of and building on it. As the town grew, the buying and selling of property became more common.[98] Though property title deeds (known as "Adsaniyya certificates" because the town notary was typically from the Al Adsani family) existed, there was no central land register in the town. Plots of land were not officially organized, and a property was usually identified in a title deed according to its neighbors and surrounding landmarks. For example, a document from 1894 recording the sale of a house by Meethah al-Murshaid to Mansour al-Fraih identifies the property under sale as being "bordered to the west by the road and the house of Sayed Fayez, to the north by the house of Al Qahtani, to the south by the road, and to the east by the houses of Al Wazzan, Al Halawah, and Al Zanki."[99] Even commercial properties were recorded this way before oil.

The establishment of boundaries for new, undeveloped land was more challenging. When the Reformed Church in America's missionaries acquired a large piece of land from Mubarak in a relatively empty area on the western edge of town in 1911, the title deed indicated that the property was a 270-by-300-foot rectangle. The boundary marks put down by the ruler's guards, however, "were just heaps of stone flung down haphazardly wherever the spirit had moved the Sheikh's servants so that instead of the site being a rectangle, it was a polyhedron with at least seven sides."[100] The missionaries and their American architects were much more meticulous than the local authorities: they remeasured the property and moved the boundary markers to conform to the dimensions specified in the deed of sale. When Mubarak found out about this, he was furious. "'What!' he cried, 'Do you mean to tell me that you have moved my boundaries—*my* boundaries?'"[101] The ruler was more insulted by their actions than concerned with the accuracy of the boundaries of a nearly two-acre seafront plot in an area that, though relatively empty at the time, was popular among merchant land speculators on account of rumors that a terminus of the Baghdad Railway might be established nearby (which never materialized).[102] The missionaries eventually got the ruler's approval on the area they wanted for their hospital. Their experience highlights that the identification of clear, fixed boundaries in the designation of private property was uncommon.

The missionaries' land tale also reveals that the distribution of empty land for new development in the early twentieth century came under the purview of the ruler. In many Adsaniyya documents of the mid-eighteenth century, Abdullah II appears as one of the signing witnesses to the transactions, indicating that the ruler had some role to play in the exchange of land and property at that time. However, it is not until Mubarak's reign that we have clearer evidence that unowned and unbuilt land in town could be allocated (either sold or given away for free) to a new owner only by the ruler. In other words, land not already owned and certified with an Adsaniyya document was state land. In 1908, for example, prominent urban notable Sayyid Hashem al-Naqib acquired from Mubarak an empty plot of land in the largely undeveloped western edge of town, where he was planning to build a new home.[103] Throughout the first several years of his reign Mubarak gave plots of land on all sides of town to his subjects for free. Lorimer observed in 1904 that these plots were, "on account of the increasing prosperity of the place, being taken up and built upon by enterprising individuals as commercial speculation."[104] By 1907 the town had grown to four or five times its original size as a result of this practice.[105] All sales of new land on the seafront included the requirement that the owner put up a sea wall along the front of the property.[106]

Notwithstanding this rudimentary attempt at urban planning, Mubarak's land scheme appears to have been financially motivated rather than an attempt to control urban development during the pearling boom. After spending the first decade of his reign giving out land grants for free all over town, in January 1907 Mubarak informed the occupants of the buildings erected on this land that they had to pay the ruler 75 percent of the cost of their holdings, as estimated by Mubarak's own appraisers, in order to maintain ownership. If the owner could not afford to pay this new "extortionate building tax," as the British Political Agent called it, the ruler would pay the owner 25 percent of the value and take possession of the building and land.[107] Mubarak certainly gained a hefty profit from this extremely unpopular policy; in the same year that this land tax was initiated, he purchased an expensive new steam yacht.[108] More important than the income he exacted from those who could afford to pay the tax, however, was the land that he appropriated from the many townspeople who could not. It was not so much that this scheme made Mubarak one of the town's biggest landowners (he had already controlled the land before he handed it out). Rather, the scheme brought into his ownership land that had been developed and built on at his subjects' expense rather than his own. He was then able to rent out the acquired property to members of the public for yet further profit, a lucrative venture at a time when more and more immigrants were coming to Kuwait looking for work. The confiscation of property as punishment for crimes, and in cases of default on debts or fraud, also became a common practice of all Al Sabah rulers from Mubarak onward, bringing more and more profitable urban land under the jurisdiction of the ruling family throughout the early twentieth century. If a debt was due to a third party, the ruler would sell the debtor's property to pay back the claimant. But if the debt was due to the ruler, he would keep the property for himself.[109] A person found guilty of a crime could also have his or her property confiscated and added to the ruler's private landholdings. The house that Stanley and Bessie Mylrea rented for thirty years was such a property; the former owner had murdered a woman in it and stuffed her body down the well in the courtyard. When the man was found guilty, the ruler took over the property, and it was thus that Mubarak became the Mylreas' landlord.[110]

By the interwar period the ruling family became the town's largest landowners, and their properties became their principal source of revenue. The *suq* in particular came almost entirely under Al Sabah control in the post-Mubarak era. By the 1930s only members of the ruling family could build new shops and lease them out (infiltrating a space formerly controlled by the town's traders).[111] Rents for both houses and shops in the town skyrocketed under Ahmed al-Jaber's reign, because the ruler did little to control his family's constant rent hikes. As one example, when an Indian tailor returned to Kuwait after several years' absence, his former landlord, Abdullah al-Salem, allowed him to bid with the current tenant to rent back his old shop; by the end of the bidding competition the rent had gone up from 40 to 90 rupees per month.[112] The 1938 *majlis* made a substantial effort to curtail these excesses: they allowed all members of the public to build new shops and reduced rents in the *suq*.[113]

Preceding the *majlis*, of course, was the Municipality, Kuwait's first official institution with a broad mandate over urban affairs. One of its first projects was numbering all of the houses in town, which helped clean up existing land disputes. Within a few weeks of the numbering, officials came across ninety houses owned by a member of the ruling family who had formerly been in charge of the *suq* guard. His ownership of some of these houses was under dispute by their original owners, so the issue was brought before the ruler, who demanded to see the documents proving his rightful ownership of all ninety properties. He could produce only seventy-one title deeds, so the remaining nineteen houses were seized and restored to the claimants.[114] The Municipality also became the first official body to allocate previously unowned land in the town, and all land transactions now had to be administered by the Municipal Council.[115] No attempt was made, however, to define plots of land by size or fixed boundaries, and title deeds continued to identify properties by recognized surroundings.

This traditional method of delineating private property soon became a hindrance, however, when the Municipality began work on Kuwait Town's earliest planned development schemes. Most of the institution's projects involved street widening to accommodate the slowly increasing number of motorcars. In 1931 a wide road leading from the Dasman Palace to the heart of the *suq* area was cut through the town. The busiest part of the waterfront road in front of the old British Political Agency in Sharq was doubled in width, and several blind streets around town were rounded off to make it easier for cars to turn corners.[116] Because all such street-widening projects involved some demolition of houses and shops, or at least partial demolition of front steps, the Municipality awarded financial compensation to affected property owners. A committee would inspect the houses and shops that the Municipality needed to acquire and evaluate how much compensation would be adequate to pay to the owners.[117] Because acquisitions for development purposes were compulsory, and because the compensations awarded were usually low due to the Municipality's fixed budget (it was still functioning on 2 percent of customs revenues), these early development schemes were extremely unpopular. One major problem that the Municipality faced was that, because there had hitherto been no organized land registration system in the town, people tended to expand their houses well beyond the original limits of their land (when rebuilding a collapsed wall or installing doorsteps, for instance). The Municipal Council decided that no compensation would be paid for any part of a property that the owner had taken over from the road. This decision brought the Municipality into conflict with the public. The notion that "whatever was taken from the road should be returned to the road without compensation," as Kuwaiti municipal historian Najat al-Jassim puts it, was at odds with public conceptions of private property.[118] In the public's assessment, if they used it, it belonged to them; the vagueness of the traditional title deeds corroborated their claims. For example, a dispute arose in 1941 between Ahmed al-Nassar and Faris al-Wogayan over the closed alley that led to and ran between their houses. The small inner streets running between homes, particularly the alleys that were not through streets, were used almost exclusively by the local residents as semi-private spaces.

Because both claimants' families used the alley, they each claimed that the street belonged to them. The Municipal Council intervened and decreed that in fact neither party had any claim over the street.[119] The discrepancy between the use value and the exchange value of land was thus coming into focus for the first time in Kuwait Town. With the advent of rudimentary town planning in the 1930s, land required clearly defined boundaries and limits and could no longer be simply appropriated and used at will. Compensation for development projects made the monetary value of land more meaningful.

From the Municipality's perspective, such conflicts highlighted the inadequacy of the existing land-registration system. In 1940 the institution therefore began registering all land transactions both inside and outside the town wall.[120] This attempt at organizing real estate in order to facilitate road widening and building projects did not, however, improve the state of urban development in the ensuing decade. A new obstacle to municipal planning emerged in the 1940s: land speculation by members of the ruling family. As part of his post-*majlis* state-building tactics, Ahmed al-Jaber used his oil income to increase Al Sabah family allowances substantially. This increase in income whetted the appetite of many members of the ruling family, who became "suddenly consumed with an extraordinary land hunger." In 1941, several Al Sabah began marking out various areas of open land in the town center "with the intention of claiming them as their private property."[121] This land grabbing was particularly acute in the main town square, named Sahat al-Safat, which the Political Agent attributed to the enhanced value of land in the vicinity of the cable and wireless station, where the new post and telegraph office was due to open.[122] "They intend to build shops on their sites which they hope will let more readily than shops situated farther from . . . the new post office."[123] This land was usually seized from its existing owners, who had no legal recourse to stand up to the ruling family member who took their land. Political activist Ahmed al-Khatib recalls in his memoirs that Ali al-Khalifa al-Sabah, the first Director of Public Security, seized his family's land near Sahat al-Safat and built shops on it. When his mother took the matter to the town magistrate, Abdullah al-Jaber al-Sabah, he told her that Ali was willing to give her three of his new shops, an offer she refused. The family's right to their land was never restored, despite their many efforts to reclaim it over the ensuing decades.[124] Many other families lost their land through similar seizures by members of the ruling family.[125] The president of the Municipality being a member of the Al Sabah family made it unlikely that the Municipal Council would reject land claims made by his relatives. By 1948 such land grabbing in prospective development areas, which was sanctioned by the ruler, extended beyond the town wall.[126]

Though the merchant-run Municipality tried to organize and control Kuwait's urban growth and development from 1930 onward, the advent of oil and the financial independence it brought to the Al Sabah gave Kuwait's rulers a more direct role to play in city formation. This role included enhancing the physical presence of the state on the urban landscape. Prior to 1938, Mubarak's *kishk*—essentially a courthouse used by all subsequent rulers until the reign of Ahmed al-Jaber (when it was used by his brother and deputy Abdullah)—was the only official state building in town, along with the customs building and the arsenal in the Nayef Palace. The 1938 *majlis* had overseen the construction of a new building to house the courts, police, and other government departments.[127] Ahmed continued this process in the 1940s and new buildings for housing state departments began to appear all around the town.[128] However, for the two centuries before these changes, Kuwait Town's urban landscape had developed autonomously into a spatial expression of its port identity rather than being designed as a spatial manifestation of state power (at a time when there was minimal government presence in people's everyday lives). Although the Bani Khalid fort that later became the ruler's palace was the *starting* point of Kuwait's settlement, the structure was not the *focal* point of the town's continuous growth over the two hundred years after the Al Sabah came to occupy it. Rather, it was the commercial and maritime activities of the town's merchants and mariners that gave the town its distinct morphology, shaped the contours of urban space, and determined the patterns and practices of everyday life before oil.[129]

2

Port City Life

The Spaces of Everyday Life

Kuwait Town's demographic and spatial expansion over the first two centuries of settlement mirrored the growth and vitality of its port economy. Through this process of natural, unplanned development, the urban landscape evolved to meet the everyday needs and desires and support the activities of the people who inhabited it. The realities of the climate, of the maritime economy, and of the absence of a strong central state combined to create an urban landscape and experience based on the spatial and behavioral integration of private (domestic) life, civic (social) life, and public (economic and political) life. The town contained three distinct morphological sectors: the seafront, the market area, and the residential quarters. However, these areas were functionally connected to one another insofar as they were mutually shaped by and intimately linked to the town's port economy. Life within these different sectors was also highly integrated, as each area encompassed a mix of economic, social, and political activities. Urban life in the various spaces of the pre-oil city was thus characterized by diversity and simultaneity (in that multiple things happened in the same space at the same time), spontaneity and possibilities for the unexpected, and a constant engagement with difference.

The town port served as the locus of spatial expansion and shaped the contours of everyday urban life.[1] The port was located at the middle of the town's shoreline where Kuwait was first settled. In time the coastline (*sahel*) grew outward to the east and west of the port, while the market area (*suq*), extended inland on a perpendicular axis leading from the port to the open-air Bedouin market known as Sahat al-Safat (see Figure 1, p. 24). Despite its economic and spatial centrality, the port was initially a minor "commodious harbor for small craft" that did not correspond to the town's high level of shipping activity.[2] As a free port, the town initially had no central customs house or fixed place for trading vessels to load and unload their cargo for inspection. Rather, when arriving back in town, Kuwait's pearling and trading vessels pulled right up to the shore, where their crews unloaded their wares and gear and prepared the ships for mooring.

The foreshore running the length of the town therefore developed into "one great shipyard of Arab dhows."[3] The coastline to the east and west of the central harbor was divided into several tidal jetties (*inga'*, singular *nig'a*) where the town's fleet could moor and undergo repairs while being protected from the waves (Figure 3).[4] Like most public services and facilities in the town, these jetties—without which "the maritime life of Kuwait would be impossible"[5]—were funded, built, and maintained by the town's ship-owning merchants, "each according to his ability to pay and according to the number and size of the boats in his possession."[6] The first row of houses facing the sea belonged to the town's *nowakhada* (ship captains, singular *nokhada*), merchants, and shipowners, and the latter usually built a *nig'a* directly opposite his house for the mooring of his own ships and others in the vicinity. Between the *inga'* and the first row of houses were several *'amayer* (singular *'amara*)—warehouses that stored and sold wood and other seafaring and building materials—belonging to merchants and shipowners.[7] Most shipbuilding and repair activities also took place along the town's foreshore, and the *dhow* yards, in the words of Australian shipwright Alan Villiers (who sailed with a Kuwaiti vessel and visited the town in 1939), gave Kuwait Town "one of the most interesting waterfronts in the world."[8]

This *sahel* grew considerably during the pearling boom of the early twentieth century. The main boat harbor in Sharq was enlarged to three times its former size; the thirty-five thousand rupees needed to complete the project were collected from the homeowners and boat owners who benefited from the enlargement.[9] The *dhow*-building yards expanded with the rising demand for pearling vessels, and the seafront became lined with more "huddle[s] of beams and planks," while the number of ships berthed in the *inga'* in the off-seasons multiplied.[10] Villiers described the scene in 1939: "All along the waterfront . . . almost from wall to wall of the town, the

FIGURE 3. *Inga'* (tidal jetties) of Sharq. *Source*: Kuwait Oil Company archives.

big ships and the little ships jostle one another. On the beach, on the tidal flats, and in the sea they lie cheek by jowl."[11] The *sahel* was one of the most important and active morphological sectors of the pre-oil urban landscape, and the *inga' 'amayer*, shipyards, *dhows*, and constant clutter of "maritime paraphernalia" covering the length of the *sahel* year round left little doubt that Kuwait was an active maritime town.[12]

Like the *sahel*, the port, or *furda*, also expanded during the early twentieth century to accommodate the substantial increase in trade that resulted from both the arrival of British steamers in the Gulf and the pearling boom. Although British ships anchored in Kuwait when the town was used as a temporary transit station by the East India Company from 1793 to 1795, the swell in shipping activity in the early twentieth century warranted the expansion of the town's docks. Three anchorages were each built with a capacity to receive ships of different sizes (fishing and pearling vessels, larger deep-sea shipping and trading *dhows*, and British steamers).[13] Also contributing to the development of the town port was Mubarak's imposition of customs dues. In 1904 he constructed a customs administration building along with a spacious and secure stone warehouse for the reception and safe storage of merchants' goods as they waited to be taxed and carried away into the market.[14] Though such warehouses were built for the merchants' "convenience," they were also needed to accommodate Mubarak's numerous new customs regulations. As of 1908, for instance, goods had to be inspected at the customs premises prior to the levying of duty, which required additional space.[15] Nonetheless, Mubarak's improvements to the port facilities were a boon to the merchants' trade: in 1912 he ordered from England a "three-ton hand-power crane for landing and shipping heavy packages at the wharves," and he extended the covered and enclosed areas of the customs premises to minimize the "old risk of loss and damage by thieves and weather."[16] With its transformation into a port complex, the *furda* finally reflected the level of economic activity passing through it. "[From] the customs yard a continual stream of horses, horse-drawn carts, and Persian coolies, laden with bales and boxes, emerged to toil laboriously up the hill towards the [*suq*]."[17]

An extension of Kuwait's role as a port was its florescence as a market town. The *suq* comprised the central part of the built-up area, with the oldest part (the Suq al-Tujjar) directly facing the port. This was the site of the town's first shops selling goods imported from Basra, Iran, India, and elsewhere. The rest of the *suq* was segmented into smaller inner markets (*aswaq*). As the town gradually grew from the early eighteenth century onward, so did the market area, which continuously extended southward from the port in the shape of a central corridor flanked by the town's residential districts. During the trading boom of the early twentieth century, most shops in the Suq al-Tujjar were converted into offices from which the merchants ran their growing businesses and in which they displayed samples of their imported commodities, which they sold wholesale to the petty traders of the expanding inner *aswaq*.[18] Initially these *aswaq*, such as the central Suq al-Dakhili (Indoor Market, because it was covered), were unspecialized, with each containing a mix of merchandise such as meat, wheat, spices, fabric, chinaware, and medicine. During the period of "remarkable growth" at the turn of the twentieth century, the market area grew considerably.[19] In 1903, Kuwait Town contained five hundred shops, and at least forty new ones opened annually.[20] In 1904 the bazaar was reportedly larger and better supplied than it had been only two years previously.[21] Several new markets opened by 1912 and, according to the British Political Agent, "all [were] thronged."[22] The new markets were increasingly specialized according to the merchandise and craft of their vendors, and the extensive *suq* became spatially organized according to commodity, trade, or both. Vendors in the mixed areas began moving to the specialized areas, and the markets they vacated became specialized themselves. The Suq al-Dakhili, for example, changed into a market catering specifically to the needs of the new Mubarakiyya School around the corner, with most vendors becoming either booksellers or tailors of school uniforms. The *suq* grew to incorporate up to fifty such specialized branches.

Over time the *suq* extended into Sahat al-Safat, an open space (*saha*) that before the twentieth century was located just outside the town limits (Figure 4). In this large, undeveloped clearing (hence the name Safat, from the root word *safa* meaning clear),[23] the Bedouin tribes of the surrounding hinterland set up temporary stalls where they traded their desert produce, such as milk, butter, ghee, horses, and sheep, with the townspeople in exchange for dates, clothing, firearms, salt, and manufactured items.[24]

FIGURE 4. The Bedouin market in the Sahat al-Safat. *Source*: Kuwait Oil Company archives.

Originally this Bedouin market was located just outside the Abdulrazaq Gate of the second wall. Desert traders pitched their tents near this clearing whenever they came to trade with the townspeople. Caravans trading between Kuwait and the Arabian interior also camped there, creating a "suburb" just outside the urban limits.[25] Sahat al-Safat (hereafter referred to as al-Safat) was a counterpoint to the *sahel:* whereas the latter was where the town interacted with the sea, the former was where the urban met the desert. Just as the number of ships berthed along the *sahel* revealed the extent of the town's maritime activities, so the number of camels crouched in al-Safat, sometimes numbering up to five hundred, emphasized Kuwait's importance in the caravan trade.[26] By the early twentieth century, urban sprawl had incorporated al-Safat into the town's expanding landscape, and it became the town's main public square.

Functionally Integrated Spaces of Diversity

Although inherently economic in nature, the seafront, *suq*, and al-Safat were all prominent social and, to some extent, political spaces. These different urban sites were explicitly public spaces, not in terms of ownership but rather in terms of the "sense of public life" they engendered, each reflecting different ways of "being with others in public."[27] There were significant overlaps between the functions and representations that these sites encompassed as urban public spaces in Kuwait, and each served multiple simultaneous purposes and activities. Al-Safat was principally the site of the open-air Bedouin market, the part of the *suq* that the townspeople visited regularly to stock up on supplies brought in from the desert. It was also, however, the kind of public space that Fran Tonkiss describes as a site of collective belonging, where the "local and everyday" combines with the "monumental and symbolic." Such sites afford "equal and in principle free access to all users as citizens," providing a sense of social and political belonging in the city.[28] Al-Safat was the main town square used for public festivities, bringing together all members of the urban population in celebration:

On the afternoon of a religious festival, rich and poor, all dressed in new clothes for the occasion, would flock to the main town square to see the sheikh's armed bodyguards perform the Bedouin war dance (*'arda*). Many women stood on roof-tops to enjoy a better view, while others mingled in the general crowd. The sheikh himself would usually be present and take part in the dance, and on his arrival women spectators would often express their delight with the traditional shrill ululation.[29]

The 'arda became a common event in al-Safat during the reign of Ahmed al-Jaber. It served to demonstrate publicly the ruler's growing power and authority, and to rally the public to support him. For instance, after Ahmed's investiture as Knights Commander of the Order of the Star of India, the ruler and his entourage went to al-Safat for an 'arda performance. The day was declared a public holiday so that the townspeople could see their ruler wearing his British decorations.[30]

The punishment of crimes was also a very public affair in Kuwait Town. In 1934, the case of a group of men responsible for a string of robberies was "tried in public amidst crowds of people, young and old, who form a procession and go singing in chorus and clapping hands, ahead of the accused as they go to Court from their cells and vice versa."[31] Al-Safat in particular was where prisoners were publicly humiliated by being mounted onto a crosspiece of wood fixed into a pole in the ground after being flogged.[32] Stanley Mylrea recounted once seeing a man charged with public drunkenness who had been "terribly beaten across the head and face being ridden through the bazaar on a donkey with his face towards the beast's tail. The man was quite unconscious. From the bazaar he was taken out to the open market place, and tied to a post, in the full blaze of the summer sun. I do not think he lived to see the sun set."[33] By being turned into a public spectacle, prisoners were ostracized by their fellow townspeople and overtly excluded from participation in urban society, which engendered a sense of social belonging among those still included. Prisoners also served as warnings to the townspeople of what might happen if they too transgressed the law or displeased the palace.

Symbolic control over al-Safat became an implicit part of the ongoing struggle between the merchant opposition and the ruler in the late 1930s. In 1938 the majlis banned dancing and drumming within the walls of the city, a move that the Political Agent interpreted as being aimed at the Al Sabah and their constant performance of Bedouin war dances in al-Safat. At the same time, the majlis permitted the playing of radios and gramophones in coffee shops in al-Safat, which the ruler had hitherto forbidden.[34] Radios (tuned mainly to Arab nationalist broadcasts from Egypt, Iraq, and London) played an important role in stimulating Kuwait's populist movement in the late 1930s, and permitting them to be played in coffee shops in the main town square was the majlis's way of spreading its ideas among a wider audience.[35] The majlis thus replaced the pro-ruler 'arda with pro-democracy broadcasts in the town's most public and widely accessible space. In 1939, however, the most notorious public execution in Kuwait Town's history took place in al-Safat, signaling that the contest between the reformists and the palace had officially swung in favor of the ruler. On March 9, Mohammed al-Munayyis, a Kuwaiti grain merchant living in Iraq, distributed leaflets around town proclaiming the Al Sabah deposed and calling upon the public to revolt. The following day al-Munayyis was arrested, sentenced to death as a traitor, "publicly shot, and subsequently hung until evening, in the main square." March 10 ended with Ahmed victoriously leading a war dance in al-Safat.[36] By the 1940s al-Safat had become a reflection of the growing power of the state under the auspices of the Al Sabah, because most government department headquarters—most notably the new Public Security building—were situated there.

But al-Safat was adopted for a new type of public use during this period. Beginning in 1942 the Basra Public Relations traveling cinema came to Kuwait for a couple of nights every few months to screen films, which were projected onto the wall of the Public Security building. At least ten thousand people attended the first of these events, sitting on the ground in the middle of the square to watch the films, and the number of attendees increased each time the cinema came to town.[37] Al-Safat thus became the site of the town's first form of organized public entertainment. Everyone, regardless of background, age, or sex, could and did attend the screenings for free.

Like al-Safat, the *sahel* was also occasionally used for public celebrations that brought the townspeople together in public for a common purpose. Such events included rare official visits by prominent personages, such as Lord Hardinge, the Viceroy of India, in 1915: "All Kuweit was agog with excitement, the beach was crowded with men, women and children of all classes of society, every one awaited eagerly the coming of the great steamer which would bring to Kuweit for the first time in its history a Viceroy of India."[38] More significant in the collective consciousness of the townspeople were the start and end dates of the annual pearling season, when the wives, children, neighbors, and friends of the mariners and divers came out to the shore to bid the pearling vessels goodbye or to welcome them home with much singing and dancing. The *guffal* (closing) celebrations at the end of the season "surpassed all others in scale" and the "atmosphere of joyous anticipation on shore defies description."[39] The *guffal* made the town whole again by bringing thousands of fathers, sons, and brothers back to their families after four difficult months at sea. It was also "a collective acknowledgement of the pivotal position occupied by pearl diving in the economy of the Gulf, bringing as it did employment to the mariners and capital to the merchants."[40]

Aside from such public celebrations, however, for the most part the *sahel* was a place of unplanned and incidental, though not entirely unexpected, encounters. It was the type of public place that the townspeople shared not so much as a symbol of collective belonging but, more simply, "as a matter of fact."[41] Because the *sahel* was, as one townsman described it, Kuwait's "gateway to the outside world," it was one of the busiest spaces in the town year round, crowded with merchants and laborers.[42] People interacted with one another along the *sahel* largely through "marginal encounters" as they went about their busy tasks in the space that guided Kuwait's maritime industries.[43] The town's shipbuilders were always hard at work in the *dhow*-building and repair yards. Depending on the season, the crew of a pearling ship might be getting ready for a voyage or preparing their ship for berthing, and the dancing, singing, and rhythmic clapping that accompanied their arduous work made the *sahel* a very lively place. It was also common for large sections of the coastal strip to be blocked off by men sitting on the ground making sails, and fishermen mending their large nets. If it was the end of the trading season, the vast array of imported goods, ranging from mangrove poles to cartons of tea and bags of rice, would be unloaded directly onto the beach, examined by the importing merchants, then prepared for storage or selling (Figure 5). Another familiar scene along the *sahel* was the mainly Persian water carriers filling kerosene tins or saddle bags with water from the Shatt al-Arab to be delivered to the houses of the town, and women often sat on the beach with empty tins waiting for the *dhows* to arrive so they could buy water for their homes.[44] Groups of women could also normally be found on the shore washing clothes against a shallow breakwater, gathering together in groups to socialize as they worked and waited for their clothes to dry in the sun, with their children swimming in the sea nearby.[45]

Some features of the *sahel* fostered a more deliberate kind of social exchange: spaces for "visiting and being visited" by friends and acquaintances.[46] A string of coffee houses along the beach and at the port gave sailors, fishermen, and ship captains a place to rest from their day's work.[47] Most seafront houses had a *datcha*, a coral and mud bench built out from the front wall and carpeted for seating. From the *datcha*, captains watched their ships and engaged with their crews, old sailors reminisced about their days at sea, merchants watched their wares being unloaded or prepared for

FIGURE 5. Merchants' cargo being unloaded onto the *sahel*. *Source*: Kuwait Oil Company archives.

voyage, all the while exchanging news of the sea and distant ports.[48] Sailors and other townspeople going about their business along the *sahel* would briefly pause to greet these men, for as Villiers learned during his visit to Kuwait in 1939, "the walker . . . must always salute the sitter."[49] Everyday life in the pre-oil town was as much something to watch and discuss as it was something in which to participate.

The most prominent public space in Kuwait Town that fostered "sociality, exchange and encounter with others" was the town *suq*, in which most daily activity was concentrated.[50] Barclay Raunkiaer observed in 1912 that most pedestrian traffic in the town every morning streamed toward the market, then returned into the residential neighborhoods at around noon for lunch and the afternoon rest, then streamed back into the market in the late afternoon until evening.[51] The *suq* was not merely a place to trade and buy one's daily food and supplies. It was also an important space of everyday sociability. "Here is where the great mass of people congregate during the days. It is the hub of the town," wrote one of the American missionaries in 1910.[52] Proprietors treated their shops as small reception rooms, and buyers were treated as guests, invited to sit down for a chat and some tea or coffee from the itinerant bazaar tea seller.[53] Every morning and every afternoon the townspeople were there, "visiting and being visited, drinking coffee, chatting, calling on this merchant and that, and greeting shaikhs and wise men, sitting on carpets outside shops or inside shops, looking on at the teeming life all around . . . listening to good yarns and bad gramophones."[54] The *suq* also played an important role in the social lives of nonaffluent urban women who shopped for their own households, and for women who worked as domestic servants for richer families. Their regular visits to the *suq* gave such women the opportunity to "learn the latest gossip and see the general activities of the town."[55] To supplement the limited incomes of their husbands, some women also worked as traders in the *suq*.

The *suq* was also the main site where the ruler interacted with the public. His *kishk* (the town's first "state" building) was located in the busiest part of the bustling market area, adjacent to the entrance to the vegetable market and occupying the southeast corner of the Money Changers' Square (Figure 6). Official notices relating important political and commercial information—such as the start and end dates of the pearling

FIGURE 6. Mubarak's *kishk* in the heart of the *suq. Source*: Kuwait Oil Company archives.

season, as well as Municipal announcements after 1930—were written out and posted on a wall near the *kishk*.[56] Whenever a new notice was put up, the townspeople would gather around and one of the literate men would read it to the crowd.[57] The *suq* thus offered one of the only means of mass communication—aside from word-of-mouth, which the market also facilitated—before the establishment of local newspapers in the 1940s. As the Political Agent put it in 1938, in the *suq* "nothing is secret."[58] It was where one went to learn the news of the world by reading the foreign newspapers available in the missionaries' Bible shop. Because of the amount of news and views passing through the markets, "no Arab would spend a whole day out of the *suq* if he could avoid it."[59]

Most important, the *suq* was where public opinion was formed and expressed. When in 1932 a young Kuwaiti nationalist took offense at something said at a daily church service in the American missionaries' hospital, he went "up and down the bazaar" complaining about the missionaries.[60] The *suq* was thus the town's primary venue of social and political commentary and debate. In addition to the news and views that spread from shop to shop and market to market, there were also particular places within the *suq* that gave form to the Habermasian public sphere: "the sphere of private people coming together as a public" to freely discuss matters of common good.[61] This "architecture of sociability"[62] included the Ahliyya Library, where dissidents met to discuss politics in the 1930s, and the American missionaries' Bible shop, which was a "casual meeting place of the hot-headed anti-Subah [*sic*] youths of Kuwait."[63] It also included the offices of the Suq al-Tujjar, where the town's social and political elite went to collect donations for their jointly funded services, such as the Mubarakiyya School. The school was also located in the heart of the *suq*, and it became a breeding ground for many of the opposition leaders of the interwar period. In these places the townspeople were free to discuss, debate, and contest the main social and political issues of the day. As the missionaries reported in 1917, they enjoyed "absolute freedom of speech" in their Bible shop, where they and their visitors could "say anything they like."[64]

The Socio-Spatial Organization of Urban Quarters

In addition to being the main centers of everyday activity before oil, the *suq* and the *sahel* also served as poles of expansion for the town's largest morphological sector: the residential areas that extended away from the sea "in two wings," to the east and west of the central port.[65] The town consisted of two main sea-facing quarters (each of which was divided into smaller neighborhoods): Jibla (Qibla) to the west and Sharq to the east. There was also a much smaller third quarter between these two, known as al-Wasat ("the middle"), that directly faced the central port and palace once enclosed within the first town wall. This district contained only a few residential neighborhoods. It was (and still is) often classified as part of Sharq. As the town's population increased, Sharq and Jibla expanded laterally along the coast more rapidly than they spread inland toward the desert, demonstrating the townspeople's need to remain in close proximity to the sea and harbors, and creating the "peculiar length and narrowness" that characterized the town's shape until the early twentieth century (see Figure 1, p. 24).[66]

Although urban growth was largely unplanned in pre-oil Kuwait Town, there was an inner logic to the socio-spatial development of the residential quarters that was in large part determined by the town's two main economic sectors: trading and pearling. Jibla, on the one hand, developed into the hub of the urban oligarchy: the Sunni Najdi merchant elite, such as the Al Ghanim, Al Marzouq, and Al Sager (to name a few), who controlled Kuwait's deep-sea carrying trade. Though as shipowners they were intrinsically dependent on the town's maritime identity as a port, these families did not necessarily make their living directly through seafaring. Rather, they were traders whose businesses were closely connected to other ports around the Gulf and the Indian Ocean. Sharq's inhabitants, on the other hand, were more directly dependent on the sea for their livelihood. Sharq was the hub of the town's pearl trade and was where most of the pearl merchants lived. The majority of the inhabitants of this larger quarter were directly engaged in seafaring, including *nowakhada*, shipbuilders, sailors, and pearl divers.[67] In other words, whereas Jibla was the mercantile quarter, Sharq was the maritime quarter. Though there were some exceptions to this rule, historical tradition preserves this general distinction.[68] Both quarters expanded considerably during the population upsurges of the pearl boom era, though as the main pearling and maritime quarter Sharq absorbed most of the newcomers. An entirely new inland quarter, Mirqab, also emerged during this period, extending southwest of the Abdulrazag Gate and stretching out towards the gypsum quarries well beyond Sahat al-Safat.[69]

The population of Kuwait Town was quite culturally diverse (discussed in Chapter 3), and divided into broad socioeconomic strata. These socioeconomic and cultural differences were not, however, deeply inscribed

onto urban space, neither in the design of residential architecture nor in
the organization of neighborhoods. Houses in the pre-oil town were not
used as projections of social status or as markers of ethnic identity, and they
only minimally displayed a family's individual taste and style. Most houses
looked the same on the outside. Because they shared boundary walls, the
size of a dwelling could really be determined only from the inside. The
houses of the most affluent families had up to five courtyards, each serving
a particular function or part of the house: one for the *diwaniyya* (plural
diwawin), the men's visiting quarters; another for the *harem*, the family
living area; and others for the kitchen, for animals, and sometimes even for
the *'amara*, or storage area. These large houses were compounds containing
many members of an extended family and were most common among the
rich merchants, such as the Al Ghunaim and Al Bader houses in Jibla and
the Al Nusif and Ma'rafi houses in Sharq. Middle-income families usually
had no more than three courtyards, and the least affluent houses often
had only one or two courtyards that had to accommodate a multitude
of functions (Figure 7). The quality of life inside the less affluent houses
was significantly lower than in the larger merchant houses. The American
missionary doctors had the opportunity to enter a wide variety of family

FIGURE 7. A regular courtyard house before oil. *Source*: Kuwait Oil Company archives.

homes in Kuwait and one of them observed in 1914, "The rich have houses that are airy, and, to a fair degree, clean. Their habits of life are reasonably hygienic, in outward things. The poorer classes, on the contrary . . . are dirty to a degree scarcely believable . . . their homes present a chaos quite indescribable."[70]

These differences were discernible only from the inside. The uniform shape and style of the urban form was due partly to the scarcity of building materials in Kuwait. The vast majority of houses were made of mudbrick, and because mudbrick was relatively weak and vulnerable to collapse (particularly under heavy rainfall) most houses were single-story because the walls could not hold up a second level.[71] The ceilings were made from mangrove poles (*chandal*) imported from east Africa that spanned the width of each room. These beams were imported precut to a uniform length of 3.6 meters, so practically every structure in Kuwait had to be built to the same maximum width. Most houses contained very little external ornamentation, and only a few markers of social difference could be traced in residential architecture. During the prosperous years of the turn of the twentieth century, the richer merchant families began constructing their homes out of coral rock (the most expensive building material at that time).[72] The color of the house was also telling: the town's more well-to-do homes along the seafront were whitewashed in gypsum plaster whereas the less affluent houses further inland maintained the original color of the mudbrick. The design of the main front doors—the type of wood and nails used, the decorative carvings, and thickness—was also an indicator of the affluence of the household behind the door.[73] Though some socioeconomic differences could thus be detected on a house's exterior, cultural differences based on ethnic or religious background were hardly ever inscribed onto residential architecture.

Nor did social and cultural differences within urban society explicitly translate into socio-spatial segregation, though some discernible trends in the distribution of urban society in residential areas certainly existed. Jibla was the town's trading quarter and was predominantly occupied by the ship-owning merchant elite. It was the most socially and economically exclusive of the urban quarters, though some middle-income families also lived there. Its inhabitants were mainly of Najdi origin, with a few Persian residents. Sharq was the town's maritime and pearling quarter. Because it absorbed most of the newcomers to the town throughout the late nineteenth and early twentieth centuries, it became the largest and most culturally heterogeneous district, housing families from the highest to the lowest of the town's socioeconomic strata. It contained Najdis, Farsi-speaking Arabs, Baharna (Shi'a from Bahrain), Kanadra, Hasawiyya (Shi'i Arabs from al-Ahsa), and recently settled Bedouin, among others. Its inhabitants were sailors, pearl divers, shipbuilders, *nowakhada*, and even wealthy merchants, though fewer than in Jibla. Mirqab, the inland quarter, was by contrast a relatively homogeneous place composed predominantly of Najdi Arabs who were mostly laborers working in land-based industries such as construction. But just as Jibla contained some less affluent families, Mirqab also contained a few well-to-do households, such as the Al Shaye'.[74]

Most of the town's rich people lived along the seafront of both Jibla and Sharq, whereas the poorest residents lived "on the sand dunes" at the back of town, away from the sea.[75] However, this distribution was not so much the result of an explicit act of ghettoization by the town's elite as much as it was engendered by the need for certain groups to retain contact with the water. People with direct links to the port and the town's fleet—shipowners, *nowakhada*, and *dhow*-builders—tended to live along or near the water in order to remain in close proximity to the harbor, their ships berthed in the *inga'*, and the *dhow* repair yards.[76] Construction workers, porters, sailors, and divers did not need constant access to the town's ships (except, of course, when the latter were at sea), so they lived further inland. Shopkeepers and petty traders lived closer to the *suq*, sometimes on residential streets behind their own shops. Many of Mirqab's residents were *juss* (gypsum mortar) manufacturers who worked in the quarries at the edge of town.[77] In other words, where one lived was often determined by the source of one's livelihood. The distribution of the town's population in certain areas was also largely an outcome of immigration trends and patterns of economic growth. When the town was first settled, it extended laterally along the coast; the oldest families therefore lived closest to the water. During the economic boom of the turn of the twentieth century, new areas were created further inland to accommodate the constantly arriving newcomers, who were primarily mariners and laborers.

Neighborhood Networks

Jibla, Sharq, and Mirqab were subdivided into smaller neighborhoods known as *firjan* (singular *farij*). The *firjan* were not separated by clear boundary lines, nor were they walled or gated like the quarters of other Arab cities. It is often stated anecdotally that the boundary of a *farij* in Kuwait Town was determined by how far the voice of a mosque's *imam* (prayer leader) could carry in the days before amplifiers.[78] Each neighborhood therefore consisted of a small cluster of ten or twelve courtyard houses. But the town's *firjan* were not just residential areas. In the absence of state services, they also played an important public role in everyday urban life. They were, however, beyond the scope of palace control. Although it was part of the ruler's purview to settle trade disputes and administer justice, private disputes within a *farij* were often settled by the *imam* of the local mosque, or by a neighborhood elder to whom the residents would turn for advice, guidance, or arbitration.[79] These individuals, such as Hamad al-Rushoud in Farij al-Sabt in Jibla, were usually selected for their intellectual capacity rather than for their financial standing. These local problem solvers settled conflicts over shared walls and other disputes between neighbors.[80] They did not, however, serve as official intermediaries between the ruler and the public, because the townspeople had direct access to the ruler in his daily *majlis* in the *suq*.[81] Only on rare occasions did the ruler intervene in domestic affairs. When Dr. Mylrea of the American missionaries' hospital learned that a teenage girl named Aziza had been locked up by her family in a small room in her house for flirting with a neighbor's son, he appealed to the ruler Mubarak I to free her. But Mubarak refused. "I never interfere in these domestic matters of honour," he said. "The decision rests with the people of the house. It is their absolute right, from the very beginning of Arab history." It was only after the Political Agent got involved that Mubarak reluctantly sent his guards to the house with orders for the girl's release.[82]

The inability of the government to intrude in *farij* affairs meant that the local inhabitants were responsible for the provision of many public services. When someone in the *farij* died, for example, the men of the area went to the local cemetery to dig and prepare the grave for burial.[83] Orphans were usually adopted into the family of the unofficial "head" of the quarter if the children did not have any extended family to take care of them.[84] Beyond the realm of general social welfare, ensuring the safety and security of the neighborhood was also the responsibility of its inhabitants. By 1930 it was reported that the town contained no police force other than the dozen watchmen who patrolled the *suq* at night.[85] The ruler's guards (*fedawiyya*) were responsible solely for guarding the ruler and palace and for meting out punishment when someone was caught committing a crime. This they sometimes did with much gusto, as in 1920 when a young man was dragged through the streets and beaten "in a degrading and brutal manner" by the guards even before he had been brought to the ruler for sentencing.[86] However, the *fedawiyya* were not responsible for actually policing the town. Rather, the monitoring of public order came under the informal jurisdiction of the *farij*. Everyone knew their neighbors and regular visitors to the area, and a newcomer could easily be spotted.[87] Strangers passing through a *farij* were looked upon with suspicion and would be closely watched until they made their way out again, and younger men ran the risk of being harassed by local youth gangs. One man recalled that during his early teens he would always take the sea road when crossing Jibla to the *suq* alone, and he would only take the shorter route, along the inner *sikik* (small streets, singular *sikka*), if his father accompanied him, to avoid getting beaten up.[88] Similarly, Ahmed al-Khatib (who became a prominent political figure in the 1950s) was once thrown into the sea, even though he was a child, by a group of boys who identified him as a stranger when he passed through their neighborhood near the seafront.[89] Treating the *farij* and its *sikik* as private spaces to be carefully guarded was not a phenomenon reserved for gangs of teenage boys. Soon after Bessie Mylrea, one of the American missionaries, arrived in Kuwait, she walked through a neighborhood where some local women standing outside a doorway stared at her and ridiculed her in voices deliberately loud enough for her to hear until she passed. Once they got used to seeing her, however, they invited her into their homes whenever she walked by.[90]

Maintaining the cleanliness of the town was also a collective task that fell under the jurisdiction of the individual neighborhoods. Nearly all travelers to Kuwait between the late eighteenth and early twentieth centuries noted that the town was extremely clean and hygienic.[91] Public responsibilities like street cleaning, garbage collection, and road repairs resided with the residents of the *farij*. Each family regularly swept the area in front of their own front door, and because houses were located very close to one another, the entire street got swept regularly. Households produced very little waste: food was rarely thrown out and the only items that needed to be discarded were organic materials such as bones and human waste. These were collected in large pits in each *farij*, then disposed of in the sea. Women handled many of these neighborhood responsibilities. According to Saif Abbas Dehrab, on the basis of his memories of his mother, "When Kuwaiti men were out at sea, it was the women who had to manage the family affairs, make sure that intruders would not come to the neighborhood, and even keep up the house renovations."[92] Education was another public service provided primarily by the *farij*. Until the establishment of the Mubarakiyya School, young boys and girls went to school in the private home of a local *mutawa'a*, or religious instructor. The *mutawa'a* schools received no official state support, nor were they under any form of government control. They were established by individual men and women and funded through small fees paid by the local parents.[93]

When he came to power in 1917, Salem al-Mubarak tried to organize the residential quarters into more official administrative units under the leadership of a guardian, or *mukhtar*, responsible for maintaining "law, order, and decency, including sanitary conditions," as well as for keeping an eye on strangers and suspicious or illicit activities.[94] Although such tasks already fell under the responsibility of each *farij*, by appointing an official *mukhtar*, Salem sought to have more direct involvement in such local affairs. However, his attempt to formally organize the town's *firjan* did not have any long-lasting results, and it was not until the establishment of the Municipality in 1930 that certain tasks such as sanitation became more coordinated. The Municipality and Education Council reduced the importance of the *farij* in providing public services at a local level. By the 1930s more people were sending their children to the larger state-run schools built for the boys and girls of the broader urban quarter—such as the Ahmadiyya School in Jibla and the Sharqiyya School in Sharq—because of their more extensive curricula and better facilities. Eventually the local *mutawa'a* schools closed down. The central cleanliness and hygiene services provided by the Municipality meanwhile improved upon the local services provided by the *farij*. Within weeks of the Municipality's inception, nearly five thousand tons of accumulated street refuse had been removed from the inner neighborhoods. A communal receptacle for the discarding of household waste was installed on street corners within each *farij*. It was then collected by a municipal cart to be permanently disposed of. The Municipal Council hired sweepers and built water-spraying carts to clean the town's streets.[95] The improvements to the townscape were immediately noticeable; in 1933 Dr. Mylrea wrote that "never in its history has Kuwait been as clean as it is today."[96]

In some instances, however, the replacement of neighborhood support with citywide welfare had its drawbacks. In 1939 a new central orphanage was established under an appointed director. Political Agent Gerald de Gaury believed that children there would be "treated more impersonally, and possibly less well" than when they were taken in by the *farij*.[97]

The Municipality and local courts also became more closely involved in the arbitration of local property disputes. When a conflict arose between Abdulrahman al-Bahar and Mohammed al-Qadha over two walls (the latter believed that both belonged to him but the former disagreed), both the Municipality and the courts had to intervene to settle the matter that previously would have been dealt with internally at the *farij* level.[98] The increased level of bureaucratic intervention in the internal affairs of the townspeople led to the reduction of neighborhood involvement in the provision of community services.

Straddling the Public-Private Divide

As residential neighborhoods, the *firjan* were technically privatized spaces, but their role in urban governance and everyday welfare created overlaps between their private and public functions. Various aspects of residential life also blurred the lines between public and private life in the pre-oil town, although the architecture and layout of the urban landscape seemed to emphasize the importance of privacy. The town's inward-oriented courtyard houses, narrow streets, and high walls are commonly attributed in popular and scholarly discourse to restrictions imposed by prevailing Islamic social mores: the requirements of family privacy, sexual propriety, and gender segregation.[99] The spatial segregation of men and women is a feature commonly observed in many Arab or so-called "Islamic" cities, but Kuwait's maritime nature added a more specific requirement to this arrangement. Because they were not involved in maritime activities, urban women were left alone in the town for several months at a time as their fathers, husbands, brothers, and sons went on pearling and trading voyages. Haya al-Mughni contends that, in addition to keeping men and women apart, Kuwait Town's courtyard houses were specifically designed by men to seclude, conceal, and protect their women during the men's prolonged absences from town.[100]

Many features of the town's spatial design seemingly "announced the basic cultural concept of the separation of male and female society."[101] Houses were spatially divided between the *diwaniyya* for the men and the *harem* for the women, with separate courtyards for each. The *diwaniyya* was the more "open and accessible part of the house," with its own entrance, usually from a main street. The private living quarters had more discrete entrances situated on the "blank plaster walls" of the *farij*'s narrow, inner lanes, which "shielded" the women of the household from the "public gaze" of visitors and passers-by.[102] This "line-of-sight" requirement, the objective of which was to maintain "visual privacy" between the sexes, gave rise to architectural features that were common in many Arab-Islamic cities: windows on outer walls situated high up, entrance doors on either side of the street not directly facing each other, long corridors and curtain walls placed inside the entrance to prevent immediate visual access to the *harem* courtyard, and so on.[103] One of the American missionary women's account of the reaction of a close Kuwaiti friend to the Mission's new residence provides some insight into the *harem's* confinement:

[She] was much interested in the arrangement of the rooms and the lovely, open view out to sea. She gasped all of a sudden, 'Oh! why don't we build our houses like this!' I told her that it was because their women were so afraid of being seen. She clapped one hand over her fist and said, 'Our men shut us up—what can we do?'[104]

Though the spatial features of the urban complex support the idea that female containment was a paramount concern before oil, there are two problems with overemphasizing the connection between gender segregation and the pre-oil urban form. First, the existing literature's focus on the built environment as a means to understand gender relations and the female condition in pre-oil Kuwait Town has distorted the realities of women's experiences.[105] Though segregation may have been the aim, many households could not afford to have two separate courtyards, one for a male-only reception area and the other for the family's living quarters. The strict separation of the sexes in residential areas was usually possible only for the town's richest families. Furthermore, everyday practice and human agency often contradicted the restrictions imposed by the built environment. Kuwaiti urban women did not always remain in spaces that could offer them "maximum protection" from public gaze and they were hardly confined to the *harem*.[106] They often went out together for picnics at the edge of town, where they would eat, dance, sing, and laugh from morning until the early evening.[107] The missionary women also received regular visits in their homes from Kuwaiti women of all social classes:

I thought perhaps the reason for their coming so freely to see me was that we were living in an Arab house, and they felt they could be as secluded there as in their own houses, but since we have moved into the new mission house, which is up on a hill with an open view, I have had a great many callers, women from our new neighborhood and some of my old friends.[108]

Some of the missionaries' visitors came to see them openly, with the knowledge of the men of their households. Others did so secretly, suggesting that these women must have had certain levels of independence within the urban complex, no doubt enhanced by the long-term absence of most of the townsmen. The anonymity offered by the traditional black 'abat (robe) and veil that women wore outside the house also allowed for some freedom in public spaces. When travel writer Freya Stark was in Kuwait in 1937, she visited some female friends whose grandfather was "a bigoted old man who objected to anyone of his family leaving the Harim at all." But as soon as he went out for the day, the women of the house were able to go out themselves, for "once clothed for the street . . . no one could possibly tell his own daughter from another."[109] As Dr. Mylrea wrote in his memoirs, "There is a great deal that goes on in the women's quarters of the house that the men never know about."[110]

Even within the confines of the courtyard house, physical barriers were not insurmountable, as demonstrated by the story of the aforementioned fourteen-year-old girl named Aziza, who was known to be "a trifle bold with the boys, calling them from the roof as they walked past the house down below [on] the street."[111] The girl's family discovered that she was exchanging romantic notes with a neighbor's son. "How a girl protected by the walls of a Muslim's hareem could find opportunity for flirting was a mystery to me," Dr. Eleanor Calverley wondered in her memoirs.[112] But the fact that Aziza could call out to boys from the roof and was able to exchange notes with a young man by way of this access to the street hardly gives the impression that the girl was entirely isolated from the outside world (nor does the fact that she was literate). Such realities contradict the grim yet common assumption that "Kuwaiti women lived under the constraining physical and social conditions often associated with orthodox Muslim female conditions of the past: secluded, veiled, and overwhelmingly illiterate, they were married at puberty to a male relative, and their social horizon was limited to the immediate neighborhood of their homes."[113]

The second problem with focusing primarily on gender segregation to explain the urban form of the pre-oil townscape is that it leaves out other key determinants contributing to the town's "extremely compact and low rise" scale,[114] such as climate or available building materials.[115] The town was built to the scale of the pedestrian because everyone walked everywhere and only a few people rode donkeys. The built environment needed to protect people from the strong sun, from the severe sandstorms that were common in the spring, and from the "sudden and devastating" winter rains.[116] House walls were extremely thick and windows to the street were scarce, which prevented the heat from penetrating the dwelling. The rooms of a house were built around a central courtyard with colonnaded *liwawin* (corridors, singular *liwan*) separating the yard from the indoor spaces. Cooling breezes were caught by wind towers, and roofs were built to slope slightly toward the street so that rainwater could flow off through wooden waterspouts projected from the top of the single-story structures. To prevent flooding, most neighborhoods contained a well for the accumulation of rainwater, which was then used collectively by the local residents for various non-drinking purposes.[117] Courtyard houses were built close together and had high boundary walls. The narrow *sikik* that this layout created provided the walker with shade from the sun and cover from sand and rain (Figure 8).

FIGURE 8. Women making their way in shade through the town's narrow, winding streets. *Source*: Kuwait Oil Company archives.

Although several studies claim that "privacy" was "the main cultural definer" dictating the creation of a particular architectural vernacular in historic Kuwait Town,[118] a closer analysis of how townspeople used their neighborhood spaces reveals that the strict delineation between public and private space and life within the *farij* was anything but straightforward. The social life of the neighborhood was intimately integrated with the private life of the home. Practical needs at the level of everyday experience made people use spaces in ways that often contradicted the alleged quest for family privacy and female seclusion. Most people in Kuwait slept on their roof in the hottest summer months, because it was cooler than sleeping indoors. Although each family was on top of its own private domestic space, sleeping in the open air with nothing but a low parapet wall between neighbors rendered the strict privacy of the individual home somewhat tenuous. The imagery used by members of Kuwait's urban population when recalling this custom reveals that rooftop sleeping was a sensory experience. Neighbors were closely connected to one another through shared nightly sounds like the rhythmic singing of sailors (who in the hot weather tended to work on their boats in the cooler night hours) along the seafront,[119] and the regular cry of "*sahy?*" ("awake?") from the *suq* guards calling out to one another to make sure no one was sleeping on duty. Residents of houses with shared walls were able to hear their neighbors' voices, so they avoided making noise while out on the roof at night (Figure 9).[120]

The *farij* thus blurred the line between public and private spaces in the pre-oil town. Residents often treated the narrow corridors between houses (the *madraban*), the inner *sikik* of the *farij*, and the local *baraha*—a small square where several *sikik* met—as "semi-private spaces" used almost exclusively by neighbors.[121] In these spaces, the children of the surrounding households played, women sold snacks to local families from mats on the ground, *farij* men met to chat with neighbors, and so on. Women often passed through these semi-private spaces without being completely covered. Janet Abu-Lughod argues that the practicalities of everyday urban life in many Arab cities often made such "spillover space" within residential areas necessary, particularly for less affluent families, who had limited space inside their own homes.[122]

Even the town's seemingly most inviolable space, the courtyard house, was not entirely private. Though the unofficial "privatization of public space" is no longer an unexpected condition found in historic studies of Arab cities, the publicizing of private spaces is somewhat less explored.[123]

FIGURE 9. Rooftops of the town's *firjan. Source*: Kuwait Oil Company archives.

As already seen, rooftops made private spaces more public. In addition to giving women greater access to the outside world and connecting neighbors with one another when they slept outdoors, rooftops also provided clear views into neighboring courtyards. One Kuwaiti woman recalled that when they were young she and her sisters and their friends regularly spied on their neighbors (members of the Al Sabah) from their adjacent roof.[124] Similarly, in 1937, from the vantage point of a neighboring roof, Stark and some Shi'i friends observed *'ashura* (a Shi'i day of mourning) rituals taking place inside another courtyard house. They secured a "perfect position for seeing" the events below while the women in the courtyard remained "unconscious of being observed."[125]

A common residential feature that diminished the absolute privacy that each house could retain was a small door known as the *firya* that led from one *harem* courtyard directly into the neighbor's *harem* courtyard. Neighborhood women and children often used the *firya* to pass from one house to the other more quickly than by using the road.[126] The courtyard houses thus became semi-public spaces used as shortcuts and accessways between neighbors. Although it was mainly women, children, and servants who used these connecting doors between the houses, it was not uncommon for men to be present in the house when female neighbors came in through the *firya*, and women did not always cover their faces around the men of their neighbor's house. One man confessed during an interview that he had thus fallen in love with his neighbor's daughter.[127] Though the *harem* might have been a predominantly private space, for close neighbors it was only a semi-private space.

Although the spatial separation of the *diwaniyya* from the *harem* might seemingly emphasize the rigid separation of private and public spheres, in fact the *diwaniyya* further blurred the public/private divide within the *farij*. On certain nights of the week a particular household would open their *diwaniyya* to male visitors. Because most of the houses in the town were not big enough to have such separate areas, the institution was more common among the affluent families and those who lived in close proximity to them. The *diwaniyya* was where men went to socialize, discuss business, ask for favors from merchants or other notables, and debate political issues. Though the *diwaniyya* was physically attached to a private home, social custom dictated that no visitor could be turned away at the door, making it a public gathering place within the *farij*. The *diwaniyya* was also a space where the town's notables debated public issues. Members of the ruling family often attended the *diwawin* of prominent families, and in these spaces the men spoke frankly about their political opinions, misgivings, and grievances, knowing that these would be disseminated to the ruler. The *diwaniyya* thus played a vital role in allowing the merchants to maintain their access to decision-making. In 1923, for example, when Ibn Sa'ud demanded the collection of Najdi customs in Kuwait as a condition for reopening trade between the two territories, Ahmed al-Jaber invited five of the town's leading notables to his audience chamber along with two members of his own family to discuss the issue. The notables believed that the question of reopening trade with Najd warranted an even wider consultation with all of the town's big merchants. The following day a larger meeting of twenty-one notables was held in the *diwaniyya* of a leading merchant, Hamad al-Khalid, without any members of the Al Sabah present in order to debate the issue before taking the group's collective opinion to the ruler.[128]

The location of *diwawin* in private homes thus integrated the public political life of the town into the social and domestic space of the neighborhood. This integration of multiple functions and daily activities in the town's various morphological sectors created a vibrant everyday life in which people were constantly confronted by a diversity of experiences, people, and ways of living. This lack of coherence in the patterns and practices of everyday life, and the blurred lines between the public and the private, compelled the townspeople to interact directly with one another in various ways throughout their daily activities. This spatial intimacy both effected and reflected the considerable social intimacy of Kuwait's urban community before oil.

3

A Cosmopolitan Community

Port City Cosmopolitanism

Everyday life in Kuwait Town before oil was characterized by the spatial and behavioral overlapping and integration of different people and activities. Daily life consisted of multiple journeys between various kinds of "group life": from the ship to the *farij* to the *suq* to the *diwaniyya*. Not everyone had access to all of these various activities and social groups, and each piece of this "city mosaic" had a distinct function and character. However, they all depended on one another for the city's overall survival. As Richard Sennett argues, "This was what made life urban," particularly in times of scarcity. He calls the multiple social regions that city dwellers had to penetrate in the course of their daily activities "contact points."[1] It was through these diverse points of contact with different people and groups that the townspeople entered into social relations in and with the city. People needed diversity in their lives because none of the institutions or groups in which they lived—their family, their *farij*, their professional or ethnic group—was capable of self-support. The family depended on the *farij*, the *farij* on the merchants, the merchants on their own family networks, and so on, and various interactions occurred within and between these groups. People developed multiple and complex loyalties and affiliations that cut across ethnic and socioeconomic subcultures. This diversity prevented the development of an easy "myth of solidarity" among the townspeople.[2] Nonetheless, they did share a strong sense of community: a feeling of being related and bound together in some way. These communal bonds were based on shared experiences. People felt connected to one another not through an image of being the same as each other, but through what they actually did in their concrete relations with each other, which were largely shaped by their need for mutual support. In this context, there was no impetus to create a sense of communal relatedness based on social or cultural similarity.[3] In fact, Kuwaiti society before oil was characterized by its hybridity, its acceptance of difference, and its curiosity and desire to explore the unknown.

"Port functions," Rhoads Murphy claims, "more than anything else, made a city cosmopolitan, a word which does not necessarily mean 'sophisticated' but rather hybrid. . . . A port city is open to the world, or at least to a varied section of it. In it races, cultures, and ideas as well as goods from a variety of places jostle, mix, and enrich each other and the life of the city."[4] The variety and simultaneity of activities that took place within the town's main morphological sectors, as described in Chapter 2, allowed for constant interaction, however marginally, with different people and ways of life. As everyday spaces of informal encounter, the *suq* and *sahel* brought diverse social groups together in a shared space. The *suq* was a public space of social and commercial exchange that was equally accessible to everybody in town—including foreign visitors. The *nowakhada* spent most of their time there when they were back in their home port, as did the poorer sailors and pearl divers who "swagger[ed] in the *suq*, dressed in their best clothes, swinging their canes and their rosaries, sitting in the coffee-shops, drinking from the hookas, visiting and exchanging stories."[5] Sahat al-Safat, as the site of the Bedouin market, was the only space that townsman and tribesman shared equally, and it was where the two communities freely mixed and interacted as mutual subjects of the Al Sabah. This intermingling of people of diverse backgrounds and classes, including foreign merchants and Bedouin traders, in the town's public spaces made Kuwaitis accustomed to negotiating difference in their everyday lives. Their travels to various ports around the region and to market towns of the interior also made them open to different cultures and religions, which shaped the town's cosmopolitanism. Kuwait traded extensively with Iran, Yemen, India, and East Africa, and its merchants and mariners spent months at a time in ports around the western Indian Ocean basin during the nine-month trading season. The Kuwaiti townspeople were heavily influenced by these various cultures, particularly in such areas as language, food, music, and architecture. They often picked up customs and habits from the places they visited, such as smoking "the Persian Nargeilah . . . and the Turkish Cheebook."[6]

Kuwait was known for being a friendly and accepting place; the success of its port economy hinged on this trait. In a highly competitive region where ports regularly rose and fell in commercial prominence, Kuwait had to be a place with which people from other regions such as India and East Africa wanted to trade. British Political Resident Lewis Pelly noted in 1865 that the town's inhabitants enjoyed complete religious tolerance.[7] The majority of Kuwait's population was Muslim, particularly Sunni Muslim, but in a way that was "tolerant to others and not over rigid to themselves."[8] Pelly found them to be "far less bigoted than in the interior."[9] A telling episode occurred during the Battle of Jahra between Kuwait and the Ikhwan tribes in 1920. When Salem al-Mubarak and his forces were besieged in the Red Fort, the Ikhwan sent an emissary with potential terms for peace. He told Salem that they had been surprised to hear the Kuwaiti forces "praying like Muslims, as they had always been led to suppose that the people of Kuwait were infidels." To bring peace, Salem must prohibit all smoking, drinking, gambling, and prostitution in Kuwait. He also demanded that Salem declare the Ottoman Turks heretics and that Kuwait adopt the puritanical Ikhwan doctrine. Salem refused to adhere to these terms, and the battle resumed, until reinforcements from Kuwait Town ultimately drove the Ikhwan away.[10] This incident reveals the difference between life in Kuwait and in the landlocked Arabian interior. Indeed, when Lebanese-American writer and traveler Amin Rihani visited Kuwait in 1922 after a trip to Najd, he wrote that "Kuwait is a city that makes you forget Riyadh. It is the Paris of Arabia. There is smoking, there is whiskey, there is a patency of women. There is a doctor and a hospital; yes, a doctor and a hospital."[11]

The hospital to which Rihani referred was founded in 1910 by the Reformed Church in America's Arabian Mission. The missionaries opened a small school to which many local families sent their children, and they held Sunday services in Arabic in a house at the center of town that local men, women, and children attended regularly. The missionaries established close ties with the community, and over the next thirty years thousands of Kuwaitis "became familiar with the sayings and doings of Jesus."[12] The missionaries faced opposition from the town's religious mullahs, or scholars, who warned the public during Friday sermons against attending their hospitals and schools.[13] This preaching had little impact on people's attitudes toward the missionaries; townspeople of all classes befriended the

American families and were curious about their cultural customs and religious practices.[14] The missionaries were not successful, however, in openly converting many townspeople, who remained vehemently opposed to apostasy. In 1920, when news that a young man had taken Communion reached the *suq*, "public opinion stiffened against him. No one would give him employment and he had difficulty in buying sugar and tea and other necessities. . . . There could be no sympathy with an apostate."[15] Nonetheless, Kuwaitis were not averse to engaging the missionaries in religious discussion and debate in public, whether during their Church services, on the verandah of the hospital while waiting to be treated, or in the Mission's Bible shop located opposite the main *suq* mosque.

Alongside Kuwait's comparatively stable political and commercial environments, this cultural tolerance regularly attracted newcomers from around the region to Kuwait. The majority of townspeople were Sunnis of Najdi extraction and mixed tribal background. But the population also included Africans, Persians (both Sunni and Shi'i but mostly the latter), Hasawiyya, Baharna, Zubairis, Beluchis, Jews, and Armenians. Added to this mix by the early twentieth century were a handful of Arab and American Christian missionaries and a small number of British political agency personnel (and, after 1934, the Anglo-American oil company staff). In 1904, Africans (two-thirds of whom were slaves) were the largest minority population, at around 11 percent of the 35,000 townspeople, followed by Persians, who made up 3 percent. In the same year, the 'Utub, the town's social elite, numbered less than 1 percent. Other groups were also very small: Jews made up .5 percent, and there were two documented Armenians.[16] Still, for religious minorities, Kuwait was something of a safe haven in the region: most of its Jewish families came from Iraq after Sadeq Khan's siege of Basra in 1776, and many Assyrian Christians fled to Kuwait from Anatolia in the early twentieth century to escape Ottoman persecution.[17]

Ethnic and religious minorities did not pay separate or additional taxes in Kuwait as they did in Arab cities under Ottoman administration, and all had the right to own property. Members of the Shi'i community reported to the British Political Agent in 1918 that they had always received impartial treatment and justice from the authorities and were considered equal to Sunnis in the eyes of the law.[18] Some unofficial lines of demarcation existed nonetheless. Although the town's residential quarters were not spatially divided into ethnic enclaves, Shi'a, Christians, and Jews had separate cemeteries, and there were also one Jewish and three Persian schools.[19] Intermarriage between religious or ethnic groups was rare. One exception was when a man from a prominent household married one of his female slaves (a move most common among members of the ruling family). There was also a mild sectarian division of labor in the town. Pearl divers tended to be of African or Bedouin origin, most shipbuilders were Baharna, the *suq* guards were Beluchi, and the majority of Kuwaiti Jews were cloth sellers and goldsmiths (as well as liquor distillers). Most of the town's water carriers and port laborers, meanwhile, were Shi'i, though not all Shi'a were "penniless laborers" and they included well-to-do merchants and middle class shopkeepers and artisans.[20] Some of these families—particularly those of the prominent trading houses, such as the Behbehani—maintained business ties to their places of origin in Iran; many also spoke Farsi.[21]

Indeed, identities of origin were important to immigrant groups and they often classified themselves and others according to where they originally came from. This sometimes applied to individual families, such as the Al Hasawi, Bastaki, and Al Najdi, as well as to whole communities, such as the Beluchis or Baharna. However, such monikers did not signal social exclusion or the absence of a sense of belonging to Kuwait Town. As Nelida Fuccaro argues, there was no single term for "immigrant" in the cultural lexicon of the pre-oil Gulf, because immigrants were diverse.[22] Neither did the term *Kuwaiti* (as a signifier of collective identity) often appear in local sources before oil. (More common was the phrase *ahl al-Kuwayt*, or the "people of Kuwait.") There was no indigenous population before the arrival of the 'Utub, unlike in Bahrain, and everyone in Kuwait came from somewhere else. Kuwaiti urban society was, in other words, made up entirely of immigrants. Dress, taste, or other forms of material culture, as well as family names, often distinguished members of particular communities, but these signals did not indicate that such groups were excluded from full participation in Kuwaiti society. Rather, they revealed "a system of coexisting communities: each community at variance with each other in its opinions, customs, and beliefs, while nevertheless respecting the autonomy of the other."[23] People were not obligated to subsume their own traditions and backgrounds in order to fit into one consensual, monovocal cultural identity. The multiplicity of languages, tastes, and styles was precisely what created the social life and cultural milieu of Kuwait as a port town. Its very identity was the fact that it was a hybrid place, and from this "imperfect cosmopolitan dissensus" emerged a tolerant and open society, bound together not by an imagined collective—and consensual—identity but rather by their everyday interactions and mutual modes of living.[24]

In spite of their cultural differences, the townspeople were "closely united, and free from feuds and factions," as British official A. B. Kemball noted in 1845.[25] Kuwaiti historical memory corroborates this claim. Ahmed al-Khatib, who was born in 1928, writes in his 2007 memoir that "social ties were based on intimate friendship and brotherhood, without conscious divisions or discrimination."[26] This sense of togetherness is often attributed to the townsmen's experiences on board Kuwait's ships. The crews of the trading and, particularly, pearling vessels were of mixed social backgrounds: in 1904 around 1,500 to 2,000 of the 9,200 men on board the Kuwaiti pearling fleet were of Persian origin.[27] These men spent up to five months together away from their homeport every year, living in very close proximity to one another and working closely as a team. The adverse conditions of the pearling experience created an intimacy and interdependence among the crew that, it is said, informed these men's social interactions on land.[28] Some of the crew members of Kuwaiti ships were not permanent residents of the town. A significant portion were semi-nomadic Bedouin who temporarily camped their families inside the walls of Kuwait Town during the pearling season. Men from other towns around the region also joined the crews of Kuwaiti vessels.[29] Their experiences at sea therefore taught Kuwaitis how to coexist with difference.

The absence of both legal distinctions and sectarian strife may also have stemmed from the size of the diverse minority groups permanently residing within Kuwait Town. The relatively small number of Shi'a, Jews, Africans, Armenians, and so on was unthreatening to the Sunni Najdi majority, making it easier (in contrast to what transpired after the advent of oil) for such groups to be accepted and integrated into the urban population. The first signs of discrimination against the Shi'a emerged only after their community grew substantially in size. In 1904 the Shi'i population constituted only a thousand of the town's thirty-five thousand people.[30] From around 1910 onward, however, Kuwait Town witnessed a large influx of Persian artisans and laborers who were attracted by the high wages of the pearl boom era.[31] By 1918 the Shi'a numbered fifteen thousand out of a total town population of fifty thousand.[32] It was during this population upsurge that the Shi'a first showed signs of social discontent.[33] It was not until 1938, however, that sectarian tensions became more tangible. The fourteen members elected to the *majlis* (legislative assembly) that year were not representative of the town's population: they were all part of the Sunni Najdi merchant elite. Only the Shi'a, whose numbers had reached an estimated eighteen thousand, appealed for representation, but the notables did all they could to block their participation, saying that "Kuwait was Arab territory, and that they wanted to keep it as such, free from Persian intrigue and influence."[34] These sentiments possibly stemmed from the Iraqi Arab nationalist influence over the Kuwaiti movement. The Shi'a in Iraq had been increasingly marginalized by the rise of Arab nationalism throughout the interwar period. According to Reeva Simon, the nationalists propagated a belief that "Shi'ism was a subversive heresy motivated by Persian hatred for the Arabs and a threat to Arab nationalism."[35] Many Kuwaiti merchants sent their sons to study in Iraqi schools during this period, and the leaders of the 1938 *majlis* movement had close links with Iraqi nationalists. Their lack of representation in the *majlis* made the Shi'a anxious. "Under the one-man rule of the Shaikh the Shi'as were at any rate no worse off than the Sunnis. . . . With the coming of the [entirely Sunni] Council however . . . they feel that they are unlikely to get a square deal."[36] These tensions dissipated once the assembly was dissolved. However, the incident was the first sign of the level of social discrimination and exclusion that was to come a decade later with the advent of oil and the rapid influx of new immigrants to Kuwait.

Mutual Support

The close unity and intimacy that the townspeople felt before oil was not based on any notions of their social similarity. People knew they were different from one another and did not hide their differences through the construction of a singular idea of being "Kuwaiti." Rather, their social relatedness and sense of community were based on their shared experiences and everyday relations with one another. These experiences were largely based on the need for mutual support. Everyday life before oil was not easy. The climate was harsh, and basic resources such as water and food were scarce. The town's main economic industries were labor intensive, and most of the town's male population was absent for long periods of time on trading and pearling voyages. The economy was also based on a debilitating system of debt, and the majority of households lived a relatively meager existence. The rulers had no revenue stream to provide the townspeople with any kind of material support. The most the palace could do was offer food every evening to anyone, resident and visitor alike, who needed a meal. Jaber I (r. 1814–59) initiated this custom that, as Lewis Pelly observed in 1863, "may perhaps account for much of the peace, good will, and neighborhood, and mercantile prosperity of this town."[37] But it was not enough. The combined aforementioned realities created a constant need for cooperation and support at multiple levels and between diverse social groups within the urban community. No group, not even the mercantile elite—who were linked by marriage and shared economic interests—had the resources to fully support themselves. The merchants provided most of the town's communal services, making them a "highly respected community in the town."[38] The townspeople also relied on the merchants to import everything they needed to survive. But this trade (and the merchants' wealth) relied entirely on the manual labor of the mariners and pearl divers. These kinds of intricate social relations produced a complex urban life.

The economic organization of the town's shipping and pearling industries played a significant role in creating the social relations that connected people before oil. These were precarious industries that left much to chance: cargo could be lost through piracy or shipwrecks, and pearling depended on the quality and quantity of the annual pearl crop, as well as international tastes and markets. Every merchant's business was vulnerable to such external forces. So, whenever a merchant or shipowner suffered serious financial difficulties, the other merchants clubbed together to alleviate his debts. Covering each other's losses was a form of mutual insurance that guaranteed the merchants' long-term individual and collective survival. In insecure times, such mutual aid "protected everyone by protecting each."[39]

Because of the uncertainty of these industries, sailors and pearl divers received (unequal) shares in the profits of the ship rather than direct wages; they also, therefore, shared in the collective risks and losses. Pearling also operated on a system of advances whereby the nokhada paid each of the divers and crew members a fixed payment before the ship's departure to tide their families over in their five-month absence. This allowance usually came from an advance payment that the nokhada received from the merchant financing the voyage.[40] Oftentimes at the end of the season the amount of each laborer's share proved insufficient to cover the cost of the advance, and the diver or sailor would be obligated to work for the same nokhada in subsequent years until his debt was paid off. Nowakhada, meanwhile, were often in debt to their financiers. In his maritime history of Kuwait,

Yacoub al-Hijji points out that to be in debt in pre-oil Kuwait was normal. The entire town, even the non-maritime sectors, functioned on a system of credit and advances, and only the richest merchants were not in some form of debt.[41] For those working on a ship, being in debt meant that their labor was controlled by their creditors: the merchant financier controlled the *nokhada*, and the *nokhada* controlled the divers and sailors.

Although this economic system appears exploitative, it created important patronage networks that ensured the townspeople's survival. Debt bondage was endemic, but few mariners or divers "ever went so far as to contest the system," because the nature of everyday urban life lessened their feelings of exploitation.[42] The town's leading pearling and trading merchants controlled hundreds of boats and the thousands of men who worked on them. Because these labor-intensive industries depended on the bodily capabilities of the sailors and divers, their general welfare was not simply a humanitarian concern but also an economic imperative. During the pearl merchant secession of 1910, Hilal al-Mutairi promised his pearling crews that if they followed him to wherever he decided to settle, he would build them houses at his own cost before building one for himself.[43] Captains and merchants bore responsibility for the men who were in debt to them. As Alan Villiers noted after his travels with a Kuwaiti trading vessel in 1939, "The crew of the *Triumph* had not yet been paid and the shares had not been cast up, but Nejdi [their *nokhada*] gave them money as they needed it."[44] Such patronage was particularly important for newcomers who settled in town during the pearling boom of the early twentieth century, because they needed to "start a new life" with very little money or social ties to sustain themselves.[45] Though debt bondage gave the merchants control over labor and production in the pre-oil maritime economy, being in debt did not necessarily mean that one was entirely penniless. When money came in it did not always go toward clearing one's name from a *nokhada's* duty roster. Nor was it expected that any money a diver or sailor received separately from his share of the ship's profits should automatically be applied toward his debt. According to Villiers, "It was hard for a sailor not to be in debt and, so far as I could see, none of them tried very much not to be. Debt was an accepted thing, and to spend a lifetime owing money was apparently usual."[46]

Even within the non-maritime sectors, employers had certain responsibilities toward their laborers. The daily meals of builders, for example, were always provided by the owner of the structure being built.[47] Domestic workers also often received their meals for free at the household in which they worked. For one woman who attended the missionaries' Sunday school, lunch and dinner was provided daily for herself, her husband, and her son by the rich woman whose house she cleaned for a wage.[48] Groups within the middle stratum of society were less dependent on the richer families but still established mechanisms of support and assistance between themselves. For example, when a member of the construction trade needed any building work done for himself—such as an extension to his house— other builders would get together on a Friday, their day off, and do the work for him for free, and he provided lunch.[49] These support networks cut across religious and ethnic boundaries. When the manager of the Mission's Bible shop wanted to renovate his store in 1947, his neighboring Muslim shopkeepers donated the materials and labor that turned it into "the best looking shop on Main Street."[50] Such mechanisms of mutual support also cut across trades and were embedded in the practices of everyday urban life. At the end of the workday the *suq* fishmongers always gave away their remaining catch for free, knowing that the poorest families would need something to cook for that night's dinner.[51]

Neighborhood Group Life

Life in a time of scarcity and general need made communal sharing— of money, food, services, and possessions—between individuals and families necessary for their everyday survival. This sharing brought people into regular, direct contact with one another and "provided a focus for concrete human activities."[52] Communal living began in the home. Households rarely consisted of one family to a house, because most families could not afford to break away and live on their own. The homes of lower and middle class families were small but normally housed relatives beyond a nuclear family: a daughter-in-law, grandparents, an unwed cousin or aunt, and so on. Even though space was scarce, the number of people sharing a house with only one or two courtyards could be as high as twelve or more. One middle class household, for example, contained six nuclear families (of the same extended family) living in a house of only 150 square meters, with each family occupying one of the small rooms off the courtyard.[53] Even the richest families, who could afford to live separately in their own homes, lived communally. When a son got married, the new couple and their children customarily occupied a room in the groom's parents' home.

Though the biggest merchant households had much more space than other homes, they could contain up to fifty or sixty people. At all socioeconomic levels, personal and familial privacy at home were very hard to come by. As Saif Abbas Dehrab puts it, "While talking about sex [was] taboo, seeing sex [was] not. Given the limited space that our families lived in, sex differentiation and identification started early."[54]

Dividing the daily workload of the home was much easier for the richer households—which contained multiple family members as well as live-in servants or slaves—than it was for the poorer families. The latter (who constituted the majority of the town's population) could not totally shield themselves from the world outside their front door, and family life was deeply intertwined with neighborhood life. The townspeople's perpetual and often immediate state of need made the links between neighbors very strong—sometimes stronger than family if the latter lived far away.[55] Today, most Kuwaitis who were members of the pre-oil urban community recall the close interdependence of neighbors positively. They describe the social dynamics of the pre-oil *farij* using such terms as *takatuf* (solidarity), *tarabut* (unity), and *ta'aluf* (cooperation). As Mohammed al-Khars and Mariam al-Aqruqah describe in their study of old Kuwaiti houses, "The residents of the *farij* lived as though they were one family." They protected each other's honor, united in the face of external threats, and assisted each other at times of crisis.[56] The word *farij* comes from the Arabic word *fariq*, meaning "team." The word was originally used to denote the social organization of families living together in a particular place and working together to form a collective; it then became projected onto the space that they occupied.[57] Though neighbors were sometimes members of an extended family, in most cases they were actually unrelated but considered members of an extended family "writ large."[58] It was common for a woman with a child still of nursing age to leave her baby in the care of a neighbor with a child of a similar age to nurse for her while she was out working or doing chores. Islamic law considers children nursed by the same woman to be "siblings." *Farij* children of the opposite sex thus often grew up without the social barriers that would normally come between them when they reached marriageable age.[59]

This closeness between neighbors was not ethnically or religiously determined. Though the town's three main residential quarters each had its own distinct characteristic (Jibla was the trading quarter, Sharq the maritime and pearling quarter, and Mirqab the inland quarter), most *firjan* within these larger districts were socially and culturally mixed. There was no distinctly Hasawiyya or African *farij*, no separate Jewish or Shi'i enclave, no neighborhood occupied exclusively by Baharna shipbuilders or Bedouin pearl divers. Even the seafront was not restricted to merchants but contained houses of *nowakhada* and *dhow*-builders. The Persian community, as a specific example, did not reside in a separate area but was scattered around the town in a manner that adhered to the socio-spatial logic of urban organization described in Chapter 2.[60] So, while the older Persian trading families, such as the Ma'rafi, lived along the seafront close to their ships, the more "humble" families of sailors, porters, and water carriers, most of whom had immigrated to Kuwait in the early twentieth century, lived in the newer Mirqab quarter.[61]

It was common for the town's many *firjan* to be named after particular tribes or ethnic groups. The inland Sharq neighborhoods that developed in the early twentieth century, for instance, had names like Farij al-Sawaber (named after a local tribe) and Farij al-Beluch. Other *firjan*, such as Farij Al Ghunaim on Jibla's coastline, were named after individual families. However, the name of a *farij* rarely dictated the identity of its occupants. The naming of urban neighborhoods and streets reflected an urban custom of projecting the identity of the oldest, largest, most influential, or most visible household, tribe, or community onto the surrounding space. Neighborhoods were often established as "immigration units," where members of a particular tribe or ethnic group clustered together when first settling in the town.[62] Though doing so sometimes carved that group's identity onto the neighborhood, it was not necessarily restricted to members of that group, nor was it uncommon for people from that group to move elsewhere eventually. The Farij al-Sawaber included many Hasawiyya, Persians, and members of other tribes such as the Awazem.[63] The Farij al-Shuyoukh ("Shaykhs' Farij")—one of the several residential areas of al-Wasat where most of the members of the ruling family resided—was not restricted to the Al Sabah and included important merchant families, some Shi'i households, and families of African origin. Neighborhoods named after big merchant families usually referred to the oldest or biggest family in the area; the name also often identified the patron household of the neighborhood, on whom the less affluent families depended.

It was the everyday interactions between neighbors rather than their shared background that shaped the group life of the *farij*. Non-merchant families, particularly those of the poorest laboring class, who were almost always in debt, lived subsistence lifestyles and were unable to deal with large, burdensome expenses such as unexpected crises (for example, flooding and the crumbling of their mudbrick houses after excessive rainfall, which was common) or ritual events (marriages, funerals, religious holidays, and so on). During Ramadan it was customary for neighbors to deliver food to one another's houses every evening, not solely due to need but also in the communal spirit of fasting. Weddings were another collective celebration in the *farij*, and poorer households relied on their neighbors to supply food and lend clothing and jewelry to their daughters. Such ritual ceremonies were normally shared with neighbors even when material aid was not needed. For instance, when a boy had read through the entire Qur'an, his parents would dress him up and parade him through the streets to announce his achievement to their neighbors. As Zahra Freeth noted, "It was yet another act which reflected the close-knit community spirit of the old town where joys and sorrows were shared, and where people were supported through times of poverty and hardship by the practical help of neighbors."[64]

The necessity of this mutual support created a pragmatic need for mixed-class neighborhoods. Wealthier families often paid for shared resources, such as the communal well for the accumulation of rainwater, and supported their poorer neighbors in cash and kind. Yousef bin Issa al-Qina'i's household in Sharq, for example, regularly cooked large pots of food to distribute to less affluent families in their *farij*. Al-Qina'i's daughter-in-law recalled her own father giving food and money to several poorer houses in their al-Wasat neighborhood.[65] All residents, not just the rich, had a responsibility to help neighbors in need. When a new family moved to the area, it was customary for a different neighbor to cook dinner for them each night of their first week so that the family could concentrate on settling in.[66] Families also placed fruit peelings outside their front door when someone in the house was ill, as a way of informing passing neighbors to bring more fruit (a scarce commodity before oil).[67] These practices transcended the social and cultural differences that existed between members of a particular *farij*. When the house of a Persian family in Jibla caught fire, neighbors of all backgrounds brought food and supplies to help the family recover.[68] Islamic scripture recognizing neighbors as "people with mutual responsibilities in terms of hospitality, sharing, and kindness" may have served as one catalyst for this neighborhood assistance, as Mandana Limbert argues it did in the Omani town of Bahla.[69] However, the obligation to share resources with neighbors was also a form of mutual insurance for each individual family at a time when urban society did not have a wealthy state to fall back on.

The close spatial proximity of courtyard houses, discussed in Chapter 2, assisted day-to-day sharing between neighbors. The *firya* doors connecting houses facilitated the sharing of food and supplies and enabled neighbors to help one another with daily chores. The proximity of rooftops also enhanced this intimacy. Farhan al-Farhan recalls that when he was a young boy his parents had him sleep at a neighbor's house every night in the summer, because the woman who lived there was too afraid to sleep alone while her husband was away pearling. He would be passed over from his family's roof to her roof, and by the time he woke up the next morning he would already have been passed back to his parents.[70] Spatial proximity also made sharing somewhat of an obligation: "Neighbors were separated by only a mud wall. The day that your neighbors grilled fish for lunch, you could smell it, and because they knew that you could smell it, they would bring you some. That was how we lived."[71]

The sharing of food was indeed an everyday custom between neighbors. This included the preparation of food—such as picking the stones out of large vats of rice—which was often a communal activity among the women of the *farij*.[72] The *farij* also offered opportunities for female employment, particularly among lower class women who needed to supplement their husbands' meager income. Some local women sold snack foods, such as fava beans, nuts, sunflower seeds, and sweets, on street corners, and their customers normally sat on the ground with the seller to eat them on the spot. Some women worked as the local *khabbaza*, or baker, to whom the other neighborhood women would bring their prepared dough to bake in her household bread oven. Dehrab's mother, for example, was a *khabbaza* who also made and sold butter, yogurt, and buttermilk to her neighbors.[73] Women of wealthier households were more strictly confined to the *harem* because they had servants to take care of the kinds of daily activities that would require venturing into the town. Other women therefore worked as door-to-door traders, selling makeup, fragrances, clothes, cooking utensils, and other items to women who did not have the option of shopping in the markets. These everyday activities were central to the social life of the *farij*, because they brought together women of diverse backgrounds on a regular basis. The *farij* made women's daily tasks more sociable and, conversely, socializing for *farij* women often entailed some element of domestic or local work.

Everyday Social Life

These multiple interactions between neighbors made the *farij* a highly sociable space before oil. But the centrality of the *farij* in everyday social life was determined not just by the need for mutual support. It was also, to some extent, shaped by even more practical considerations. The time it took to travel two or three miles by foot along the town's many winding streets made people less inclined to visit friends or family who lived across town,[74] so normally they would do so only on special occasions. As Dr. Lewis Scudder of the American missionaries' hospital observed during the Eid al-Fitr (the feast commemorating the end of fasting during the month of Ramadan) in 1941, "There is an interesting custom in Kuwait, which probably had its origins in the peculiar length and narrowness of the town as it sprawls along Kuwait Bay. To facilitate visiting, and by common consent, the West is visited by the East on the first day of the feast and the East by the West on the second."[75]

At the everyday level, people's social lives tended to be fixed within their own neighborhoods. The main activities of a typical day were organized around the five prayer times: after the early morning prayer, people headed out to work, which ended at around noon for the midday prayer and rest, then recommenced after the afternoon prayer and ended for the day at sunset. The hour-and-a-half of twilight between the sunset and the final night prayers, which brought the day to its official end, was the only period people really had in which to socialize outside the context of home and work. Because there were no streetlamps, people had to get home before darkness fully descended and therefore could not venture very far away. As one man described it, "If one didn't go to visit his neighbors [after work], he wouldn't go anywhere."[76] Men and women tended to socialize separately in the *farij*, unless visiting family. *Farij* men of more affluent households usually visited local *diwawin* to socialize, exchange news and views, and make business deals. For men of the lower classes, the space within the *farij* most commonly used to gather and visit neighbors and friends after work was the local *baraha*. An open space where multiple streets met, the *baraha* connected several *firjan* with a central meeting ground (similar to Italian piazzas). It was an ideal social space for neighborhood men who were unable to visit each other at home because it could intrude on their families' private life. Simultaneously, it enabled them to satisfy the need to stay in close proximity of their homes before dark.

Women also socialized in the *baraha*, as did the local children, who played games in the square whenever they were not in school.[77] The rhythms of daily activity as determined by prayer times also ensured that most men were back in their own *farij* in time to pray in their local mosque, which enhanced the social intimacy between neighbors. As one Kuwaiti man described it,

We would see each other five times a day in the mosque, and twice a day in the *suq*, and the eighth time in the *diwaniyya*. . . . And when one would meet his neighbor or his friend or his relative eight times a day, whatever problems would arise between them would dissolve quickly and they would soon reconcile.[78]

The fact that the townspeople are normally described as cohesive and peaceful does not mean that tensions and conflicts did not exist between them. Rather, "the multiple contacts necessitated by dense . . . social conditions" helped diffuse hostility between people. By engaging each other daily in diverse concrete interactions, people had to deal with conflicts directly rather than "[store] up their grievances in private."[79]

The *farij* was even more significant in the social lives of women, most of whom spent significantly larger portions of the day (if not the entire day) close to home (if not at home). Neighborhood women lived very much in each other's company, joined together into what Haya al-Mughni calls "a community apart" due to the prolonged absence of the town's men.[80] They therefore made the effort to cultivate their friendships with one another. One day soon after her family's arrival in Kuwait in 1911, Dr. Eleanor Calverley of the American missionaries' hospital was called out to the house of a notable family on the western edge of town, far away from her own house in the town's center, to treat a sick daughter. Dr. Calverley found the women in the *harem* extremely unwelcoming and unfriendly. Five years later the missionaries' residence was relocated to the same neighborhood to which the doctor had been called that night. Suddenly the women of the same notable household became extremely friendly toward her and regularly invited her over and visited her home. Now that she was a neighbor it was important for them to establish a relationship with her family, and they treated the Calverleys as one of their own, asking after their daughter when she was sick and constantly sending over food.[81]

Of course, living in such close proximity to one another within the *farij* had its drawbacks. One downside to the intertwined morphology of the residential quarters was that it facilitated the spread of disease among the townspeople. Although Kuwait was considered a very healthy town, when there was plague or other epidemics the disease spread rapidly. In the summer of 1933, for example, a smallpox epidemic broke out—one of the worst the town had seen—that claimed thousands of lives. Dr. Stanley Mylrea attributed the rapid spread to the close-knit houses "with their innumerable rooms almost airtight and light tight."[82] The close proximity of neighbors also facilitated the spread of another (though not as likely to be fatal) dreaded reality: rumors and scandal. The missionary women regularly had to avoid mixing groups of female visitors in their homes, "for the slightest cause of jealousy, even jealousy of our friendship, will cause one woman to start rumors about another."[83] And as one of the hospital nurses once noted, information traveled rapidly "from harem to harem."[84] This was what four women who visited Bessie Mylrea at her home in 1915 were forced to learn when it was discovered after they left that a silver fruit knife had gone missing. The news quickly leaked out to women all over town, and for weeks the four visitors lived in fear that the men of their households would hear about the scandal.[85] As Limbert explains, neighborhoods thus "functioned as the primary means for the social regulation of everyday behavior."[86]

The neighborhood Qur'anic schools played similar regulatory roles. Children usually went to school in double shifts—in the morning and after the midday rest—and teachers often became responsible for making sure that the students in their charge behaved outside of school hours. One anecdote repeated by many men who grew up before oil was that teachers marked the hands of young boys with ink to make sure they did not swim in the sea between school sessions.[87] The boys were also made to do chores in the teacher's house; drying shrimp, boiling locusts, and crushing and storing dates were all tasks that Dehrab remembers doing for his teacher for one rupee a month.[88] Schools thus reflected the multiplicity of roles, activities, and interactions that a single space or institution could embody in the pre-oil town.

Dissonance

These diverse types of day-to-day contact within the *farij* created a strong sense of community among the townspeople—one based on shared concrete experiences and multiple contact points. This is not to say, however, that all members of the urban community had access to all of the town's activities and members. Sahat al-Safat, the *suq*, and the *sahel*, described in

Chapter 2, enabled the townspeople to be together in public in various ways, and the simultaneity of activities in these spaces allowed for constant encounters and interactions with difference.[89] But though people of all social and cultural backgrounds theoretically had access to such common spaces, not everyone had equal access to the multiple activities that took place within them. All members of urban society could attend celebrations and ceremonies in al-Safat, and all religious groups had the right to worship in Kuwait, but only Sunni rituals were performed in public. Minority groups conducted their own ritual ceremonies in private. The Shi'a did not hold 'ashura processions through the town as was common in Iraq and Bahrain but rather held their mourning rituals in private homes, separately for men and women.[90] Similarly, the African community had its own private social club in a courtyard house where members performed ritual dances every Thursday.[91] Meanwhile, the extent to which urban women had access to public spaces varied according to social class, because "a townswoman of some social position never went to the market."[92] Less affluent women, on the other hand, had to do their own shopping in the suq and their own laundry on the beach, which gave them access to the kinds of social encounters and interactions that took place in these public spaces.

Also, though everyone had access to public places like the suq and sahel regardless of background or class, lines of separation and exclusion existed within these spaces. The Bu Nashi coffee shop near the Suq al-Dakhili was a relatively exclusive place frequented by the town's merchant elite and members of the ruling family; sailors, porters, and other laborers usually went to coffeehouses along the sahel. Women could engage in commercial activities in the suq, but they had a separate market of their own, known as the Suq al-Harim ("Women's Market"), in which to do so. As Fran Tonkiss argues, "While the idea of public space is founded on principles of equality and access, the exclusions which operate in real public spaces point to the limits of belonging in the city."[93] Though women, laborers, and religious minorities were all visible in public spaces and participated in different aspects of urban life, such marginalized groups all faced limitations in their everyday urban experiences.

Furthermore, the fact that such groups were visible in public spaces did not mean they were also engaged in the public sphere.[94] The realm of social and political debate and decision-making was dominated by the town's male merchant notable elite, as were the spaces in which the public sphere operated, such as the diwaniyya. When nonelite townsmen attended *diwawin* it was usually to request assistance or arbitration from the host rather than to participate in the social and political discussions that these spaces embodied. Women of all classes did not have access to *diwawin* at all. But whereas women were thus excluded from participation in the public sphere, men were largely excluded from the private sphere of their fellow townspeople's family lives. Women's access to the private lives of their friends and neighbors therefore gave them an important public role to play in urban society. As Peter Lienhardt puts it,

Living so much in the company of other women, they learn a great deal more than their husbands usually do about family situations, particularly since the social proprieties of what can be discussed are less of a restraint on them than on men. It is, in general, improper for men to speak about women, whether those of their own families or of other peoples', and it would be difficult to discuss family affairs without mentioning the women. Hence men tend to learn more about private affairs from their womenfolk than they do from other men.[95]

Such "private affairs" included births, engagements, marriages, and divorces, as well as scandals, gossip, and rumors. In a society as small as pre-oil Kuwait, where a marriage (or divorce) between two high-profile merchant houses could have great economic significance, and where most business deals were made on the basis of reputation and mutual trust, such information could often be critically important for the men to know.

Though not all members of urban society had equal access to public spaces, or equal rights to participate in the town's diverse activities, these different groups depended on one another intimately for the town's overall survival. The group life of the city was shaped by the multiple contacts and interactions that the townspeople had to journey between in the course of their daily lives in order to survive: the *farij*, the *suq*, the *diwaniyya*, the merchant patron, the neighborhood schoolteacher, fellow craftsmen, other women in the neighborhood, the mosque, and so on. This complex and diverse urban life created a powerful sense of community between its residents, shaped by their concrete activities and relations and mutual modes of living. The sudden affluence that came with oil dramatically altered Kuwait's urbanity by removing the sense of need that created this social relatedness, while simultaneously opening up new avenues whereby people could more "easily conceive of their social relatedness in terms of their similarity rather than their need for each other."[96]

4

Oil-Era Modernization

Oil and the Transformation of Society

Oil was discovered in Kuwait in commercial quantities in 1938, and the first barrels were exported in 1946 (the delay caused by World War II). The oil income went straight into the hands of the ruler, and it was his responsibility to distribute the wealth among the population. With the accession to power of Abdullah al-Salem in 1950, Kuwait entered a period of enormous state-building and centralization. Oil revenues brought about a major shift in the social pact between the rulers and the ruled. Kuwait's escalating oil production capabilities coincided with production declines in Iran after Mohammed Mosaddeq nationalized Iranian oil facilities in 1951. Abdulla al-Salem used Kuwait's growing hydrocarbon leverage with the British to increase the terms of the concession with Kuwait Oil Company (KOC) (based on a nine-cents-per-barrel royalty) to a 50–50 profit-sharing agreement in 1951.[1] Kuwait's oil revenues shot up exponentially. Whereas in 1948 the oil income was approximately $5.6 million, by 1953 it had reached $169 million, and it kept increasing annually.[2] With this substantial rise in oil revenues, the balance of power between the merchants and the rulers was forever disrupted. In 1955, the British Political Resident noted that "the checks and balances of mediaeval society have been upset. The Shaikhs with, comparatively speaking, unlimited wealth have become independent of the merchants."[3]

Without taxes, Abdullah had sole control over public spending. Despite this new autonomy, the ruler was determined to share the oil wealth with the people of Kuwait.[4] During his first year in power he spent nearly a fifth of the country's revenues on health and education.[5] The British political agent recognized that this ruler was "more modest than his predecessor and appears to be more sincerely devoted to the interests of his people."[6] The country's first British master planners similarly observed that Abdullah wanted to use the country's newfound wealth to make Kuwait "the best planned and most socially progressive city in the Middle East."[7] Though the ruler's desire to invest the country's newfound wealth "in the betterment of the lot of the people" was most probably genuine,[8] it may also have stemmed from his own involvement with the merchant opposition in 1938. One of the *majlis*'s main grievances was that Ahmed al-Jaber was not spending any of his oil concession revenues on improving conditions in the country during the economic crisis that lasted until the end of the 1930s.[9] The immediate launch of Abdullah's modernization schemes upon his accession to power preempted any opposition to the state's control of the country's ever-increasing oil revenues.

Abdullah al-Salem's modernization program hinged on the twin pillars of urban development and social welfare. Urban development entailed building new neighborhoods, houses, schools, hospitals, and roads; laying down water pipes and sewer lines; and building water desalination plants and electric-power stations (all at the government's expense).[10] Social welfare included free education and health care, guaranteed state employment, state housing options for all income groups, marriage loans for young couples to start their own families, subsidized electricity and water, and more. The distribution of the oil wealth through such welfare services contributed "in large measure to the stability of the State and making it more difficult for extremism or agitation."[11] Kuwaitis became entirely dependent on the state—rather than on the merchants or the *farij*—for their moral and material well-being. The government replaced the merchants as the principal employers of national labor and as the providers of public welfare.

Abdullah al-Salem continued his predecessor's policy of institutionalizing the political functions of the ruling family by delegating responsibility to and sharing power with his relatives. All of the principal state departments and high offices of power were held by members of the Al Sabah.[12] But if the 1938 *majlis* movement taught Abdullah anything, it was that the merchants would not easily agree to remove themselves from the political and economic affairs of Kuwait. The ruler would therefore have "to buy the merchants out of politics rather than simply drive them out."[13] This goal was achieved through two means. One was the development of a land acquisition scheme and the sanctioning of land speculation, through which the merchants became extremely wealthy (discussed later in this chapter). The second means was the creation of favorable trade conditions and investment opportunities for the merchants. This method included privatizing some government industries to be taken over by merchant businesses, awarding contracts for public works to their newly established construction companies, permitting only international companies to work in Kuwait in a 50–50 (later 51–49) partnership with local firms, and compelling foreign manufacturers and car companies to sell their products through Kuwaiti agents. Abdullah also built a new large port in Shuwaikh to help facilitate the significant growth of merchant trade.[14] Through all of these schemes the historic trading families of Kuwait became evermore rich in the early oil years. In Peter Lienhardt's words, "for all the abrupt economic change that Kuwait was experiencing, business had not made a fresh start."[15]

To safeguard and enhance their new economic interests, the merchants increasingly stayed out of oppositional politics. The merchant-run Municipal, Education, and Health Councils of the post-*majlis* era still existed and were tied to their respective government departments when Abdullah al-Salem came to power in 1950. Under his reign they became elected councils, but only the Education Council actually functioned properly.[16] In 1954 the merchants petitioned Abdullah to form an advisory council, but instead the ruler announced the formation of the Higher Executive Council, consisting of members of the ruling family and a few of their well-known loyalists.[17] Reelections for the merchant councils were never held, thus ending the merchants' collective dominance over participatory politics in Kuwait. The first popularly elected National Assembly of 1963 contained very few merchants.

From 1954 onward the merchants sustained their role in decision-making through appointments to high positions in government departments (called ministries after independence in 1961) or committees, through which their interests became intrinsically tied to the state. Those who held posts within the state administration used their privileged positions for their own economic gain as well as that of their associates rather than for political opposition or leverage. Before oil, the merchants unproductively invested a large part of their wealth in the town, particularly in the provision of social services and facilities. This gave them social prestige and political leverage vis-à-vis the rulers, but little financial gain. After the advent of oil, these same powerful groups began to seek a financial return on their investments. For example, in 1955 the merchants protested the government's newly built central kitchen that provided midday meals for all schools. Though the kitchen bought meals by tender from the local merchants, the merchants "apparently [feared] that the provision of meals by the Government would in some way deprive them of a channel for profit."[18] Merchant frustrations with the government in the post-1950 period became less overtly political and focused primarily on delays in development projects in which they had a financial stake.[19] In 1954 a lull in development disgruntled merchants who had large stocks of construction materials ready to unload on the government.[20]

Immigration, Citizenship, and Employment

The launch of the oil industry led to a substantial increase in immigration from the desert and neighboring Arab countries due to new employment opportunities in the oil, construction, and service sectors.[21] This influx, coupled with the establishment of state welfare programs, necessitated the creation of a nationality law by which eligible families would formally become Kuwaiti citizens. At the time, local residents and newly arriving foreigners alike assumed that immigration would not be permanent. Rather, "the laborers would have to return home once the construction work was finished, while young Kuwaitis now at school or in universities abroad would soon be able to take over the work of the better educated immigrants."[22] Kuwait's first nationality law, passed in 1948 at the start of the immigration wave in an attempt to control the expected influx, was therefore relatively inclusive. In addition to families who had been residing in Kuwait since 1899, children born in Kuwait to Arab or Muslim fathers and people who had lived in Kuwait for at least ten years were eligible to be naturalized.[23] Nearly a decade later, in 1957, however, the country's first census revealed that non-Kuwaitis constituted 45 percent of the total population, and by 1961 they had reached 50 percent.[24] With the realization that the newly defined national population was fast becoming a minority, and that immigration was far from slowing down, in 1959 a new law was introduced in which Kuwaiti nationality became much more narrowly defined.

According to the new law, "original" Kuwaiti nationals were those whose families had settled in Kuwait by 1920.[25] Children of Arab or Muslim fathers born in Kuwait were no longer eligible for citizenship, and naturalization became much more restrictive.[26] The law thus established new political and legal distinctions between locals and newcomers. Though immigration continued as it had before oil, new arrivals no longer had the ability to integrate and become part of the permanent local community as they had before. The nationality law also created distinctions between existing members of Kuwaiti society. Access to citizenship was not as straightforward for tribes as it was for the townspeople due to the requirement to prove settlement (with land ownership deeds, birth or death certificates, and so on). Though some Bedouin managed to obtain nationality by origin according to the 1959 law, many were denied that status and were naturalized only after independence in 1961 in exchange for joining the army, particularly after Iraq's threat against Kuwait that year.[27] Tribes whose question of residency was too ambiguous to be decided upon became classified as *bidun jinsiyya* (without nationality, or stateless).[28] The long-term impact of the nationality law is discussed further in Chapter 7.

With the growth of the welfare state, a large portion of the national population became a bureaucratic class of public sector workers. Increased education opportunities for women, including the chance to study abroad (mainly for those from well-to-do families), meant that more women entered the workforce, and most went into the public service sector.[29] Pearl divers, sailors, and porters were all able to find more steady work in the oil industry or in government service, with fixed wages and higher incomes than in their previous modes of employment.[30] Though variations in income still existed between members of the population, Kuwait no longer contained a national laboring class as it had before oil. Manual labor (primarily in the construction industry) was handed over to a new migrant workforce, mainly from Iraq, Iran, Egypt, and south Asia. Palestinians, Lebanese, Egyptians, and south Asians worked as technicians, schoolteachers, nurses, doctors, and dentists, and in other professions for which Kuwaitis were not yet properly trained.[31] As the national laboring class was eliminated and the middle stratum widened to take in the vast number of government employees and midlevel businessmen, only the thin upper crust of the merchant elite remained in place at the top of the socioeconomic hierarchy. Meanwhile, beginning in the late 1940s, the pastoral tribes and villagers who had obtained citizenship gave up their previous economic activities of herding, farming, and fishing and entered the urban workforce (mainly in the oil sector, army, and police, and to some extent in government bureaucracies). In the late 1960s the government began a Bedouin settlement scheme that ultimately resulted in the full sedentarization of Kuwait's nomadic sector. Kuwait's entire population thus became urbanized.

The Modernist Project

The redevelopment of old Kuwait Town into a modern city was a key element in the state modernization project after 1950. By the late 1940s the old town enclosed within the *sur* was unable to accommodate the country's rapid demographic growth. Motor traffic had become commonplace, and cars struggled to navigate Kuwait's small winding alleys and uneven dirt roads, and to enter and exit the town's gates. Big American cars, buses, and trucks imposed an unbearable strain on the existing road system.[32] Kuwait Town became almost completely outdated overnight, and as Stephen Gardiner put it, "A new era, a new life . . . had to be constructed from scratch."[33] The decision was made to demolish the old town to make way for "a more beautiful and dignified town center."[34] David Harvey describes this process of creative destruction as a necessary condition of twentieth-century progress and one that has been essential for the implementation of any "modernist project." "How could a new world be created, after all, without destroying much that had gone on before? You simply cannot make an omelet without breaking eggs."[35]

However, convincing the public of this would not be easy. To justify the wholesale demolition of the pre-oil town and the creation of a new world (over which the state was in complete control), the past had to be portrayed as a period of suffering and hardship. That is, the promise of "progress" needed to be confirmed by the memory of "poverty."[36] This constructed dichotomy between past and present became an essential part of state development discourse after 1950:

Since the State is the only party controlling the oil sector, government interference was imperative from the very beginning because it shoulders the burden of developing the society, modernizing the economy, and fulfilling the individuals' well-being to make up for years of suffering in the pre-oil phase, and to take a short cut towards the establishment of a prosperous up-to-date society.[37]

This discourse was also a key component of the universal modernist project. With its focus on building a new future, modernism required the negation of existing social conditions. In this way, modernism "as an aesthetic of erasure and reinscription" was closely linked with modernization "as an ideology of development in which governments . . . seek to rewrite national histories."[38]

During these transitional decades, many Kuwaitis did in fact come to reject the past in favor of the new and modern. The government convinced people that their old houses were dirty, unhealthy, and infested with insects, and they promised to build them new, cleaner, and better houses outside the city.[39] Some people had already started to see the tangible benefits of urban modernity in the KOC town of Ahmadi. Nearly forty kilometers south of the city, Ahmadi had been redesigned according to British planning principles in 1947. As a former KOC employee told Reem Alissa, "Early on, people used to be jealous of those who lived in Ahmadi because it was so quiet, well-planned, clean, aesthetically pleasing, the garbage was collected nicely, the colors of the houses were always clean and vibrant."[40] Kuwaitis were also now traveling to Paris, London, and Beirut; according to a man who experienced the changes, "they didn't want their old town anymore."[41] Zahra Freeth, a British woman who grew up in Kuwait in the late 1920s and early 1930s, visited the country in 1956. After she had taken photographs of some of the older houses in the town, her Kuwaiti friends grew "impatient at my interest in the Kuwait of the past, and asked why I wasted time on the old and outmoded when there was so much in Kuwait that was new and fine." When Freeth mentioned that many of the old buildings were due to be demolished, one young woman exclaimed, "Let them be demolished! Who wants them now? It is the new Kuwait and not the old which is worthy of admiration."[42] This sentiment had not changed by the end of the 1960s. When a group of British planners consulted "informed local people" in Kuwait about sites of architectural or historical importance in the town, it was "clear from the response that most Kuwaitis do not value old buildings as highly as we are inclined to, and some even welcome the idea of ridding Kuwait of everything to do with the past."[43] To most Kuwaitis the old town became associated with a life of hardship and need whereas the new city symbolized unprecedented wealth and progress. As Gardiner accurately described, "People are overtaken by events, and the optimistic prospect of a gleaming new city to replace the muddle, poverty and primitive conditions would have seemed irresistible."[44]

The Advent of City Planning

The state strategy launched at the start of the 1950s—the complete transformation of the obsolete old town into a modern city center—was based on the fundamental belief that rational, modern planning would make Kuwait the most advanced city in the region.[45] Now that urban development and public welfare were entirely funded by oil revenues, the state became the primary agent of urban growth and social change. The general public was not involved in how their city was transformed or how their lives changed after 1950, because they no longer paid any taxes. When a team of British planners began working on Kuwait's second master plan in 1968, they proposed introducing a program of public participation in the process. However, "this was rejected by the client in favour of a process of obtaining 'informed opinion' from representatives of government departments and selected industrial and commercial undertakings."[46] Although the Municipality conducted a few social surveys in the 1960s and 1970s to assist the foreign planners in their studies, these surveys had very little impact on how things actually developed. Throughout the ensuing four decades of urban planning and development, the government expressed little concern (even in the construction of public housing) for how the city would meet the needs and satisfy the demands of the different people compelled to use the spaces they produced. Urban planning focused more on endowing the city "with a pleasing appearance of order" than on "knowing what sort of intimate, functioning order" it would have—that is, it focused on how the city looked rather than on how it worked.[47] Furthermore, Kuwait's configuration as a city-state meant that without local governments to serve as independent decision-makers at the district level, planning was an entirely top-down and centralized process. The elected officials of the country's new suburban municipal governorates could make only minor decisions in their own districts about such issues as sanitation and street maintenance.

The first step in the state-orchestrated urban development project launched in 1950 was the production of "all the services that had not been there before—metalled roads, pavements, sewers, piped water, electricity and telephone cables and new buildings—and to produce them all at once."[48] The city had to accommodate the country's rapid population growth alongside the increasing number of cars. It was also important that the city visually reflect the country's newfound prosperity and modernity—something the existing pre-oil landscape failed to do. Under the advice of Abdullah al-Salem's British planning advisor, Major-General William Hasted, in April 1951 the state's Development Board commissioned the English town-planning firm of Anthony Minoprio, Hugh Spencely, and P. W. Macfarlane to prepare a report for the "re-planning" of Kuwait Town. The planners visited Kuwait for three weeks in July of 1951, and they submitted their plan to the ruler that November, who formally approved it in 1952 (Figure 10).[49] Although the plan was put together rapidly, it served as the "guiding principle for urban expansion" in Kuwait and fundamentally transformed both urban space and everyday social life over the ensuing decades.[50]

The master plan had four main objectives: (1) the development of an efficient road system, (2) the redevelopment of the central area of the old town within the wall to allow for commercial growth, (3) the expansion of the city outside the wall with the construction of new residential areas and development of the existing villages, and (4) the creation of specialized industrial, educational, and health districts outside the city center.[51] The British firm had no experience in town planning outside the United King-

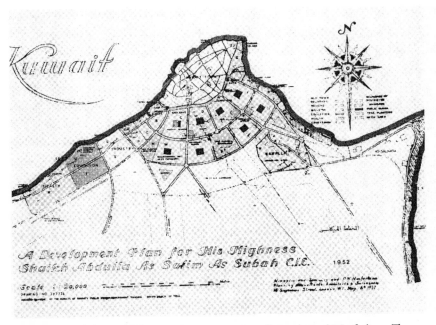

FIGURE 10. 1951 Plan for Kuwait Town by Minoprio, Spencely, and Macfarlane. The perimeter of the old town is clearly preserved, with new ring roads and neighborhoods beyond. *Source*: Kuwait Municipality.

dom. In an interview with Gardiner in the early 1980s, Anthony Minoprio admitted, "It was a difficult commission. We didn't know anything much about the Muslim world and the Kuwaitis wanted a city—they wanted a *new* city, hospitals, schools, housing and good communications. . . . All we could give them . . . was what we knew."[52] The planners therefore exported from Britain for their master plan for Kuwait a combination of postwar planning principles that they believed were "in accordance with the highest standards of modern town planning."[53]

Their primary inspiration was the British "new town" planning movement with which the men were themselves closely involved. In 1947 Minoprio had finished a plan for the new town of Crawley, and in 1945 he had worked on a plan for the postwar reconstruction of Chelmsford.[54] The British new-town plan grew out of the Garden City ideal first conceived by British social reformer Ebenezer Howard at the turn of the twentieth century. Howard believed that decentralization was the solution to the overcrowding, unsanitary conditions, and social problems that industrialization had bequeathed to all large cities. He sought to bring together the best that the city had to offer (the availability of work and cultural facilities) with the best of the countryside (open space, fresh air, recreation, a beautiful natural environment) in a single community.[55] The community would be surrounded by a greenbelt to prevent encroachment into the surrounding countryside, which would provide the city's residents with agricultural resources. Howard's Garden City model inspired a wide range of decentralization schemes in British, American, and European cities, and across the decolonized world, throughout the twentieth century. The "new town" plan of postwar Britain was one such interpretation, though, as Helen Meller argues, "the administration and development of the new towns owed very little to that historical origin."[56]

In his analysis of Kuwait's 1952 master plan, Gardiner identifies three main "abstractions" that mutated from Howard's Garden City ideal into the conventional British new town.[57] One was the debasing of the concept of the greenbelt from surrounding farmland into a "containment strategy" that separated the urban core from new areas of growth beyond it.[58] A second abstraction was the ring road system. New-town planners used Howard's theory—that old towns grew out from a central nucleus in a sequence of rings—to devise a system in which a series of concentric circular or "ring" roads radiated out from the town's center. These roads were then intersected and connected by a set of radial roads that cut across the concentric rings and converged onto the center of town.[59] A third feature of the new town that was part of the "planning orthodoxy of the time" was the neighborhood unit: a planned residential area with shops and other amenities to accommodate a community of five to ten thousand inhabitants. These neighborhood units were connected to each other via the ring and radial roads and surrounded the urban core.[60]

These were the main principles driving town planning in Britain at the time that Minoprio and his colleagues brought to Kuwait.[61] Howard's Garden City, and by extension the new town model it inspired, was "conceived as an alternative to the city."[62] But in Kuwait's context, the model replaced the existing city. Rather than planning a "new" city for Kuwait on undeveloped land, per the government's instructions the firm grafted the plan onto the existing town, which became the new "city center." The firm had initially wanted to keep the 1920 wall (*sur*) intact, because they believed it would make a strong edge for the new core. However, according to Minoprio, "the chief difficulty about this was that it would then have done its job—it would have kept the cars out—you can't drive limousines through a gateway made for carts and goats."[63] The Development Board therefore demolished the *sur* in 1957. Its memory, however, was preserved in the semi-circular shape of the new Green Belt: a park that marked the perimeter of the new Kuwait City. The urban boundary created in 1920 thus remained a permanent line of demarcation for the city center (see Figure 2, p. 25).

In the vast empty desert beyond the Green Belt would be the new residential areas that were a principal feature of the 1952 plan. As in most British new towns, these neighborhood units were planned to house around six thousand people each and to surround the urban core.[64] Just as the *sur* had once served as the dividing line between town and hinterland, so the new Green Belt created a "clean break in the urban area [that] defines the point at which Town changes to suburb and emphasises the character of each."[65] This buffer zone made it easier to conceive of the "city center" as a separate and clearly identifiable space. Though intrinsically dependent on the city and connected to it by a new ring-and-radial road system, the new neighborhood units that came up on the other side of the Green Belt were distinctly separate from the city center (Figure 11).

Inside the Green Belt, Minoprio and his team found it difficult to design a city with modern facilities within the existing layout and organization of the old town. Next to modernist ideals, the dense and intricate

FIGURE 11. New roads and suburbs built in the desert. *Source:* Kuwait Oil Company archives.

layout of the pre-oil urban landscape looked disorderly and chaotic (though in reality there was an organic logic to the winding streets and blind alleys that the townspeople understood). Aerial photos of the town taken by Hunting Aerosurvey in 1950 in preparation for the master plan gave the planners the all-important "God's-eye view" with which to visualize their project field.[66] These images confirmed that the existing townscape did not conform to a consistent geometric pattern that could be legible to outsiders. Furthermore, the morphology of the pre-oil town had evolved in a manner that planning discourse would classify as mixed-use, with commercial spaces such as the *suq* and industrial areas such as the *dhow*-building yards located adjacent to residential neighborhoods.

In keeping with the most fundamental principle of modernist city planning, Minoprio and his colleagues believed that the city should be divided
into a number of functional zones, "each suitable for a particular kind
of development."[67] The plan therefore kept heavy commercial traffic and
industrial activities away from houses, schools, and clinics.[68] Meanwhile,
the compact scale of the existing urban landscape was incapable of accommodating the rapidly increasing amount of motor vehicle traffic inside the
city. The planners therefore recommended that the old courtyard houses
be demolished "as soon as possible" to make way for "new roads, public buildings, and open spaces."[69] In order to orchestrate this "wholesale
reconstruction" of the old town into a modern, planned city, the state
needed to be in complete control of the space it sought to develop.[70] This
requirement necessitated bringing all urban and desert land under state
authority. A new land acquisition scheme (*tathmin al-arady*) was launched
whereby the state purchased the bulk of the land inside the town wall from
its existing owners, who were relocated *en masse* to new neighborhoods
outside the city center.

The state purchased land both inside and outside the town wall at deliberately and artificially inflated prices.[71] This strategy was meant to serve
a dual purpose. On the one hand, official government publications claim
that the policy was implemented as a means of quickly and easily distributing the state's newfound oil wealth among its citizens.[72] On the other hand,
the plan also provided an incentive for the townspeople to vacate the city
center and move out to the new suburbs. The Municipality started acquir-
ing land inside the old town in the 1930s in response to early development
needs such as wider roads when cars were introduced. Though townspeople whose property was acquired received compensation at that time, the
value offered was usually so low that the policy was extremely unpopular
and often resisted.[73] Under the acquisition policy launched after 1951, compensation came out of state oil revenues rather than the Municipality's
small share of customs receipts. The owner of the acquired land therefore
received a much larger compensation than before, at a price that was well
above the market value of the land or property being purchased. Families
could use this *tathmin* money to build modern houses for themselves on
state-allocated land in the new suburbs. The policy thus became more attractive to the general public. In fact, to speed up the process of emptying
the city center, the government made it possible for people to request that
their properties be acquired even before the area was set for expropriation.

In 1951 the Political Resident heard that "owners are clamouring for their property to be included in the areas marked out for demolition."[74]

As Ghanim al-Najjar has expertly shown, land acquisition significantly bolstered the economic standing of what he calls the "upper echelon" of the existing power structure in Kuwait: the ruling family and the merchant notable elite. Most of the bodies involved in the land acquisition process were appointed, and included members of the Al Sabah and high-profile merchant families or their bureaucratic clients. For a percentage of the profit, these bureaucrats leaked information on areas earmarked for expropriation to their wealthy patrons, who would then quickly buy this land for a fraction of the price before the expropriation was announced.[75] The evaluation of the price to be paid for each piece of land was under the sole jurisdiction of an Appraisals Committee appointed by the Municipality whose valuations could not be questioned or overturned by any other institution. Because the committee worked without a set pricing standard, payments for land were arbitrarily unequal. Land in Jibla, for example, tended to be acquired at prices much higher than the prices paid for land in Sharq, for no reason other than that the merchants there had stronger influence over the process.[76] Al-Najjar found that by 1972 only 1 percent of the population had obtained 90 percent of the total amount spent by the state on land acquisitions while 99 percent of the population shared the remaining 10 percent.[77] Between 1952 and 1967, the government spent just over 582 million Kuwaiti dinars (KD) on land acquisitions,[78] and another 688 million during the 1970s.[79] Al-Najjar's findings challenge the publicly declared objective that land acquisition served to redistribute the oil wealth as widely and equitably as possible among the Kuwaiti citizenry. Jill Crystal convincingly argues that Abdullah al-Salem used the land acquisition scheme as one of several means of satisfying the demands of ruling family members who had appropriated massive tracts of land outside the city, as well as a means of buying the loyalty and dependence of the merchants.[80] The payment that the remaining 99 percent of the population received for the acquisition of their property was much-needed seed money to help them get started out in the suburbs. But it did not make them rich. As one man put it, "If we had known what was happening in the planning process, we would have used the extra money we had to buy real estate. Other people knew and bought land and got rich. We didn't know, but the merchants did."[81]

The acquisition scheme also officially transformed land into real estate in Kuwait—that is, into space most coveted for its exchange value rather than for its use value. After 1951, landownership acquired significant economic importance. When in the late 1920s a man bought a small house in town for only 15 rupees, it cost less than the donkey he bought from the same person at 18 rupees. When he sold the same property thirty years later, in 1958, he got 180,000 rupees for it.[82] The small size of the private real estate market kept the cost of land high. In 1954 the Higher Executive Council established what became known as the Private Ownership Line (POL) to demarcate the planned urban areas of the country, incorporating the city center, the new suburbs, and the coastal strip to the oil town of Ahmadi. All land outside this line (97 percent of Kuwait's total territory of 17,818 square kilometers) became classified as state land and was not open to private ownership.[83] Land within the POL (the remaining 3 percent) could be privately owned and therefore purchased by the state through the land acquisition scheme. By 1979 about a quarter of this "private" land also came under state control (the bulk of the remainder being new residential areas).[84] Most of the state's landholdings inside the POL were within the city center, 75 percent of which was state-owned by 1977.[85]

The Crisis of the City

The land acquisition scheme thus successfully cleared the city center of its former inhabitants and allowed the state to play a central role in "shaping the form of the new city."[86] However, the "meteoric rush" to modernize the city without first establishing a sound planning administration inadvertently created an institutional chaos that plagued the planning apparatus in Kuwait for decades.[87] The different state departments involved in urban planning and development lacked clearly defined objectives and roles, which resulted in clashing responsibilities and competing prerogatives within and between the various institutions charged with implementing the 1952 master plan, namely the Municipality (headed by the Municipal Council), the Development Board, and the Public Works Department (PWD).

Though in the past the British had never imposed advisers on the Al Sabah rulers, the discovery of oil made Kuwait's political and economic stability a matter of British concern.[88] By the end of his first year in power, Abdullah al-Salem agreed to appoint Colonel G.C.L. Crichton as Financial Controller and Major-General William Hasted as Controller of Development.[89] These advisers established the Development Board in 1950 to oversee state spending in urbanization, approve new projects for implementation, and organize all planning and building. The Board consisted of the directors of the Finance, Municipality, Education, Health, Awqaf, and Public Works Departments, along with a small group of English advisors led by Hasted. The latter's objective was to steer Kuwait's development boom toward British planners, architects, and contractors.[90]

The British advisers immediately came into conflict with two "particularly strong forces" within the ruling family: Abdullah al-Mubarak, head of Public Security, and Fahad al-Salem, the ruler's brother, who was simultaneously head of the Municipality, PWD, and Health Department.[91] Fahad had veto power over all development work in the country, which created a schism between his administrative empire and the Development Board. This schism significantly impeded urban development during the critical first years. Hasted was handing over all construction contracts for early state projects such as schools, water desalination plants, and power stations to five British contracting firms who monopolized Kuwait's development in the early 1950s. In opposition, Fahad arbitrarily cancelled many Development Board projects, such as the new state hospital in Shuwaikh, before completion.[92] He also used his own Arab engineers for development work as part of his campaign to cross Hasted.

Fahad managed to assume control over the Development Board in 1952, resulting in the "complete stoppage of work" and increased confusion within the planning administration.[93] Under Hasted, the Development Board consisted mostly of British technical staff. When Fahad took control, he replaced these people with individuals from whom he could guarantee allegiance—predominantly Arab technocrats such as Majduddin Jabri, the former mayor of Aleppo, whom Fahad made Chief Engineer of the PWD in 1952.[94] Hasted was increasingly relegated to a technical advisory role, until he eventually quit his position and left Kuwait in 1954. The five British firms soon followed suit, and when Jabri came into conflict with Fahad in 1955, he too quit.[95] By the mid-1950s, the Municipality and its cooperating institutions were left without much experience in or knowledge of how to effectively build the new city that was laid out in the master plan, particularly because the plan was based entirely on foreign planning principles that were alien to Kuwait's own urban heritage.

The inefficiency, maladministration, and chaos that continuously plagued the state's planning administration had a significant impact on how the city developed during this crucial first decade. Development projects outside the city center generally proceeded apace (though with some blockages from Fahad). By 1959, three ring roads and eight suburbs had been completed. Other major projects constructed outside the Green Belt included a new port complex in Shuwaikh and new industrial, health, and education zones along the coastal stretch connecting the city to Jahra. These projects were built on empty land, which made development outside the city relatively straightforward. Development inside the city, by contrast, was a much slower and more complex ordeal precisely because the new city was being superimposed onto the existing townscape.

A major hindrance to the development of the city center was the land acquisition scheme and its artificial inflation of real estate values. In the absence of a fixed pricing standard, the Municipality's Appraisals Committee would take the existing market value of land in a given area as an indicator, then set its price for an acquisition in that area well above that base value. This price would in turn cause the market value of land in the area to soar. Suspicions that the government was planning to acquire a particular area led to land speculation. Land values therefore fluctuated dramatically and randomly throughout the first four decades of the oil era.[96] In 1952 an average square meter of land without a house inside the city center cost KD 4; by 1960 the price had risen more than thirty-two times to KD 129. Land with houses cost approximately KD 13 per square meter in 1953, and increased to nearly KD 200 by 1966.[97] This skyrocketing of real estate values inside the city center made development untenable.

The goal of the land acquisition scheme was to bring about "the amalgamation of tiny plots of land in private ownership into larger state-owned blocks suitable for re-development."[98] When the Municipality demarcated a particular section of the city to be developed, it first had to identify the multiple landowners in that area and then to acquire the land from them. Once all existing houses or structures were demolished, roads were built and the area was reorganized into development blocks. Though some of these plots were used for government buildings, high land values precluded the state from building for public needs inside the Green Belt.[99] New residential development was almost entirely absent, as were projects geared specifically toward the public interest. The 1952 master plan had cordoned off a large part of the city center for the new state university, but this plan was scrapped in the 1960s and the university was situated outside the city instead. Except for the state-run Amiri Hospital, established in the early 1950s, the city contained no centers for public services. Rather, over the ensuing decades the city was transformed into a landscape of wealth and power, at the expense of meeting the needs and desires of everyday users.

After spending so much revenue on land acquisition, saving money and making a profit became principal goals of state authorities, "irrespective of the consequences bequeathed to the city."[100] Fahad al-Salem, for instance, insisted on the "automatic acceptance of the lowest tender for all development work," which regularly resulted in substandard work.[101] In order not to spend more money on actually building up land in the city center, the government sold or leased most of its urban landholdings to the merchant-run private sector for commercial development, at a fraction (around 4 percent) of the cost to the state.[102] As Fakhri Shehab (Abdullah al-Salem's chief economic advisor in the early 1960s) noted in 1964, the merchant capitalist elite amassed enormous private fortunes by first selling land to and then buying it back from the state.[103] However, the constant fluctuation of land values made speculation a much more lucrative venture for the private sector than actually building projects on this valuable real estate. Therefore, by the end of the first decade of oil, much urban land remained undeveloped and was increasingly used for car parking or the disposal of construction waste, or was still occupied by dilapidated court-yard houses awaiting demolition.

The complex process of sorting out "the old, crazy-quilt patterns of property ownership" inside the city also took up too much of the time and concentration of the survey and town planning sections of the Municipality, "not leaving them the adequate time to pay closer attention to what was going on in site planning, civic design, architecture and land-economics."[104] When land inside the Green Belt was in fact used for commercial development, the owner's desire to quickly generate a profit often led to a "meteoric rush into construction which often precluded thorough design." Development activity inside the city throughout the 1950s was therefore "piecemeal and spasmodic."[105] The few government and private office buildings and commercial complexes constructed during this period were randomly placed, with little spatial coherence linking them with one another (Figure 12).

The first part of the new city developed with a certain amount of site planning was Fahad al-Salem Street, a project initiated in 1957 to modernize and enhance the city's commercial qualities.[106] The new, broad commercial thoroughfare led from Sahat al-Safat to the Jahra Gate. After 294 old houses were demolished, the Municipality reordered the area into 103

FIGURE 12. The "piecemeal and spasmodic" growth of the 1950s. *Source*: Kuwait Oil Company archives.

blocks of 166 square meters each, which were then sold to private developers to construct the buildings that would line the street.[107] Most of the owners of this land came from the biggest merchant houses in Kuwait, such as the Al Ghanim, Al Fleij, and Al Shaye', as well as members of the Al Sabah.[108] The Municipality and Development Board fixed real estate prices along the thoroughfare to avoid the skyrocketing of land values that was occurring elsewhere in the city, which revealed the importance of the project's success.[109] When completed, the street was 1,240 meters long and 40 meters wide, and it was flanked by seventy five-story buildings comprising 960 ground-floor shops along colonnaded pathways with 2,200 apartments above (mainly targeting middle-income expatriates).[110] The building owners stood to make a hefty profit from the rents of these shops and apartments.

Fahad al-Salem Street was promoted to the public as a model of the most up-to-date and superior building techniques, complete with tree planting, street lamps, and ample parking.[111] The PWD even established a Jahra Street Facade Committee to ensure that the street-facing side of each building adhered to uniform and harmonious design requirements and color schemes.[112] On the surface, the street looked like the ultimate symbol of Kuwait's modernity and prosperity (Figure 13). But there was no government quality control over the actual building process. Hurried con-

FIGURE 13. The uniform building heights and facades of the new Fahad al-Salem Street corridor, with the more sporadic buildup of the 1950s in the background and the Sheraton Roundabout in the foreground. *Source*: Kuwait Oil Company archives.

struction by private developers resulted in cheap buildings that began to obsolesce before they were even completed.[113] Rather than being a beacon for future city growth, the project turned out to be little more than a way for private landowners to make quick profits.

More Planning

By the early 1960s, it was clear that Kuwait was outstripping the capacity of the 1952 master plan, which had been designed for a population of 250,000 people. Kuwait's population was already reaching 300,000, and the Municipality had to extend the physical limits of the plan to encompass additional residential and industrial areas outside the Green Belt.[114] The government needed someone with the planning experience and expertise that state institutions were severely lacking to take Kuwait into the next stage of the development process (a prospect made easier now that Fahad al-Salem had died). But rather than turning to Britain when Kuwait was in the throes of brokering its independence, in 1960 the ruler appointed Palestinian-American architect and town planner Saba George Shiber to be planning adviser and official architect to Kuwait's PWD. That same year Abdullah al-Salem froze all construction inside the city center until a comprehensive solution to the incongruous and irrational build-up of the urban center could be conceived.

Shiber's main criticism when he arrived on the scene in 1960 was against the intrusion of the foreign "experts" he felt had led Kuwait down the wrong path of urban development. He lamented the destruction of the organically formed pre-oil town and its replacement with abstract planning and architectural influences that had no place, precedent, or purpose in Kuwait or the Arab world. He believed that "Kuwait and Kuwaiti society—different from all known planning precedents—were overlooked and their problems lightly disposed of by pencil and T-square." Kuwaitis had become "victims, of 'modern' planning."[115] Shiber decided to use Kuwait's own urban past rather than some abstract and remote British planning principle as the guiding force behind his plan to repair the damage. His main contribution was the development of a new central business district (CBD) in the heart of the city, an area that headed inland from the Seif Palace (as Mubarak's palace complex in the center of the town's seafront, or *al-seif*, came to be known) and the *furda*, incorporating the *suq*, al-Safat, and parts of Mirqab and Jibla. Over the preceding decade this historic core of the pre-oil town had "grown to be the thorniest and most unwieldy" part of the city.[116] Like the planners before him, Shiber called for a rigid separation of spatial functions and insisted that industry and residences "be weeded out of the [CBD]."[117] Despite his criticism of the planning methods of the previous decade, the reorganized blocks of the CBD met with the same fate as those parts of the city that were developed in the 1950s. Beginning in April 1961, the government acquired land in the CBD to be demolished, re-planned, and sold to the private sector at public auction by January 1963.[118]

Once again, the main beneficiary of this area's redevelopment was the commercial elite. On the site of the former Merchants' Market, which faced the old port area, Shiber constructed large blocks to serve as modern headquarters for the merchants' ever-expanding businesses. Behind these sea-facing blocks, new imposing structures housed banks, other financial institutions, and the new merchant-run Chamber of Commerce, all of which linked closely with the merchants' private enterprises. The completed parts of Shiber's CBD constituted the most compositionally coherent part of the city since redesign began in the 1950s. For the first time, "the relationship of one building to another—basically urban design, city architecture or townscape—has been introduced" (Figure 14).[119] Unlike Fahad al-Salem Street, Shiber's buildings were three-dimensional structures with shaded walkways connecting one building to the next and ample off-street parking (whereas the rest of the city suffered from a lack of parking). The buildings were well made and durable, using Arab architectural influences such as *mashrabiyya* (latticework window screens) and colonnaded *liwawin* to protect people from the sun and heat. Despite these differences, the area was again a commercial development that privileged merchant business over public needs.

Only half of Shiber's CBD plan was ever implemented. Initiation of development in the country's most expensive real estate zone once again triggered speculation, making land values in the area skyrocket and the continuation of the project unfeasible. After the plan was halted in 1965, Shiber left Kuwait. Once again the Municipality lacked sufficient staff to guide

FIGURE 14. One of the completed blocks of Saba George Shiber's Central Business District. *Source*: Kuwait Oil Company archives.

development, and building was still sporadic. Hamed Shu'aib, a Kuwaiti, became the Municipality's chief architect. In 1968 the Municipality signed an agreement with Colin Buchanan and Partners (CBP), an English planning consultancy established in 1964 by Colin Buchanan, known in Europe for his role in modern transportation planning. The hope was that a more comprehensive and long-term master plan for Kuwait would "control the chaotic situation and prepare for a better future."[120] Between 1968 and 1971, CBP produced a master plan covering three main areas: a physical plan for the entire country; a plan for the urban areas, excluding the city center and extending south to the oil town of Ahmadi; and a separate plan for the city center. The planners produced both a long-term and a short-term strategy: the former was based on a projected population of around two million to be reached between 1985 and 1995, and the latter was based on a more immediate period of growth, with a population estimate of 1.258 million to be reached between 1978 and 1984.[121] While the Buchanan team worked on their master plan, four international architectural firms—Peter and Allison Smithson from England, the Greek architect Georges Candilis, Reima Pietilä from Finland, and the Italian firm Belgiojoso, Peressutti, and Rogers—were invited to translate CBP's strategies for the city center into an urban-architectural reality. The terms of reference that the firms received admitted that "the character and coherence that the Old City possessed is vanishing but development by modern buildings has not replaced this by anything that can yet mark the new City of Kuwait as a great capital city."[122]

Despite the time and expense that went into its production, the CBP master plan (and therefore, by extension, the four city plans produced alongside it) was almost immediately rendered defunct when it was completed at the end of 1971, and it was only minimally implemented over the next decade. A weak planning administration coupled with high land values once again contributed to the plan's failure. Under normal circumstances, each new zoning proposal or planning regulation drawn up by the Municipality's City Planning Department had to be sent to the Municipal Council for individual approval.[123] The initial intention for the new master plan was that a newly established Master Planning Department (separate from the City Planning Department) would break down the thousand-page plan into the necessary planning regulations on which the Municipal Council would need to make specific decisions. But upon the completion of the study the staff of the Master Planning Department disintegrated. Three years after the plan was submitted the Municipality had not yet succeeded in dissecting it, and without approval it technically remained a confidential document, locked up in a room in the Municipality building.[124] As one high government official said to Ghazi Sultan (Director of Master Planning in the Municipality from 1968 to 1971), "What is the use of drawing up plans when you know that neither the will nor the machinery exists to implement it!"[125]

In September 1970 another key minister in the planning process predicted "that all things will come to a full stop when the plan is presented to the government in December, for the simple reason that no-one in Kuwait is capable of or is willing to make such long term policy decisions that will affect the growth of the country for the next 20 years."[126] Specifically, the Municipal Council was not used to giving, nor would it be willing to give, formal approval "to a document that would have such wide ranging effect on the market prices of land in Kuwait."[127] Normally the Council would never make a decision that would identify all areas to be developed over the next five years. Rather, it would make a more specific decision as to whether, for instance, a particular commercial street should be extended. This policy was not surprising given the level of land-grabbing and real estate speculation sparked by the land acquisition scheme. Identifying as yet untouched areas as earmarked for future development always led to increasing land values, often to the point that the original plans would have to be scrapped. "What this meant was that someone had to go through the master plan with a tooth-pick and literally reduce it to a day-to-day document valid for the next 20 years." The City Planning Department was incapable of this task, "so the plan lies safely locked up where it is."[128]

Soon after the plan's completion, the quadrupling of world oil prices during the 1973 oil embargo led to an economic boom throughout the Gulf. Kuwait's annual oil revenues shot up from $1.9 billion in 1973 to $8 billion in 1974.[129] In 1976 the government gave in to private sector pressure to increase floor area ratios inside the city center in order to combat higher building costs due to substantial inflation. However, this change in turn pushed up land values so high that the move became "to some extent self-defeating." It also made the potential for commercial development (let alone less profitable development such as housing or public services) inside the city center entirely unfeasible.[130] In 1970 the most expensive urban land, located in the *suq* and al-Safat area, was valued at approximately KD 450 per square meter; by 1977, land prices in the same area rose to between KD 4,000 and 5,000 per square meter. Elsewhere in the city, land values were equally high: up to KD 2,500 per square meter in al-Baluch in Sharq and around KD 3,000 per square meter west of the *suq* area. It was thus concluded in 1977, "There is little evidence that, at these prices, commercial development can be viable in the short to medium term."[131] Kuwait was already surpassing the limits of the 1971 master plan's short-term strategy, which was set for a capacity of 1.258 million by no earlier than 1978. By 1975 the population had reached one million due to a new influx of immigration after the 1973 oil boom. With increased affluence, Kuwaitis required more service (particularly domestic) workers, and migrants from countries negatively impacted by the hike in oil prices (particularly South Asia) increasingly turned to the Gulf for employment opportunities.[132]

Buchanan recommended regular revisions of the master plan to adjust it to the country's constantly changing circumstances. Shankland Cox Partnership conducted the first review in 1977. The revised plan adjusted the long-term population projection to 2.76 million by the year 2000. It also proposed the construction of two new towns: Subbiya on the northern tip of Kuwait Bay, and Khairan on Kuwait's southernmost coast. The plan was never properly implemented, however, due to the debilitating crash in 1982 of Kuwait's Suq al-Manakh, an illegal but thriving stock market in which trading in companies banned on Kuwait's official stock exchange was based on the use of postdated checks. When someone tried to cash a postdated check and it bounced, a financial crisis immediately ripped through the country. Practically every economic sector was hit, and the private sector stopped investing in construction and urban development projects as it struggled to cope with the crisis. In 1983, CBP conducted a second master plan review and further adjusted population estimates, housing needs, and so on. By the end of the 1980s, their proposals for new commercial centers, industrial areas, and the new towns that Shankland Cox had recommended had still not been implemented.[133] A third master plan review began in January 1990 but was interrupted by the Iraqi invasion that August, after which it was decided that postliberation Kuwait would require an entirely new master plan rather than a review of the 1971 plan, which was considered "no longer appropriate."[134]

Landscape of State Power

Although the 1971 master plan was never implemented, the 1973 oil boom stimulated major construction activity in Kuwait. Rising land values and high inflation meant that development once again focused heavily on profit and satisfying the demands of the economic elite. One difference during this period, however, was the simultaneous transformation of the cityscape into a spatial reflection of the growing power and presence of the government. Although the authority of the rulers and the functions of government had grown significantly after 1946, very little changed throughout the first two decades of oil to increase the presence of the state on the urban landscape. By the 1970s there was a concerted effort to enhance the "practical and symbolic focus of national administration" in the city center.[135] The timing of this new desire for a "great capital city" was significant. Kuwait's role in the 1973 oil embargo left the government in a strong-enough position to sign an agreement with KOC in 1974 that gave Kuwait 60 percent ownership of its oil (with the remaining 40 percent nationalized the following year). The government now played a much larger and more central role in managing the country's economy, and the administration expanded and became more complex.[136] The state therefore needed a capital city to reflect its now complete autonomy (expanding the process that Mubarak had begun at the turn of the century). With the help of their international advisers, over the next decade the government put together "a veritable Who's Who of the international giants" in the field of architectural modernism to produce spatial declarations of state power in a vernacular that the world could recognize as truly modern.[137] Pietilä worked on an extension to the Seif Palace complex; Kenzo Tange from Japan designed the country's new international airport; Jørn Utzon, of Sydney Opera House fame, designed Kuwait's Parliament building; and the renowned Danish modernist architect and designer Arne Jacobsen was commissioned for the Central Bank.

Perhaps the most symbolic project of this period was the large water-supply system designed by Swedish architect Sune Lindström that consisted of thirty-one "mushroom towers" divided into five clusters located in key zones around the country.[138] A sixth cluster, known specifically as the Kuwait Towers, was distinctly situated on a small promontory jutting into the bay at the eastern extremity of the city center. The towers were designed separately by Danish architect Malene Bjørn and became the country's national landmark.[139] The international architectural community praised the entire project, completed in 1976, for its impressive combination of functionalism and aestheticism. In 1980 the designers won the prestigious Aga Khan Award for Architecture for excellence in design.[140] But the water towers symbolized an even greater achievement for Kuwait than architectural excellence. They represented an irreversible break with the hardships of the past: whereas once fresh water was scarce and had to be imported by ship, now hundreds of thousands of gallons of desalinated water were easily accessible. Because the mushroom towers were the country's tallest structures, and the Kuwait Towers constituted (at that time) the highest point in the urban center, the population would be constantly reminded of this achievement as they went about their daily routines within Kuwait's new urban landscape. Water was also heavily subsidized by the state and was practically free for the entire population. The towers became a poignant symbol of the new role of government in providing for the public's material well-being.

Kuwait City was thus transformed into a legible state capital that permanently inscribed the new social, political, and economic centrality of the rulers and their state apparatus onto the city. This transformation thoroughly reversed the trend of the pre-oil period, when the marginal activities of the rulers left very few visible markers on the urban landscape. The buildings constructed during this period, such as the Central Bank, the Ministry of Foreign Affairs, the Ministry of Justice courthouse, and the massive Ministries Complex—all completed between 1975 and 1985—were "more than mere homes for government leaders."[141] They were emblems of the new modern state that had appropriated the most historically significant, spatially privileged, and economically valuable spots in the city. The new Ministries Complex, which housed several state institutions, took over one of the main entrances to the city, the Nayef (or Shamiya) Gate, just beyond the Nayef Palace; the Central Bank was adjacent to the old Suq al-Tujjar; and the Ministry of Planning stood on the site of the demolished Tell Bhaiteh, where the town was first settled.

Most significant was the three-part expansion of the historic Seif Palace, which housed the offices of the executive branch of government. The first expansion took place between 1962 and 1964 when the rest of the town was undergoing mass demolition. A large reception hall was constructed adjacent to Mubarak's old palace, along with a golden-domed clock tower. By the end of the decade the government sought once again to "improve the setting" of the Seif Palace area.[142] The Council of Ministers, Ministry of Foreign Affairs, and National Mosque—all classified by CBP as "buildings with ceremonial linkages"—were to be integrated into the Seif Palace complex.[143] This much of an expansion required considerable space. The Seif Palace was flanked by the historic Sharq *dhow* harbor to the east and the old *furda* to the west. The CBP planners urged that the town harbors be retained as part of the urban landscape due to their historical associations and pleasant aspect. Nonetheless, more than half of the Sharq harbor was swept away for the Seif Palace's eastern extension, work on which began in 1978.[144] Whereas in the pre-oil period the harbors constituted the focal points of the urban landscape, by 1981 the seat of government had become "the most important part" of the city.[145]

Pietilä's designs for this second extension corresponded to the height and style of the existing palace buildings in order to ensure continuity and harmony between old and new.[146] However, the "humble scale and character [of Pietilä's structures] did not satisfy the ambitions of the government." In 1984, only three years after the project's completion, the Seif Palace was earmarked for a much larger transformation.[147] The new plan expanded the executive offices that were still housed in the old palace and in its 1962 extension. This new extension completely wiped out the entire historic port complex to the west of the palace (by now the bulk of the country's cargo was handled by Shuwaikh's modern port facilities), and the former hub of Kuwait's historic urbanism became a heavily guarded private space from which the general public was barred. The old port town was officially remade into a state capital.[148]

Despite the demolition of the source of the merchant's historic power, the changing cityscape after 1973 continued to reflect their ever-increasing economic power. The only other major construction projects during this period, alongside state buildings, were the buildings that housed the country's financial sector, which was growing rapidly due to the increase in oil income coupled with Lebanon's decline as the Arab banking center during the civil war.[149] Two major additions to Kuwait City in the late seventies and early eighties were the Kuwait Stock Exchange building, designed by well-known British architect John Bonnington, and the American firm Skidmore, Owings & Merrill's banking complex (which housed the Industrial Bank, the Real Estate Bank, and the Bank of Kuwait and the Middle East). Both were located within the site plan of Shiber's CBD. New luxury commercial centers, such as the joined Le Méridien Hotel and Salhiya Complex just off Fahad al-Salem Street, also began appearing around the city.

The new partnership between state and private sector interests was thus reflected in the cityscape during this period of "architectural enlightenment," at the expense of public interests.[150] Of all the major projects inside the city center that were commissioned to international architects during this period, the one that was scrapped altogether was a massive national housing project designed by Georges Candilis. Furthermore, the city remained as compositionally incoherent as it had been in the preceding decades. Neil Parkyn, an architect who lived and worked in Kuwait in the late 1970s, noted on a return visit to the city in 1983 that these new buildings each stood "in isolation, having no 'back' or 'front,' often no planned linkage to the next one."[151] As Lawrence Vale puts it, they were "isolated islands in a sea of parking lots."[152] The spaces behind and between these new masterpieces remained undeveloped and neglected, occupied by the ruins of the few remaining pre-oil courtyard houses and the rapidly obsolescing "dusty walk-ups from the 1950 building boom."[153] Outside the Green Belt, however, development was proceeding apace with the construction of the new suburbs to which the townspeople were relocated throughout the first three decades of oil.

5

The Move to the Suburbs

Importing Suburbia

Suburbanization and the mandatory vacating of the city center by its former inhabitants constituted the most considerable urban transformation of the early oil years and played a critical role in determining how both the city and urban society changed as a result of oil. As Saba George Shiber succinctly put it, "The story of new Kuwait is the story of the 'exodus' from 'ad-Dira.'"[1] Life in the new, privatized suburbs significantly altered the townspeople's everyday lifestyles and social relations. Suburbanization in Kuwait was not a response to existing social problems such as squalor, overcrowding, or poor health and hygiene in the city center as was common in British and other European cities in the nineteenth and twentieth centuries as well as in other Arab cities such as Cairo. Nor was it premised on the kind of "dream of upward mobility" that accelerated the suburbanization of working class white Americans in the post-World War II decades.[2] Rather, "the great exodus" in Kuwait was first and foremost a means of clearing away the old town for the development of a new city to be built in its place.[3] Dislocation from the urban center was not optional for city residents, and the state constructed new residential areas away from the city purely to accommodate the displaced townspeople. The specific method of suburbanization employed in Kuwait was brought in through the 1952 master plan and constituted the most important part of the plan's implementation in the ensuing decades.

Like the midcentury British neighborhood units on which Minoprio, Spencely, and Macfarlane based their plan, Kuwait's new residential areas were constructed along lines similar to America's publicly sponsored postwar housing developments and subdivision suburbs. The neighborhoods were designed as homogenous residential areas, emphasizing detached single-family living on allocated plots. The areas had some basic amenities, but the assumption was that residents would commute to the city center for work. Despite these similarities, there were also several differences and contradictions in the ways that Kuwait adopted and adapted this imported suburbia. Perhaps the most significant difference was that, whereas American postwar housing developments involved a public-private alliance (with federal interventions in municipal zoning and government-insured mortgage financing paving the way for the construction of large-scale developments by private builders such as Levitt and Sons), in Kuwait the entire process of suburban growth and development was in the hands of the government. Though the design and construction of government housing projects was sometimes tendered out to private contractors, the vast majority of housing schemes for Kuwaiti citizens were state-led and heavily subsidized (and prevented the establishment of a mortgage market). Housing for non-Kuwaitis followed a different model that more directly involved the private sector. However, like African Americans in postwar US cities, non-Kuwaitis were systemically excluded from the suburbs (except as servants) and from homeownership, and were restricted to the rental market in the city center or other commercial areas.

Even for Kuwaitis, homeownership was not infused with the same ideological connotations as it was (and still is) in the United States, where, as a key component of the American dream of upward mobility, it gave the suburbs not only economic but also moral value. As Barbara Kelly describes, "Housing, home ownership, the American home itself, became the mobilizing themes for a wide range of interest groups, each of which presented ideological arguments stressing the need to preserve the American way of life."[4] Suburbanization in Kuwait, by contrast, explicitly introduced and encouraged the adoption of a completely new way of life. As described in the previous chapter, in order to facilitate the state's wholesale redevelopment plan, Kuwaitis were encouraged to shed the past and "embrace modernity."[5] Part of this process entailed conforming to new ways of living in new and improved residential areas. Kuwaitis accepted these changes because the new suburbs materially elevated people's lives in very immediate

and tangible ways. Houses were bigger and cleaner, and had more amenities that made everyday life much easier. The speed and ease with which
Kuwaitis embraced suburban living reflects their pragmatic approach to
life, ability to adjust to change, and willingness to absorb new lifestyles—
legacies of their port city heritage coupled with their history of scarcity.

Though housing is not specified as a state obligation in the Kuwaiti
Constitution as are education and health care, from the advent of the welfare state the government pledged to provide all citizens with a new subsidized dwelling. Like the American housing schemes after which they were
modeled, the suburbs (along with other key components of the welfare state
such as employment, education, and health care) would uplift or reform
Kuwaiti ways of living. However, whereas suburbs like Levittown (the archetypal midcentury American subdivision) and British new towns were often
described as "planned" or "model" *communities*, Kuwait's new suburbs were
known in official discourse as *al-manatiq al-numuthajiyya*, or the "model
areas," and little reference was given to the social worlds they were meant to
embody or foster. The suburbs were important vestiges of Kuwait's advanc-
ing urban modernity, showcasing all the features of the country's newfound
prosperity and progress: state-of-the-art health clinics, advanced schools,
wide roads, lush gardens and trees, luxury housing, and of course rational
planning. But aside from the promotion of nuclear family living, the planning discourse involved in the development of the suburbs contained no
expressions of the social values or norms these areas were expected to rep-
resent or promote. The specific way in which suburbia was constructed in
Kuwait, as a key component of the oil welfare state, thus made these new
residential areas as spatially, socially, and ideologically distinct from their
Western counterparts as they were from Kuwait's own pre-oil *firjan*.

Constructing Suburbia

The new suburbs were constructed just beyond the Green Belt as
"super-block" developments, each about 2.25 square kilometers and housing six thousand people.[6] The 1952 plan emphasized the need for definite
boundary lines—created by the new ring and radial roads—to contain
each unit "so that buildings do not straggle into the desert."[7] The imported
concentric ring road plan actually fit well onto the existing structures of
Kuwait's pre-oil urban milieu. The First Ring Road, located immediately
beyond the Green Belt, was designed to echo the semi-circular path of the

sur, and the additional rings followed this same general shape as they emanated further away from the urban center. Although the *sur* was demolished in 1957, its five gates were physically preserved and it was from these gateways that the radial roads connecting the ring roads extended. The *sur* thus served as the basis for Kuwait's highway system and established the boundaries for the new suburban areas (see Figure 10, p. 99).

Between 1954 and 1959, eight new neighborhood districts were constructed within the first three concentric ring roads; by 1960 a fourth ring was added to the road system and an additional seven new suburbs were completed by 1965 (Figure 15). The need to empty out the city center as swiftly as possible to begin work on new development projects within the Green Belt necessitated direct government involvement in the townspeople's relocation, which began in 1954. In addition to receiving

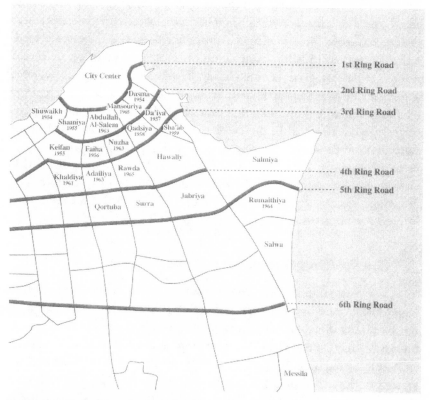

FIGURE 15. Map of the suburbs and commercial areas between the First and Fifth Ring Roads. *Source*: Patrick Semaan.

financial compensation, Kuwaitis who sold their land to the government for development purposes were also entitled to a plot of residential land in one of the new neighborhoods on which to build a new home. This land was distributed at a nominal price—about 10 percent of its actual value.[8] Kuwaitis of limited income who could not afford to build their own homes—such as low-paid government employees, families who did not own property in the city center, or those who did not make enough from the acquisition of their property to build alternative housing—were eligible for a "limited-income group" (LIG) government-built house in lieu of a plot of land. An LIG house was provided at an average price of 30 to 40 percent of its actual value, to be paid through interest-free installments.[9] By 1958 a third option, known as the Plot and Loan Scheme, gave limited-income families the option of an empty plot of land in conjunction with an interest-free thirty-year government loan to build their own home.[10] These various public housing schemes created clear socioeconomic distinctions between members of the urban community. Nonetheless, the LIG housing projects for less affluent urban families were "integrated closely with the areas of private housing" within the first three to four ring roads. Nine of these fifteen neighborhoods contained both government housing and allocated plots.[11] Due to the substantial government subsidy involved in all of these relocation options, by the end of the 1970s most of the pre-oil urban population was rehoused outside the city center.

These suburbs were centrally developed and managed by the government. They did not have neighborhood councils or any other form of local government through which the requirements and needs of the residents could be transmitted to central state authorities.[12] They were "developed primarily for residential uses," and were designed to be relatively self-contained, with their own schools, mosques, post offices, police stations, and health clinics.[13] The suburbs became the spaces in which the government could easily distribute the services of the new welfare state. Public participation in the management of suburbs was limited to neighborhood cooperative societies. Local co-ops, funded and managed by members of the local community for the benefit of their fellow residents, were responsible for the sale of food and other commodities and the provision of some public services.

The first cooperative society in Kuwait predated the move to the suburbs and was established by a group of students from the Mubarakiyya

School who, under the direction of their teachers, put together money to open a small grocery store in 1942. They then divided the proceeds evenly between them. Three other schools established similar cooperative supermarkets by 1952, as did the employees of the Education Department in 1955. In 1962 the government passed a law to regulate these cooperative societies, giving them the official stamp of approval. Residents of the new suburbs then began putting together the capital needed to fund, open, and run their own co-op shopping centers in the middle of their residential area to provide local residents with such necessities as groceries, household tools, and kitchen utensils.[14] The first of these co-ops, in Keifan and Shamiya, opened with starting capital of KD 41,021 and KD 38,411, respectively. Residents became members of their local co-op by paying an annual subscription fee of their choice. The amount paid was not equivalent to shares in the co-op. Rather, a member's annual profit was calculated as a fixed percentage of the amount of money the member spent buying goods from the co-op that year, which was then awarded as a refund.[15] This method of sharing in the profits on the basis of the amount of one's own purchases created the incentive to shop locally, thereby ensuring the long-term continuity of the co-op. By the 1980s about half of the national population were members of their local cooperatives.[16]

The cooperative societies also provided a certain amount of cleaning services within the residential areas, and they spent some money on local cultural facilities such as libraries. They also distributed food and money to local families in need.[17] They were run entirely by elected boards of local residents, and in some ways they formalized the traditional role of the *farij* in providing public services at a local level, thereby offering some continuity with the past in the new suburbs. However, the central government also had a role to play in the creation and running of these cooperative societies. The Municipality and Ministry of Commerce monitored the co-ops closely to ensure that they satisfied national food consumption and trade regulations. The government built the co-op premises in the center of each neighborhood unit at its own expense and rented the space to the local society at a nominal price. In exchange, it used the co-ops to distribute government-subsidized foodstuffs to which each Kuwaiti household was entitled, such as rice, salt, and cooking oil.[18] Such government involvement represented significant discontinuities with the past, when the state played next to no role in shaping the *farij* or contributing to the well-being of its residents.

Housing Distribution

Housing plots in the new neighborhoods were allocated largely by lottery. Applicants drew lots and the winners' names were put on a priority list for plots in a newly completed residential area.[19] Although applicants could choose the plot they preferred from among those available for distribution in a particular area, it was difficult for most people (aside from some prominent families with influence in the housing administration) to specify such preferences as the precise neighborhood in which they would like to live. This fixed procedure left little scope for the majority of the population to choose their residence according to family ties or to know in advance who their neighbors would be.[20] Furthermore, plots, housing loans, and government-built houses were all allocated on a single-family basis, meaning that extended families were divided up into smaller nuclear families who were then dispersed across different areas. In a 1969 social-residential survey conducted by the Municipality, only 30 percent of the people polled in Shamiya stated that either of their immediate neighbors were relatives.[21] In 1982, Kuwaiti social geographer Abdulrasool al-Moosa conducted a social-residential survey as part of the third review of the Buchanan master plan. He too found that two-thirds of his respondents were unrelated to their neighbors.[22]

The inequalities of the land acquisition scheme played a principal role in the dispersal of the townspeople into new residential areas. The timing of acquisitions largely determined the areas to which families moved. Those whose properties inside the town were acquired by the state early on—namely families who lived in the most sought after real estate along the coast or near what became the central business district, and those who had the most influence within the development apparatus—moved out to the first eight neighborhoods to be fully allocated by 1960. Those whose properties were acquired later moved out to the areas allocated in the second wave between 1961 and 1967. The amount paid for an acquisition of property in the town also usually determined whether a family went for a plot only, a plot and loan, or a government-built house. It was not uncommon for neighbors or inhabitants of neighboring *firjan* to receive unequal payments for their property in the town due to the arbitrary pricing of the land acquisition scheme. New disparities in wealth between members of the same family and between former neighbors of relatively equal socioeconomic standing contributed to the scattering of pre-oil urban communities.[23]

Meanwhile, the fact that people could petition the government to have their land acquired resulted in great discrepancies between people who had government connections and those who did not. These discrepancies were related not only to how much a family received for their property but also to how quickly the acquisition took place. Although petitions for acquisition had to meet certain criteria specified by the Municipal Council—most of which were under the broad heading "in the public interest"—people with strong influence in the government could often exert sufficient pressure to sidestep these requirements. In 1962, twenty-one prominent merchants signed a petition requesting that the Municipal Council acquire their properties in Jibla. Though none of their stated reasons sufficiently met the criteria for acquisition at that time, the Council complied with the request and the merchants' houses were duly acquired.[24] At the other extreme, in 1964 a man named Mohammed Ali Abu-Hamad was still living in the city in a house that the state had requested for demolition in 1956 but that had not yet been acquired. Abu-Hamad lived in this house with twenty-eight people and was penniless. He could not afford food to support his family let alone rent for a better house while he waited for the state to fulfill its request to acquire his property. Without sufficient influence or personal connections in the planning apparatus, Abu-Hamad was stuck living in his dilapidated house in the town indefinitely, whereas most of his former neighbors had already moved out to the new suburbs.[25]

Architectural Changes

The form of the new suburbs contrasted sharply with that of the pre-oil *firjan*. House plots were allocated at 750 or 1,000 square meters while government-built houses in the same areas were constructed on plots between 400 and 750 square meters, depending on the number of bedrooms and family income.[26] This spacious layout was completely different from the structure of the *firjan* of the old town, which had consisted of "courtyard houses huddled together in a closely knit texture."[27] Also, unlike the houses of the pre-oil period, which usually contained many members of an extended family, villas in the new neighborhoods were restricted to single-family use. The average urban household in 1970 was estimated to contain seven people, creating the extremely low density of fifty-five square meters per person, with "many small families occupy[ing] large houses."[28]

Residential architectural styles and tastes also changed substantially. Before oil, climatic considerations coupled with the limited availability of building materials had dictated a uniform architectural vernacular in Kuwait Town. Because many houses shared outer boundary walls and because entrances were conspicuous, it was not always easy to determine where one house ended and the other began; the size of a particular house (and therefore the affluence of the family occupying it) could really be determined only from the inside. With the advent of oil, however, the environment was no longer an obstacle to construction, and Kuwaiti merchants imported a vast array of building equipment and materials.[29] Technology's ability to regulate temperature with air conditioning in the summer and heating in the winter meant that houses no longer needed thick, high, windowless walls to block out the climate. The suburbs' self-built houses were designed around "Western" models. As single-family villas, they inverted the plan of the old courtyard houses "by relegating the house's centrifugal social space to the perimeter."[30] Also unlike their predecessors, they fronted the main street, and low boundary walls left parts of the garden, front entrance, and facade of the house open to public view (Figure 16). The new villas were thus much more exposed to the outside world

FIGURE 16. A typical new villa in the suburbs, open to public view. *Source*: Aga Khan Trust for Culture. Courtesy of Aga Khan Trust for Culture.

than the houses of the old town had been, making the visual aspect of one's residence important for the first time.

The only condition imposed on families building their own houses in the suburbs was that the structure had to be a single-family detached villa. They could therefore design their homes according to newly developing styles, creating what Huda al-Bahar described in 1985 as "a Disneyland of residential manifestations."[31] Geometric shapes, sharp askew angles, asymmetrical lines, sloping roofs, cantilevered balconies, and "unfunctional decorative slabs of concrete punched with various openings, aided by technicolour elevation" became common features of residential architecture in the 1950s and 1960s.[32] These modern villas, though certainly an eclectic "hodge podge of architectural forms" (as al-Bahar described them), vividly represented the excitement and experimentation of the early oil years in Kuwait.[33] Such novelty and uniqueness in residential architecture—built at great expense and sometimes bordering on the "outlandish"[34]—was important to the residents of the suburbs. According to al-Bahar, "people perceived their house as a symbol of their affluence and status in society."[35] As previously discussed, guaranteed government employment after 1950 had expanded the Kuwaiti middle class by eliminating precarious laboring jobs and giving all citizens access to an equitable income and lifestyle. With the decline of the old social tiers, homes now replaced occupation or trade as measures of social standing. This change added a new dimension to the social interactions between neighbors in Kuwait: competition and keeping up appearances.[36] As Zahra Freeth noticed while driving through some of these new suburbs in 1970, "Keeping up with the Joneses in Kuwait tends to take the form of demolishing and rebuilding your house as soon as the neighbors put up something bigger or more modern."[37] In addition to changing tastes and styles, these villas also expressed the new levels of wealth and extravagance that many families were now enjoying, particularly those in the earliest neighborhoods, who benefited most from the land acquisition scheme. Even families of more moderate incomes were able to utilize attractive government loans to build large houses with eclectic designs. This is one way in which the new Kuwaiti suburbs contrasted sharply with the mid-century American subdivisions on which they were based. One of the sharpest criticisms of Levittown and other similar suburbs was that they were architecturally bland and uninspiring in their cookie-cutter repetition.[38] Although residents of these American suburbs were given the opportunity to make structural and design changes to their homes, the ethos of these housing developments emphasized conformity and moderation rather than individuality and extravagance (especially during the mid-twentieth-century period of anticommunist paranoia, when social nonconformity or difference was labeled deviant and therefore politically threatening).[39] In Kuwait's earliest suburbs, individuality and extravagance were the order of the day.

The suburbs between the First and Fourth Ring Roads also included many government-built houses constructed in the 1950s and, to a lesser extent, the 1960s. Shiber called this "urban, or in-city" limited-income housing, as opposed to the LIG housing constructed later, "beyond the so-called planning limits of the city."[40] Built on smaller plots than the privately built villas, the government houses were designed according to one of two possible styles—"Eastern" (*sharqy*) or "Western" (*gharby*)—to be chosen by the recipient. The Eastern-style house was built in an L-shape adjacent to the boundary wall of the plot; the Western-style house, like the self-built villas, was a street-facing house set back a proscribed distance from the boundary wall. There was no set policy in the distribution of these two styles of houses, and both styles could be found mixed into the different neighborhood units.[41] However, the government houses were built in clusters according to a single, simple, functional design, more closely resembling American tract housing. Although integrated into the same neighborhoods as the privately built villas, these government houses contrasted sharply with the eclectic house styles of the more affluent families living nearby. The residents of the government households could make major structural and personalized changes to their homes only after all installments had been paid, which usually took around ten years.[42] New levels of social inequality created by the land acquisition scheme in the early oil years thus became stamped onto residential spaces within the suburbs. However, once the house was fully paid for, LIG housing recipients in these areas could apply to the Credit and Savings Bank for "second-story" loans to make structural and decorative changes to their houses. This allowed them to tailor their homes to suit their specific needs and styles, particularly once the loan value was increased from KD 7,500 to 10,000 in 1976.[43] These lower-income families were thus able to raise their homes to a "new socio-economic level" and erase some of the visible differences between themselves and their more affluent neighbors.[44]

The architectural experimentation of the early oil years that characterized the new suburbs reveals that urban Kuwaitis fully embraced the quest for modernity and change that the state had promoted in the production of the new city. As al-Bahar observed firsthand:

Kuwaitis began to experience a sense of freedom from the constraints of the traditional way of life and a sense of affluence toward a modern living environment. . . . Many of their attempts were in search of a new identity that had no link with the past, and rather than develop, enhance and refine the traditional character in the context of the new, they simply discarded the old and started to build the new on very shaky and superficial grounds.[45]

Architectural styles such as California space-age Googie, brutalism, Bauhaus modernism, and Streamline Moderne were freely fused with diverse stylistic features such as colonial verandahs, Arab *mashrabiyya*, and Art Deco pillars. Such attempts to mimic international modernism through trial-and-error reflected the cultural experimentation of a society rapidly changing and eagerly searching for the ultimate statement of its newfound prosperity.

Nonetheless, al-Bahar, like Shiber and Freeth before her, viewed this process of architectural change in the early oil years as a disruption to Kuwait's architectural identity. She blamed the structural and aesthetic failures of the era on expatriate Arab architects who did not understand Kuwait's environment or how best to interpret the "confused thoughts" of their Kuwaiti clients.[46] However, this perspective overlooks the fact that, as "consumers of suburbia," the townspeople were not simply "innocent bystanders" in this process.[47] The new architecture was not entirely suited to the local climate: roofs were not always properly canted for rain, and cracks in the concrete from the extreme heat often caused leaks.[48] However, the abandoning of traditional architectural styles in favor of "westernized" modes of residential living was not merely "a symptom of striving after novelty at all costs."[49] It also reflected the changing everyday needs and values of the users of these spaces. Architectural fantasies were buttressed by social pragmatism. Where old social customs persisted in the suburbs, the architectural features that corresponded to them were retained. One example of this was the *diwaniyya*. Bigger houses in the suburbs meant that families of all classes, beyond the merchant elite, now had enough room for separate visiting quarters for men. The institution therefore survived the move to the suburbs and in fact became a common feature of most homes. Villas in the suburbs continued to be designed with separate entrances for the *diwaniyya* and the main part of the house.[50]

When traditional social customs changed, however, residential architecture evolved to reflect these changes. Several spatial features for the visual concealment of women, like high boundary walls and curtain walls behind main doors, were abandoned. Kuwaiti urban women in the early oil years went through numerous social changes. Travel, new education opportunities, and paid employment fundamentally altered female roles and expectations in Kuwait, particularly among merchant class women, who before oil had less freedom than women of the less affluent classes. The emancipation of women was a vital component of Kuwait's *nahda*, or "awakening," in the social discourse of the early oil decades, among women and men alike.[51] The defining moment came in 1953 when a group of girls took off their black *'ibiy* (singular *'abat*) and burned them in the schoolyard.[52] Over the next three years the question of the unveiling of Kuwaiti women dominated the public sphere. By 1956 the government dropped the headscarf as part of the uniform in public schools, and by 1961 women were permitted to work in the public sector without being covered.[53] With the removal of the veil, there was no longer a need to block women from sight in their own homes. Although the *diwaniyya* continued to be a male-only domain, men and women in the new suburbs began entertaining in their homes together, "in the European way. . . . The wife welcomes her guests at the door and moves freely among them. . . . Often at parties there will be dancing to the record-player, and some Kuwaiti girls, with their husband's consent, will go so far as to partner other male guests."[54]

In 1978, Ghazi Sultan, then working as a private architect, participated in a design bid for a government housing project, which by then was targeting the sedentarizing Bedouin rather than limited-income urban Kuwaitis. When Sultan's team presented their house designs, the representative from the Ministry of Housing, which Sultan claimed had been taken over by "devout Muslims," protested that the house had an opening between the dining and living rooms:

Suppose you are having dinner and a guest comes in. What should your wife do? Go upstairs and have her dinner? You cannot have that. You have to put four walls on each and every room, and you must be absolutely sure that the woman of the house can walk from one part of the house to the other and be totally sure that no strangers will see her.[55]

Although Sultan trained in America, as a Kuwaiti architect he was sensitive to the social and cultural requirements and needs of his local clients. He was adamantly against the "[blind] use of western space standards" and he believed that local architecture needed to "respond positively to the realities of climate and orientation."[56] He also avoided "individuality for individuality's sake," and he believed that "uniqueness is not necessarily a positive criterion for design."[57] In other words, Sultan was not of the mind-set that guided the architectural experimentation of the early oil years, which critics like Shiber and al-Bahar believed were antithetical and insensitive to Kuwaiti social values. Rather than being a deliberate neglect of local customs, Sultan's abandonment of gender segregation in his house design suggests that this was no longer a social norm among the (sub)urban Kuwaiti clients for whom he had been designing homes for more than a decade. Whether or not this was something that the Bedouin sector of society still desired, or whether separated spaces for men and women were being imposed upon them by the housing authorities, is difficult to ascertain. As discussed later in the chapter, all Bedouin housing projects were constructed according to what was known in planning discourse as "Eastern" or "Arab" style. The recipients of these houses often complained that they were not given design choices, even though "the families occupying these houses are all different from one another."[58] Nonetheless, for urban Kuwaitis, changes in the architectural vernacular of residential spaces in the early oil years did often reflect changing social needs.

Socio-spatial Segregation

In sharp contrast to their pre-oil predecessors, but true to their American subdivision counterparts, the new suburbs were created as socially homogenous enclaves that differentiated between sectors of the population by background. Although the suburbs within the first four ring roads contained the same heterogeneous population that once occupied the town's residential quarters, new lines of demarcation between certain sectors of the urban population were drawn in the new suburbs. Furthermore, the fact that other sectors of the population—namely non-Kuwaiti immigrants and the formerly pastoral Bedouin and villagers—were excluded from the inner suburbs homogenized the diversity of the former townspeople by turning them into a clearly demarcated social group, increasingly referred to as *hadar* (or sedentary urbanites) to distinguish them from other newly urbanizing Kuwaitis.

When the suburban relocation program was launched in 1954, the first neighborhoods immediately outside the town wall that were allocated to displaced townspeople were Shuwaikh and Shamiya to the west and Dasma to the east. Jibla residents were given plots of land in the two former areas while Sharq residents were moved to the latter. Some of the social characteristics of Jibla, the more socially elite quarter of the pre-oil town, were thus transported to Shuwaikh and Shamiya. Of the first eight suburbs constructed between 1954 and 1959, only Shuwaikh did not contain any government-built LIG housing.[59] The more socially heterogeneous nature of Sharq, meanwhile, became a defining attribute of Dasma. Although detailed information on the residents of each district was not provided in the 1957 (the country's first) or any subsequent census, some ideas about the social composition of these areas can be gleaned from the results of the 1963 and 1967 parliamentary elections (noting that, since the inception of Parliament, Kuwaitis predominantly vote along sectarian lines).[60] The elected Members of Parliament (MPs) of Shamiya and Shuwaikh were practically all of Sunni Najdi background, while the MPs from Dasma included men of prominent Sunni families of Sharq, such as the Al Nusif and Al Rodhan, as well as prominent Shi'i families, such as the Al Kathmi and Dashti.[61]

The creation of an exclusive merchant enclave out in the suburbs was not entirely new because Jibla's coastline had also been a relatively elite zone. What was more unusual was the creation of Kuwait's first Shi'i enclaves as a result of state relocation policies. A prominent former member of the Municipality (who wished to remain anonymous) claims that a large portion of the Shi'a were deliberately the last to have their property in the city (primarily in Sharq) acquired by the state. They were therefore among the last of the townspeople to be relocated out of the city, because first priority for plots and LIG housing went to people whose properties had been acquired.[62] Although such a policy is not officially documented, election results are once again telling. From the 1963 elections onward, at least four of the five MPs in the Sharq electoral district were Shi'i. Though before the oil boom most of the town's Shi'a lived in Sharq, the district itself was not a Shi'i-majority area that would have produced four out of five successful candidates in any election. But by 1963 most of Sharq's Sunni residents had been relocated to new suburbs. Though many Shi'i families—particularly the more prominent ones, such as the Ma'rafi—had also moved out to new areas such as Dasma, the election results reveal that enough of them had indeed been left behind in the 1950s to turn Sharq into a Shi'i-majority area by 1963. Most of these residents were less affluent families waiting for government-built housing.

Between 1961 and 1965, seven new neighborhoods were completed. Only two—Rumaithiya and Rawda—contained LIG housing as well as plots and therefore took in a large number of the limited-income families still waiting in the city to be relocated. The majority of Rumaithiya's LIG housing recipients were Shi'a, and when the boundaries of new national electoral districts were drawn in 1981, Rumaithiya became a Shi'i-majority district. In other words, through land acquisition and relocation tactics the state guaranteed the Shi'a (traditional government supporters) representation in Parliament. Whether this was intentional or not is debatable. Jill Crystal argues that after independence the rulers searched for allies outside the old merchant elite, and "[one] forum for this search was the National Assembly. There the amirs balanced the merchants with beduins, Shias, and progressives, in turn politicizing each community."[63] The creation of Kuwait's first Shi'i enclaves—first in Sharq and then in Rumaithiya—might therefore have been an intended outcome of state housing policies as alleged by the aforementioned Municipality official.

The only former townspeople who did not move from the old town to the new neighborhood units beyond the First Ring Road were members of the ruling family. Rather than receiving plots in the new suburbs alongside the former townspeople, the Al Sabah staked out large plots of land well beyond the old town wall for the building of their new palaces. Most of these residences were located along the coast in Sha'ab, Salmiya, Salwa, and Messila, which fell outside the urban displacement scheme and were otherwise developed by the private sector. Although over time new neighborhoods were developed in close proximity to these palatial estates, their detachment from the suburbs both effected and reflected a growing social distance between the townspeople and members of the ruling family. Lienhardt noticed this distance when he visited in 1953: cars belonging to the Al Sabah carried special license plates that identified them as "shaikhs" and they expected to be "given respectful precedence in traffic, but, more importantly, they were on no account to be overtaken." Cars and residential neighborhoods alike thus "[suggested] an element of growing distinction and separation within the community."[64]

Some social segregation thus occurred within the suburbs to which the townspeople were relocated, but more significant was the segregation between the former townspeople, non-Kuwaiti immigrants, and the villagers and Bedouin who gave up their pastoral lifestyles to become part of Kuwaiti urban society. Most geographical studies on Kuwait that acknowl-

edge the separation of these three sectors in discrete residential zones attribute the phenomenon to a natural inclination of people of different social
backgrounds to self-segregate.[65] However, before oil, Kuwaitis did not have
a tendency to self-segregate. Furthermore, from 1950 onward it was the
state's responsibility to come up with a solution to house the entire population in newly developed areas. Socio-spatial segregation in post-1950 Kuwait was thus less the result of spontaneous settlement (as had been the
case when Bedouin and other immigrants settled in landward neighborhoods such as Mirqab before oil) and more an outcome of state housing
policies. The KOC town of Ahmadi may also have served as an inspiration
for this new method of socio-spatial engineering. Ahmadi's 1947 plan, designed by British architect James Mollison Wilson (also of the Garden City
school), divided the oil town into three sections: one area for British and
American senior staff; another for Indian and Pakistani clerical, financial,
and technical staff; and the "Arab Village" for indigenous workers (Kuwaitis, Bedouin, Arabs, and Iranians).[66] The Arab Village was "meant for
the exclusive housing of natives with the aim of keeping them physically
and socially separated from expatriate staff areas."[67] In Ahmadi in the late
1940s and early 1950s, locals were considered inferior to the foreign staff;
their area was therefore at the bottom of the oil town's spatial hierarchy.
Outside of the context of KOC's social world, however, by 1950 affluence
put Kuwaitis at the top of the country's social hierarchy. The development
of Kuwait's suburbs therefore mimicked, but inverted, KOC's hierarchical
model of ethnic segregation. The neighborhood units constructed beyond
the Green Belt in the 1950s and 1960s—bordered by the First Ring Road
to the north and the Fourth Ring Road to the south—were also "intended
exclusively for the Kuwaiti section of the population." However, unlike
the Arab Village, these "model areas" were privileged enclaves from which
other social groups were barred. Stringent controls ensured that state-
distributed plots were developed as detached single-family villas only.[68]
Apartment buildings were strictly prohibited within the neighborhoods,
as was renting of any kind (including rooms, floors, or outhouses within
a villa).[69] Non-Kuwaitis were prohibited from owning property in Kuwait
and therefore could only rent accommodations in privately owned, multi-
occupancy buildings. Such buildings were restricted to commercial areas
being developed by the private sector, such as Salmiya, Hawalli, and the
city center, which together housed 80 percent of the 28,000 households
living in rented accommodations in 1965 (see Figure 15).[70] By 1969, 72 per-

cent of the population living in the neighborhood units between the First and Fourth Ring Roads were Kuwaiti, while 81 percent of the inhabitants of Salmiya, Hawalli, and Kuwait City were non-Kuwaiti.[71]

From the late 1940s onward, male low-income migrant laborers made up the majority of Kuwait's non-national population and became the most segregated and isolated sector of society. These men lived mainly in distant "bachelor" camps managed by their employers (mostly large companies with major state contracts such as for cleaning), in temporary accommodations located on project sites as in the case of many construction workers, in shantytowns on the outskirts of the built-up area until the 1980s, or increasingly in dilapidated old houses awaiting demolition inside the city center. In the case of the latter, between 1965 and 1970, eight thousand Kuwaitis and twelve thousand non-Kuwaitis moved out of the city while the number of single male non-Kuwaitis living in shared accommodation in the city increased from nine thousand to nineteen thousand.[72]

By the early 1980s, the strict separation of Kuwaitis and non-Kuwaitis slightly diminished. During the 1970s a fifth ring was added to the road system and a new band of neighborhood units was developed between the Fourth and Fifth Ring Roads (see Figure 15). Though similar in design and services as the earlier suburbs, the government shared the responsibility of creating these areas with the private sector. As it did in the inner suburbs, the Municipality divided up the land into standard residential blocks subdivided into housing plots and created public areas such as roads and public schools. However, the government did not actually acquire this land from its existing owners before developing it as it had done before. Once the land was ready for distribution, each existing landowner received a number of plots equivalent to the size of their original landholding, which they could then sell.[73] The objective was to ease the burden on state authorities to provide citizens with land or housing (or both) by opening up a private real estate market, because by the 1980s the state's supply was falling far short of public demand. Citizens could forgo waiting on the list for a plot or government-built house by using state housing loans to buy land in these new areas. Because land in these neighborhoods was not state-allocated, rented accommodations were permitted. Two areas, Jabriya and Salwa, contained a large number of apartment blocks as well as villas, and they became Kuwait's first socially mixed neighborhoods (though Salmiya was also partially mixed).[74] Surra and Qortuba, however, became Kuwaiti-majority areas.

Just because the neighborhood units between the First and Fourth Ring Roads were exclusively for Kuwaitis did not mean that all Kuwaitis were welcome to settle there. Although residents of the former villages and the newly sedentarizing Bedouin were eligible for state housing, they were settled in different outlying areas developed specifically for that purpose. In 1964, the government developed new housing schemes within the villages of Jahra, Farwaniya, and the southern coastal Adan district, where smaller numbers of Kuwaitis lived (Figure 17). Like the townspeople, village residents received state compensation for their existing landholdings along with a state housing option. By 1968, eight of these villages contained new government-built LIG houses and all but one also contained allocated plots. Though this housing scheme was similar to those between the First and Fourth Ring Roads, village residents could obtain new housing only in the same village in which their previous property had been acquired, which limited their ability to move away from the outlying areas into the more central suburbs.[75]

An entirely different policy was established for rehousing the Bedouin who had obtained Kuwaiti citizenship. These tribes did not have access to

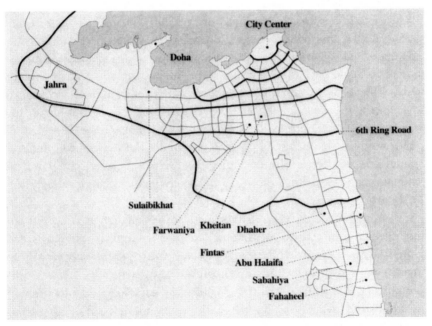

FIGURE 17. Map of the villages and outlying areas beyond the Sixth Ring Road. *Source:* Patrick Semaan.

tathmin (land acquisition) income because they had not been permanently settled before oil and therefore did not own land. In the late 1940s, local tribes began settling down in or near urban and industrial areas as they became aware of new employment opportunities in the oil sector and in the military and police forces. They established spontaneous shanty settlements on the outskirts of the oil town of Ahmadi or in the city center, abandoning their tents for new homes built out of palm thatching, wood, and corrugated iron.[76] These shanties were viewed by the state as an affront to Kuwait's modernity and progress: "a slur on the social conscience of the community" and "aesthetic blotches on the landscape."[77] After the 1959 nationality law was passed some shanty residents became Kuwaiti citizens. The remainder were *bidun* and non-Kuwaiti laborers. In 1962 the government launched a Bedouin settlement program (*tahdir al-badu*) to house shanty residents who were entitled to state accommodation in order to clear some of the informal areas, a process that took at least two decades to complete. Large-scale government-built projects for Bedouin settlement were constructed in "separate areas" far away from the townspeople's suburbs, beyond the boundaries of what became the Sixth Ring Road.[78] The creation of these new Bedouin settlement districts—known in official and popular discourse as *al-manatiq al-kharijiyya*, or the "outlying areas"—"collectively [amounted] to the wholesale creation of a completely new suburbia in the desert" (see Figure 17).[79] These distant projects were planned and constructed not just as massive housing estates but also as self-contained townships. They included shopping complexes, community and leisure centers, main bus terminals, and offices (in the case of Jahra), in addition to the standard services found in the inner suburbs such as schools, clinics, and police stations.[80] The townships' residents would not need to commute to commercial or service centers within the Kuwait City metropolitan area (though many would do so for work), thereby reducing traffic congestion in the urban center.[81]

Though it is difficult to determine if socio-spatial segregation was an intended or unintended outcome of state policy, keeping different social groups away from each other did serve the state's political interests. The main potential threat in mixing urban Kuwaitis with non-Kuwaitis was the spread of Arab nationalism and other ideologies deemed threatening to and by the rulers.[82] The Kuwaiti nationalist opposition of the 1950s and 1960s was heavily influenced by the presence in the country of Arab expatriates who served as teachers in local schools and held influential positions in government agencies where Kuwaitis worked. To have Kuwaitis and expatriates living in the same neighborhoods may have presented too much of a threat. So the government put in place strict controls prohibiting rentals in the inner neighborhood units in order to prevent non-Kuwaitis from moving in.

The rapidly increasing number of foreigners immigrating to Kuwait in the early oil years coupled with the inefficient provision of adequate housing for these groups by the private sector resulted in extreme overcrowding in non-Kuwaiti areas in the 1950s and 1960s.[83] This was particularly true of labor housing, which also suffered from poor maintenance and hygiene and from a lack of public services—including insufficient water and electricity. Over time some less affluent Kuwaiti families tried to rent out floors or rooms in their homes within the suburbs to expatriates. A few went so far as to build their houses deliberately as flats to be rented out to non-Kuwaitis.[84] The Buchanan planners believed that this practice, though illegal, could in fact alleviate two problems: an abundance of wasted space in the inner suburbs and overcrowding in non-Kuwaiti areas. Furthermore, renting out rooms or floors of villas reduced the financial burdens of low-income Kuwaiti families who were struggling to meet their loan repayments or house installments. One young teacher, for example, had spent his entire government loan along with his "humble" savings and borrowed money to build his new house. His salary was not enough to pay off these debts; he therefore decided to rent out his entire house in order to make back some money.[85] For non-Kuwaitis, it was increasingly cheaper to rent space in Kuwaiti villas because rents in apartment buildings soared in the 1970s due to inflation. For instance, a car mechanic who could no longer afford his building rent managed to secure a floor in an LIG house for himself and his family for KD 70 per month.[86] Despite its potential to solve existing problems on both sides, the practice was met with severe government crackdowns on rentals in the so-called "model areas" in the early 1970s.[87] In her comparative study on Arab housing policies, Rula Sadik argues that the Kuwaiti government's policy against rentals in the inner suburbs ensured that government loans would be used solely for housing and not for income-generating purposes.[88] Whatever the motivation, the outcome of their spatial separation was a growing social distance between nationals and non-nationals. In 1969, 78 percent of the polled residents of Shamiya said they did not visit with non-Kuwaitis, and 83 percent of Hawalli residents said they did not mix with Kuwaitis.[89]

The Bedouin were similarly isolated. Officially, state-planning records declared that the Bedouin had certain "special needs" that necessitated the construction of their housing areas some distance away from the "non-*bedu* sector."[90] Their areas would need to provide easy access to grazing land and would have to cater to "the emotional need to be in an environment which is not completely cut off from the desert open spaces."[91] The viability of this argument is questionable, however, given the fact that many tribal families who were allocated houses in areas far away from the city such as Riqqa, Omariya, and Sabahiya actually rejected them due to their distance from the urban center where they worked.[92] The Undersecretary of Social Affairs and Labor even admitted in 1971 that the majority of applicants for government housing put the city down as their residence of preference.[93]

Housing the Bedouin in separate outlying areas may instead have been more politically motivated. In 1967 the government naturalized tens of thousands of Bedouin from Saudi Arabia in exchange for their political loyalty to the ruling family in order to counter the groundswell of dissent and opposition to the Al Sabah in the urban-majority Parliament.[94] The provision of permanent housing to these newly naturalized tribes as well as to existing Kuwaiti tribes who were longtime shanty dwellers became a principal tactic throughout the 1960s and 1970s to ensure complete Bedouin loyalty.[95] It was therefore not in the state's interest to socially integrate them with the rest of the population. The government's fear of losing the loyalty of the Bedouin through political contamination by the former townspeople was made visibly clear during the "Monday *diwaniyya*" movement of 1989 that protested the ruler's unconstitutional dissolution of Parliament in 1986. For seven weeks in December 1989 and January 1990, public gatherings took place every Monday night in the private *diwaniyya* of a different member of the defunct assembly to discuss the restoration of the Kuwaiti Constitution and Parliament. When the Monday gatherings were held in the inner suburbs, the government tolerated them. But when the fifth meeting was planned for MP Ahmed al-Sharei'an's home in the outlying district of Jahra, the National Guard and police used barbed wire and direct force to prevent crowds from getting to the *diwaniyya*. Nine men were injured. Yousef al-Mubaraki, who attended all of the Monday *diwawin* in 1989, attributes the extreme measures taken that night specifically to the fact that the gathering was held in Jahra, one of the main sites of the Bedouin settlement program and considered to be a pro-government stronghold.[96] The presence of the opposition's gathering in this loyalist district could stir up the attention of its inhabitants. It was thought that the use of extreme force against the protesters would deter Jahra's residents from joining the pro-democracy movement. When the police picked up al-Sharei'an two days later in an attempt to arrest him for holding the gathering, they took him to the Faiha police station in the inner suburbs rather than to the station in Jahra, where the alleged crime took place, as was legally required.[97] The authorities were aware that if they tried to arrest a Jahra parliamentarian in the heart of his constituency, there was a chance that the pro-government residents might switch their loyalty to the opposition.

Another plausible explanation for why the Bedouin areas were built far away from the city center is similar to the argument made earlier about the Shi'i enclave in Rumaithiya. Housing the Bedouin *en masse* in outlying areas would allow for the eventual creation of separate Bedouin-only voting districts, which could produce more pro-government representation. The Parliament had been unconstitutionally dissolved in 1976. When the ruler, Jaber al-Ahmed, called for new elections in 1981, he increased the number of voting districts from ten (with five representatives per district) to twenty-five (with two representatives each). With the addition of fifteen new districts—mainly the recently developed outlying areas—after the 1981 elections Bedouin representation in the National Assembly increased and the government was able to buy the loyalty and support of these delegates when passing legislation.[98]

By the early 1980s, most mudbrick houses, tents, and shanties had been removed from Kuwait's modern landscape, and the task of rehousing all citizens in new residential districts using the country's newfound oil income was complete. In 1984, the National Housing Authority standardized the options available to all subsequent housing applicants: residential plots and government-built houses were allocated in integrated areas that no longer differentiated citizens by income bracket or background.[99] However, the economic slump of the 1980s coupled with the Iraqi invasion of 1990 and its aftermath meant that the Housing Authority did not start allocating such standardized government housing to newly applying citizens until the late 1990s.[100]

Return to the City

In Britain, the United States, and everywhere else that new towns and subdivision suburbs were developed in the postwar period, the relegation of housing to the periphery was "the exact opposite of what [Ebenezer]

Howard was after—a busy, socially rich, self-supporting town where all parts interlocked." This modern planning strategy "hastened the death of cities" by creating decayed centers, rush-hour commuter traffic jams, "and an increasing sense of isolation" in the suburbs.[101] These same problems eventually presented themselves in Kuwait. By the late 1970s most existing residential space inside the city was in poor condition. Overcrowding was common, and residents received next to no public services. In 1980 there were only 4,500 Kuwaitis still living within the Green Belt, constituting 7 percent of the city's resident population at that time (approximately 64,285).[102] The majority of city residents were single male laborers who largely worked outside the urban center (on construction sites, in the industrial area of Shuwaikh, and so on). These thousands of laborers lived in overcrowded, dilapidated courtyard houses awaiting demolition, as well as in the rapidly obsolescing 1960s apartment blocks that originally housed small- to medium-sized non-Kuwaiti families. Without the right to demand better living conditions or services, and without the right (or time) to engage freely in public life outside of particular areas, the laborers' residence in the city center could not do much to enhance the physical state or social life of the city. Their dire economic standing aside, as non-Kuwaitis these communities of city residents legally had no stake in the city; they could not own businesses or establish community organizations, which Jane Jacobs argues are so vital to the creation and maintenance of vibrant and livable urban districts.[103]

Colin Buchanan and Partners, and the four firms designing architectural plans for the city between 1968 and 1971 unanimously agreed that Kuwaitis must return to the urban center, and the overall standard of urban accommodation must be improved, "if life there was not to fade away in the future."[104] The Buchanan planners believed that once their plans were implemented, a large number of Kuwaitis would want to return to the city. They therefore suggested that new dwellings be constructed that targeted families of young, educated professionals working in the city in government service, banking and finance, and other high-level positions. Bringing Kuwaitis back into the city would, on the one hand, improve traffic circulation in and out of town (which was hindered by the fact that those who lived inside the city worked outside and those who lived outside worked inside). On the other hand, their plan for one hundred thousand people to be living and working inside the city center coupled with an improvement of general living standards would inject life back into the historic urban core after two decades of demise (discussed in Chapter 6).[105] Aside from improved traffic flows and urban revitalization, there was a clear advantage to bringing Kuwaitis back to live inside the city center: as citizens they could demand better services and an improved quality of life from which the city's non-Kuwaiti residents could then also benefit. However, this effect was never mentioned as an incentive for increasing Kuwaiti residence inside the Green Belt.

Despite the planners' strong advice, building government housing estates for nationals inside the city center proved impossible in the 1970s due to the extreme rise in real estate values coupled with high inflation and the rising cost of building materials, all of which made urban housing extremely unprofitable. With the average price of a square meter of land inside the Green Belt at nearly KD 5,000 by the late seventies, a government house constructed on a five-hundred-square-meter plot would have been worth KD 2.5 million.[106] Consequently, all plans for government housing inside the city introduced by the 1971 master plan were scrapped. But demands for public housing increased after 1973 as inflation brought about by the oil boom made the cost of building their own homes untenable for "average-income" urban Kuwaitis even with the assistance of government loans, and the housing authorities began running out of space in developed areas beyond the city. In their review of the master plan in 1977, Shankland Cox insisted that the government would have to reconcile its desire to make a return on its investment in the bulk of the country's prime urban land with the necessity of providing housing and public services such as schools and clinics on that land despite the unprofitability of such ventures.[107] By 1977 the housing authorities finally agreed.

However, their decision was not based solely on the growing housing crisis. Government officials had started to view the fact that the country's capital city was almost entirely occupied by non-Kuwaitis as, in Rula Sadik's words, "a national affront."[108] A government housing project constructed inside the city center would resolve both the absence of Kuwaitis within the Green Belt and the lack of space for public housing outside it. The housing authorities decided to build an apartment complex restricted to average-income urban families in the former Farij al-Sawaber. Apartments meant that the government would not have to use up too much of its premium real estate on housing.[109] Work on the Sawaber Complex began in 1981, and it was the government's first (and only) multiple-occupancy public housing project inside the city center. It was conceived as a single solution to multiple existing problems:

The Sawaber project is intended to attract young educated Kuwaiti families to take up residence in the heart of their city. By creating a comfortable community which appeals uniquely to Kuwaiti families, the population balance of Kuwaiti and non-Kuwaiti would be restored and a part of the downtown area revitalised. The Sawaber project would also begin to alleviate the enormous and costly traffic problems caused by the growing number of commuters travelling to and from work in the city.[110]

It took five years to build Sawaber, which consisted of thirty-three residential buildings with a total of 524 luxury apartments designed to house up to 950 people. All units were relatively equal in size (about three hundred square meters) but had the capacity to "provide a sense of identity for each family within the project community."[111] Each family would be able to tailor its unit to suit its own individual taste and style, much like in the houses in the suburbs. The complex also included a wide range of modern amenities, including health clinics, schools, parks, retail units, and a fire station. The Sawaber Complex was thus conceived to be a city within the city. The project was pitched as "an urban oasis where Kuwaiti families can feel at home," with a "distinct and prestigious identity as a relatively self-sufficient community."[112] In other words, Sawaber was as much of a privatized, enclosed, and independent enclave as the suburbs. The large housing estate would place its middle class Kuwaiti residents physically inside the city while shielding them from the city itself, and from its non-Kuwaiti, largely labor class inhabitants.[113] Being self-contained meant that Sawaber's residents did not actually need to venture into the surrounding space, just like the residents of the suburbs did not need to "come into the city except to work because everything was there."[114] Though it was hoped that Sawaber would help restore the population balance between Kuwaitis and non-Kuwaitis inside the Green Belt, the project was not designed to restore the kind of mixed residential patterns that had been characteristic of the pre-oil town. Nationals and foreigners would be sharing the city, but the latter would remain as rigidly segregated from Sawaber's residents as they were from Kuwaitis living out in the suburbs.

Either way, after three decades in the suburbs, Kuwaitis were not interested in moving back to the city, or in moving from villas to apartments. When in 1986 the National Housing Authority began accepting applications for Sawaber apartments even before the building's completion, they received next to no interest. According to Sadik, "Even those who had been on the waiting list for a considerable amount of time . . . preferred to remain on the waiting list while they waited for the 'right location' or the 'right' housing unit (a villa in the suburbs)."[115] The brand new luxury apartments lay vacant for nearly four years, reaching only 10 percent occupancy by the time of the Iraqi invasion in 1990. But Kuwaitis' aversion to moving to the city was related not only to their new penchant for villa living. It also possibly had to do with the state of the city center itself by the 1980s. Lefebvre describes suburbanization as a "violently anti-urban planning approach."[116] The decanting of people and various aspects of everyday city life to the suburbs and other peripheral areas contributed significantly to the fragmentation and dismembering of daily life, which ultimately led to the decline of the urban core. This fragmenting process was well under way in Kuwait by the time Sawaber was constructed in the mid-1980s, and arguably was what doomed the project to failure.

6

The Privatization of Urban Life

Modernization and Privatization

From the 1952 master plan onward, Kuwait's suburbs were planned entirely separately from the city center and were designed to be self-sufficient so that there was no longer any reason to go into the city center except for work.[1] By separating people from the physical space of the city, suburbanization not only de-urbanized Kuwait's traditionally urban society; it also contributed to the rapid decline of the city center itself. Saba George Shiber warned Kuwait's planning authorities in the early 1960s that if they were not careful the city would become a place of such discomfort that citizen and merchant would freely depart from it, and the pre-oil integration of man and his city would be lost. This is indeed what happened. The incorporation of most common urban spaces into the state's modernization projects after 1950 accelerated the erosion of their public qualities and hindered the city's ability to support the kind of urban social life that existed before oil. Whether a particular urban space is considered public or private relates to the nature of activities performed within it, as well as to who creates, owns, manages, or controls it. In the pre-oil town, the demarcation between the public and the private was blurred. After 1950, increased concern with property ownership coupled with new modes of detached-villa living in the suburbs effected a clearer demarcation between public and private realms. With the new role of the Municipality and other state institutions in creating and controlling urban space, certain public functions such as maintaining the cleanliness and security of common spaces were no longer a community concern. Furthermore, planning authorities rarely sought public input into how common spaces should be produced or utilized. As expressed by an official in the Department of Agriculture in 1979 in his assessment of urban parks, the public was not involved in producing urban space because they did not pay taxes or support these spaces in any way.[2] Public opinion was usually a minor concern when it came to the production of spaces that, in theory at least, were designed for public use.

The creation of three new public parks in the city center by the early 1970s illustrates this point. The government designed these parks to beautify the city; their public use was a secondary concern. All three parks were closed during the daytime so that they could be irrigated, cleaned, and maintained.[3] They were open to the public only from 4:00 P.M. to around midnight daily, which limited the uses to which they could be put. The Municipality Park, for example, was located in the heart of the city adjacent to the central business district (CBD) and therefore had the capacity to attract a large number of city employees during the day (on lunch breaks or before and after work). It was precisely during working hours, however, that the park was closed. By the time the city parks opened, the vast majority of people who worked in the city had already ventured back to the suburbs and were not coming back into the city until the next workday. Most of the people who lived in the city center were male laborers who worked long hours with very little leisure time to enjoy the parks around them. Furthermore, during the hours in which the parks were open they were extremely controlled spaces. The Municipality and Green Belt Parks had two-meter-high boundary walls and employed full-time guards "to protect the park from vandalism and misuse."[4] Strict rules and regulations governed how the parks could be used: running, sports activities, ball games, and bicycles were prohibited.[5] On the basis of interviews with Municipality officials in 1979, Subhi al-Mutawa asserts that these rules served "to protect the park first and the people second. Since it is difficult to maintain good landscaping in the park, the rules should be restrictive in order to keep the park in good shape."[6]

State development projects like these sought to modernize the city center into a rational, controllable, sanitized, and beautiful space to serve as the symbol of Kuwait's newfound prosperity and progress after 1950. Achieving this landscape required the removal of some of the traditional features of the old town that before oil had been active venues of public encounter and interaction but no longer served any function in the modern city. One such place was the Bedouin market in Sahat al-Safat, one of the oldest and most widely used public spaces before the oil era. The presence of a camel and sheep market in the heart of the city was considered unbecoming for a modern cityscape. By the late 1940s and early 1950s, new fixtures of modern living began to appear around al-Safat, such as Kuwait's first Ford and Chevrolet dealerships, as well as the British Bank of Iran and the Middle East, which boasted both air conditioning and the first revolving door in Kuwait when it was built in 1949.[7] The animal markets were relocated to Shuwaikh, beyond the urban limits.[8] In their place came a large steel water reservoir tank constructed in the mid-1950s, which diminished the space's potential to be used for public celebrations and festivals as it had been in the recent past. Al-Safat also ceased to be the space where prisoners were publicly punished. In the late 1950s, the old arsenal at Nayef Palace became the new headquarters of Abdullah al-Mubarak's Public Security Department, where executions took place in the yard—still open to the public but now shielded from the city's view by a wall.[9]

Many of the traditional functions of the urban *sahel* were also removed in the early oil years. The changes in occupations and trades practiced by the Kuwaiti population led to the gradual decline of the maritime activities that were once permanent fixtures on the town's foreshore.[10] Most of the historic shipowning merchant families had moved on to more lucrative enterprises. In Zahra Freeth's estimation, to these "men grown rich from new sources their sailing-ships were no longer a matter of special pride."[11] In 1970 a number of representatives of seafaring and merchant families were invited to a meeting of the Council of Ministers to give their views on the banning of traditional *dhows* from the seafront of Kuwait City. Freeth recounts a conversation between her mother, Violet, and one of these men, Nasser al-Qatami:

But when V. said, "I hope you told them that we all want the boats along the sea-front, as this is one of the most delightful and picturesque features of Kuwait," Nasir looked slightly taken aback, and said, "No; we all agreed that it was a good idea to get rid of them from new Kuwait. Then we can have an elegant promenade along the front, and not the untidy mess that the boats make when they come into harbour."[12]

An official order was passed that year to move what was left of the *dhow*-building and repair yards twelve miles west of the city to the village of Doha, forever removing from the landscape of the city "the industry which before oil gave [the] town its chief claim to fame."[13] The opening of a new, larger container port in Shuwaikh diverted shipping activity away from the *furda*.[14] Despite the removal of the seafront's maritime functions, in the 1950s and 1960s people still used the area for leisure: for having picnics, taking walks, line-fishing, and so on.[15] Over time, however, the city's seafront became a dumping ground for rubbish and construction waste, neglected alike by the planning authorities and the population, who were both too "caught up in building and developing their country" to pay attention to what was happening to the old *sahel*.[16]

The *suq* was also subjected to modernization schemes, though it retained its primary pre-oil function as a place of commercial exchange. Throughout the first two decades of oil urbanization, large segments of the market area were demolished to make way for the modern buildings of the new CBD, where indoor and air-conditioned shopping blocks replaced clusters of specialized *aswaq*.[17] Though some of the historic markets survived demolition, the *suq* was significantly reduced in size. The constant closing down or relocation of shops diminished the market's historic characteristic as a familiar and reliable place to shop. Well-known cloth merchant Abdullah Abdulghani, nicknamed *shaykh al-suq*, or chief of the market, had to relocate his shop (established in 1915 in the Suq al-Dakhili) three times after the oil era began, because each *suq* to which he moved was eventually demolished. In the mid-1960s he finally settled into the new three-million-dinar cloth market building.[18] Similarly, the block that housed Violet Dickson's favorite goldsmith's shop was demolished in the late 1960s, and it was a full year before she suddenly stumbled upon his new shop while walking through the market.[19] The townspeople were accustomed to regularly buying particular items from specific shopkeepers, and the disruption to the *suq*'s layout made it difficult to hold on to the traditional social quality of commercial exchange. Also hindering the *suq*'s public nature was that new shops and market streets were built with plate-glass window displays. As Lienhardt observed in 1952, these windows made it impossible for shopkeepers and passers-by to greet each other as they did in the older parts of the market, where the shops still opened directly onto the street.[20] The newer parts of the *suq* were therefore much more privatized and impersonal, focused solely on commercial rather than social exchange. Freeth noted in 1970 that it was only when she and her mother wandered into "the more primitive parts of the *suq*" that they would meet old friends and be invited to stop in a shop and have tea like in the old days.[21]

The removal of the past from the cityscape was the first step in the modernization project. The next was to replace this past with clear indications that Kuwait was growing into a modern metropolis. In line with Le Corbusier's modernist ideal, street widening and improvement was a primary concern. The 1952 master plan determined that "Kuwait is destined to be one of the largest and most important towns in the Middle East and its roads . . . can be one of its finest features. Every important town has its fine roads."[22] The plan therefore made no provision for a public transportation network, and the city was "condemned to worship the automobile."[23] A decade later, Shiber asserted that the dominance of the car was both "the forte and liability of Kuwait's planning to date."[24] The advent of the automobile in Kuwait did not help stimulate suburbanization as it did in many American and European cities. Rather, it was the wholesale creation of the suburbs in the 1950s that made cars an absolute necessity. Whereas the pre-oil town had been built to the scale of the pedestrian, distances in the new city—in both the center and the suburbs—were comparatively immense. The geographic separation of places of residence, work, and leisure meant that society was rendered "totally dependent on the car."[25] When Freeth asked an old family friend in 1970 if he was happy with his new life in the suburbs, "he said that his new house was modern and comfortable, but he did not like living so far from his work. This had involved him in the extra expense of buying a car to come daily into town."[26] With the move to the suburbs, women lost their immediate access to the public spaces of the city center. One woman who experienced this shift noted that when they lived in town she and her mother walked to the *suq* regularly because "it was right there." After her family moved to Faiha in the 1950s, the only way to get to the *suq* was by car. Because none of the women in her household knew how to drive, they simply stopped going.[27] Many Kuwaiti women eventually learned how to drive, but the distance between the suburbs and the city contributed to a reduction in the everyday use of spaces like the *suq* and *sahel*.

The transformation of roads into busy traffic arteries changed how people used streets and hindered their traditional sociability. Higher value was given to streets than to sidewalks in planning both the city center and the suburbs, giving cars priority over pedestrians. Most city sidewalks were unpaved and therefore largely unused, and the city in general was not conducive to walking.[28] Lack of paved parking in urban areas exacerbated the problem. The 1952 plan made no parking provisions, so sidewalks and

other spaces of casual encounter such as *baraha*s were spontaneously transformed into parking lots. Within only ten years of the creation of the 1952
master plan, walking was made "a lost and dead art."[29] Al-Mutawa argues
that this lack of opportunity to walk on city sidewalks was why most parks
created in the 1970s provided walking paths: walking had become a recreational activity.[30] People's dependence on the car effected an increasing
social separation within the community and a retreat into private life. Fran
Tonkiss describes streets as "the basic unit of public life in the city," because
they require people to constantly negotiate and interact, however marginally, with other people.[31] However, as "private ground in public places,"
cars made people accustomed to the privacy of the journey from one point
to the next.[32] In the pre-oil period, the journey itself constituted a social
act, with people stopping to greet one another, speak with men sitting out
on their *datcha*, and so on. After 1950, as Lienhardt noted, cars prevented
people in Kuwait from "being accessible to casual encounters."[33]

The Eradication of Public Space

Road widening for cars also impeded access to various public spaces
in the city, further contributing to the declining use value of such sites.
Al-Safat had previously been the area onto which many main roads in the
town converged, particularly those leading in from the Jahra and Nayef
Gates. When these roads were expanded into major traffic arteries extending from the radial roads that connected the suburbs to the city center,
al-Safat became the principal point where traffic from these roads merged.
This transformation of the open Sahat al-Safat into a traffic circle significantly contributed to its demise as an accessible public space. As traffic
congestion inside the city increased, and as the area around al-Safat developed into the CBD, the open space was no longer used for public gatherings. It became another one of the many mass parking lots that filled up
practically every unbuilt space in the city center from the 1950s onwards.[34]
The last recorded mass celebration to take place in al-Safat was Abdullah
al-Salem's accession to power in 1950.

Street widening also cut the city off from the space that once constituted the focal point of the town's urbanism: the *sahel*. In the 1940s a small,
single-lane road was constructed parallel to the *sahel* where there had previously been a footpath. Shiber, the Colin Buchanan and Partners team,
and the four architectural firms working in conjunction with the latter all

advised against expanding this road into a more substantial traffic artery. Nevertheless, by the end of the 1960s, the Ministry of Public Works began to construct a new coastal thoroughfare known as the Arabian Gulf Road. This much larger, limited-access, divided highway officially "sealed the city's separation from the natural beauty of the harbor."[35] The former port town was thus transformed into what Margaret Cohen, in her analysis of the transformation of Paris's working waterways, calls a "landlocked" city. The visibility of the waterfront became obscured from daily city life, both effecting and reflecting its diminishing importance in practices of urban sociability.[36] When Freeth returned to Kuwait in 1970, the Gulf Road had already become a "busy main road, and the traffic roars past in an incessant stream." As she noted from her mother's verandah facing what was left of the Sharq *dhow* harbor, "There is no room here for the colourful scenes I had witnessed in a more leisured age."[37]

By the late 1960s, planning authorities began to focus on making the space inside the Green Belt look more like a "great capital city."[38] Many parts of the city had been neglected or only minimally developed during the first two decades of oil urbanization. Some of these spaces, such as Sahat al-Safat and the *sahel*, were strategically located but were hindering the city's modern image due to their dilapidated state. They therefore became the new focus of the planning authorities' urban beautification schemes. Such schemes further hindered these sites' ability (and that of the entire city) to support and absorb a vibrant public life.

In 1982 the Municipality initiated plans to convert al-Safat from a "non-descript parking area" into a modern urban plaza linking the *suq* to its north with Areas 10 and 11 of the CBD to its south.[39] The plaza was designed as a sunken space to deflect the din of the adjacent traffic and thereby enhance the area's "oasis character."[40] Despite its four-million-dinar facelift,[41] the new oval-shaped al-Safat remained a main traffic junction. It was detached from most of its surroundings by major roads and was now recessed to sit literally below the city, inaccessible and largely concealed from street level (Figure 18). Though one section of the oval was connected to the *suq* and could be reached by pedestrians, nothing in the design plan sought to incorporate the space into the existing pattern and function of the adjacent markets. By transforming the space into a scoop, the objective was isolation from rather than integration into the surrounding cityscape. The plaza's visual qualities were enhanced with trees, a large fountain, and a shaded monument area. Less attention was given to its public usability.

FIGURE 18. The first glimpse of the new recessed Sahat al-Safat under construction in 1987. *Source*: *Al-Seyassah* newspaper.

Although the space was meant to offer *suq* shoppers and employees of the CBD a place to relax and socialize in the heart of the bustling city, its public use was predominantly conditioned by consumption: visiting its café or shops. The "physical amenities for social interaction" that were meant to attract people to al-Safat were designed to shield the visitor from the surrounding city.[42] Shops were enclosed within twin pedestrian underpasses where there were elevators that went up from al-Safat into two buildings of the CBD. The square's outdoor café was encircled by a shaded platform that was higher than the rest of the basin but still lower than the city above.[43] Whereas once al-Safat had been fully integrated into the landscape of the town, the new Sahat al-Safat kept the surrounding city at bay.

The isolation of the new city square turned it into a "dead public space."[44] Its pedestrian underpasses were used daily by city employees to access part of the CBD that could not be easily reached from the street level. However, these pedestrians did not use al-Safat as a public space in the way the planners had hoped. In a 1990 newspaper article, one Kuwaiti man described a moment when he unintentionally wandered into al-Safat. He marveled at the trees, fountain, and monument and found that the space was prettier than he had ever realized. It was as though he was seeing the renovated square for the first time, though he admitted that, "like most of us," he walked through it more than once a week.[45] It is clear that during all those times he passed through it he had never before sat at the café or by the fountain. Sahat al-Safat never returned to being the vibrant and sociable space it used to be. Within only three years of its opening, the body in charge of its maintenance experimented with new ways of injecting life into it. In 1990, an exhibition of Kuwaiti crafts and manufactured goods was held in the square. The Public Utilities Management Company (a shareholding company that manages and maintains various public buildings and spaces in Kuwait, including al-Safat) even suggested in 1990 that an annual festival be held in the square to commemorate its history, though this idea was never realized.[46] These efforts did little to reintegrate al-Safat into the life stream of the city. A 1995 article recounting the square's importance in the town's history and social life before oil ended with this pointed question: "So where is Sahat al-Safat today?"[47] Its design, though visually appealing and unmistakably modern, significantly hindered both its accessibility and its public usability.

Even more important than al-Safat in the minds of the planning authorities during this period was the redevelopment of the *sahel*. In their 1971 master plan, the urban coastline was one of the parts of the city that CBP claimed "urgently [needed] dealing with." Beaches proved to be popular sites of public recreation all over the world, they said, yet Kuwait's seafront was "untidy in appearance and [failed], as yet, to make much use of the sea."[48] The waterfront redevelopment of the 1970s and 1980s is a vivid example of how the privatization of public spaces contributed to the eradication of the city's social life. The economic and cultural privatization of space (the former relating to ownership and the latter to urban experience) often relates closely to consumption: of food and commodities, or recreation and leisure. The need to consume in order to use certain spaces erodes their public nature, turning them into "pseudo-public spaces" (as seen in the new Sahat al-Safat).[49] During Kuwait's second building boom of the 1970s, state planners and private developers worked together to privatize formerly public urban spaces in order to enhance their economic productivity.

The shoreline adjacent to the city center was government owned. However, most of the seafront land beyond Ras Ajuzah (which marked the eastern end of the city's coastline, where the Kuwait Towers now stand) came into private ownership after the advent of oil urbanization, largely through land grabbing by prominent families in the early days of the land acquisition scheme. These families had been allowed to build houses along the coastal strip right up to the water's edge, "making it impossible for the general public to enjoy the delectable sandy beaches along this coast." As Freeth claimed in 1970, "One has to go nearly twenty miles out of town now to find freely accessible beach."[50] In their 1971 master plan the Buchanan planners recommended that the government acquire this privately owned seafront property outside the city. Though they proposed that a portion might be developed into a private sea club, they believed that as much of the seashore as possible should be made public.[51] By 1974 several coastal improvement schemes were under way in Kuwait, with rhetoric in the press about a "return to the seashore."[52] The government acquired much of the coastal land between the city and Salmiya, part of which was used for a government-owned beach club in Ras al-Ardh (which charged an entrance fee) and an Officer's Club in Bneid al-Gar. Private owners of land beyond Ras al-Ardh also opened more prestigious beach resorts such as the Gazelle Club in Messila (Figure 19). Membership in the private clubs

FIGURE 19. The private and exclusive Gazelle Club. *Source*: Kuwait Oil Company archives.

was expensive, and government-owned clubs were restricted to families.[53] An inherent segregation thus emerged in public seaside use: middle- and upper-class Kuwaitis and expatriates joined the private clubs, less affluent families willing to pay entrance fees went to the government clubs, and expatriate men living in Kuwait without their families (mostly laborers) were restricted to the diminishing and unkempt public beaches (which very few people used). Furthermore, because most of these clubs were located beyond the city's coast, they contributed to the removal of leisure spaces to specially designated zones away from the urban center.

In 1975, a design competition was held for the comprehensive development of the twenty-one-kilometer stretch of waterfront from Shuwaikh to Ras al-Ardh (which included the stretch of coastline adjacent to the city center). Ghazi Sultan (working as a private architect), the Kuwait Engineers Office, and the American landscape firm Sasaki Associates collectively won the bid. The government's objective, according to Municipal Council member Bader al-Obaid in 1986, was to "restore the liveliness of the *sahel*" that had once played such an important role in the life and history of the Kuwaiti people and their city.[54] Sultan and his team insisted that the area be used for recreational and cultural functions rather than for housing or commerce, "as the means for giving the coastline beyond the highway back to the people."[55] Despite its emphasis on the public, the master plan perhaps inadvertently enhanced the cultural and economic privatization of the space between the road and the sea. In the pre-oil period, the coastline, as an unquestionably public space, incorporated multiple simultaneous functions; it was used for housing, industry, and commerce, as well as social interaction and leisure. With its redevelopment into a planned public corniche, the seafront became associated with organized recreation rather than free social interaction, as a "civilized and domesticated space" rather than a vibrant, multifaceted, and truly public space.[56]

By 1988 the first two phases of the waterfront master plan were completed. Both projects were located south of Ras Ajuzah and thus outside the city limits. The biggest undertaking was the man-made Green Island leisure space. Smaller-scale projects included the Sha'ab Recreation Complex, which housed swimming pools, tennis courts, and yachting facilities. These activity areas were government owned and open to the general public, but like the sea clubs of the previous decade, access was subject to membership or entrance fees. These areas were also entirely cut off from the rest of the city by the multilane coastal highway, and most of the activities they housed took place indoors or behind boundary walls. Indeed, new-found concerns for cultural privacy played an important role in how this area was developed. According to Brian Brace Taylor, who reported on the project in 1989, "there are very clear guidelines governing social behavior in public which had to be respected. One had to imagine places for recreation in public that could offer privacy if needed as well."[57]

The planners themselves admitted, however, that their waterfront scheme was not designed to suit the needs and demands of existing users, because when they were coming up with their design the seafront was not actually being used much by members of the public. Without sufficient human activity on the beaches to guide the planners' ideas, the plan was in fact, according to Sultan, conceived for "non-existent users."[58] It is there-fore unclear whether the plans indeed reflected a growing preference for privacy in public spaces, or whether the creation of semi-privatized spaces along the public seafront helped foster this social predilection. The Bu-chanan planners pointed out that although there were "usually some peo-ple to be seen" in city parks and beaches on holidays and in the evenings, there was no sign of "over-use or overcrowding" in these areas despite the fact that there were only a few such spaces available to the public.[59] In other words, not many people were using the city's few accessible public spaces at the time, suggesting a possible growing preference for private leisure. However, in the 1960s and 1970s many people who lived in al-Dira (which in this context refers to the Kuwait City metropolitan area, includ-ing the suburbs) enjoyed driving down to the KOC town of Ahmadi on the weekends to enjoy its public facilities. In 1973, the KOC magazine al-Kuwayti noted that Ahmadi's public gardens contained "children run-ning, adults singing and loud music beaming from the radio, and ladies preparing food. All at a large picnic surrounded by sheer happiness."[60] So perhaps it was the poor state of the public parks and beaches in Kuwait City, compared to the well-maintained gardens of Ahmadi, that resulted in their underuse.

As part of the cultural development of the coastline, in 1986 the Qaryat Youm al-Bahhar (Seaman's Day Village) opened on the far western end of the city to commemorate Kuwait Town's maritime heritage. The village showcased reenactments of scenes such as shipbuilding, the return from pearling, and women washing clothes in the sea, along with replicas of historic spaces such as the traditional *firjan* and the popular seafront coffee shops.[61] These sights had all been deliberately and painstakingly removed from the urban landscape over the previous thirty years. The Seaman's Day Village thus swept Kuwait's historic *sahel* up the coast to the edge of town and condensed it into a confined, artificial, and controlled space. The historic lifeways that once made the seafront an active public space were frozen into a museum-like display while the rest of the coast was gradually developed into a modern promenade. The village poignantly, though inadvertently, symbolized the transformation of the formerly public *sahel* into a revenue-generating, privatized space of consumption and domesticated leisure. But the public genuinely enjoyed it, and many people visited the village regularly. To both the planners and the public, Youm al-Bahhar was more than simply a nostalgic *aide-mémoire* of the old town and lifestyle that "oil wealth has swiftly swept away."[62] By inviting Kuwaitis "to experience their past in actuality," the village showed people just how much life had changed in such a short time.[63] Realizing what Richard Dennis refers to as "the evocation of a counter-modern other at the heart of the modern city," the remaking of Kuwait's past as heritage served as continuing proof of the superiority of the new modern city that was fast "superseding and surpassing the old mercantile city."[64]

By the mid-1980s, complaints and critiques on the state of the city emerged in the local press. Common criticisms were that sidewalks and roundabouts were unpaved, that there were not enough trees in the city, that building facades on main roads were overcrowded with signs and advertisements and were poorly maintained, and that the city streets were generally unclean.[65] These critiques contributed to the launch of a series of city beautification schemes that primarily entailed the construction of colorful monuments to decorate the country's many roundabouts, and the painting of murals on several bridges by a local artist.[66] In 1986 a beautification plan for the CBD included the provision of better paving, lighting, and parking, in addition to more plants, park benches, fountains, and umbrellas.[67] In October 1987 the government spent eight million dinars on new bricks and tiles to beautify the city's roads with colorful patterned pavements.[68] Though in large part these developments in the 1980s pertained to the public parts of the city, such as streets and sidewalks, what is most noticeable about the criticisms voiced by the city's users and about the beautification schemes that those criticisms provoked was that they did not actually address how the city worked. Rather, they focused on how the city looked. The 1986 plan for more benches and better lighting in the CBD aimed not to improve public use of the space but to improve the city's appearance.[69] Even public complaints about the lack of paved sidewalks were more concerned that the city looked dull and dusty without them than that paved sidewalks and squares might improve and increase public use of these spaces. One article in *al-Nahda* newspaper in 1989 juxtaposed photos of buildings cluttered with signs and advertisements with a photo of the clean and ordered (and empty) new Sahat al-Safat, with the latter serving as the model for what the rest of the city should become.[70] Such sentiments, coupled with the general lack of reaction to the erosion of public spaces, suggest that the public bought into the image of the city that had driven the modernization projects of the first three decades of the oil era and had become less concerned with their own lived experiences in the city.

The survival of a vibrant city life relies not only on the availability and condition of particular urban public spaces, but also on the existence of multiple activities taking place simultaneously within and across the city—what Jane Jacobs simply calls "diversity." Cities must generate enough mixture of uses if they are "to sustain their own civilization."[71] Even if usability had been the Kuwaiti authorities' main impetus in improving lighting and paving in the city's public spaces, without the existence of multiple activities and functions to bring people into the city at various hours of the day, these spaces would remain minimally used and effectively dead no matter how well planned or attractive they looked. Suburbanization coupled with the removal from the city center of the everyday activities that once turned places like the *suq*, *sahel*, and al-Safat into the pre-oil town's "intricate architecture of social life" ultimately killed off the city's historic urbanism.[72] No new activities or uses (aside from work) were brought into the city to replace these functions (or to compensate for their removal) and rekindle the city's sociability. Houses, schools, hospitals, and even the new state university—originally planned by Minoprio, Spencely, and Macfarlane to be situated inside the city center—were all relegated either to the suburbs or to discrete zones outside the city limits. Leisure shifted outside the city to new beach and sports clubs. By the 1970s most commercial activity was also relocated outside the city center. The town of Salmiya, located about ten kilometers south of the city along the coast, emerged in the 1970s as the prime new shopping and entertainment district,[73] and neighborhood cooperatives reduced the need to go into the city markets for everyday needs. In 1969, 87 percent of the polled residents of Shamiya did their daily grocery shopping in the nearby co-op or at a neighborhood store, and only 11 percent still went to the town *suq* on a daily basis (though more went on a weekly and monthly basis).[74] With suburbanization and urban planning, daily life was divided into fragments; work, residence, transport, commerce, and leisure became separate pieces in the life of the newly "dismembered and dissociated human being."[75] The relegation of political life into its own discrete sphere further contributed to this social fragmentation.

The Politicization of the City

Ash Amin and Nigel Thrift argue that the erosion of public space in the modern city and the increasing preference for private life does not always result in the demise of the public sphere (where private people publicly discuss matters of commom concern).[76] This was certainly true of Kuwait after 1950, when newspapers, magazines, and journals of diverse political slants proliferated, due largely to increased political freedom under Abdullah al-Salem. These publications gave members of the public ample means not only of hearing the news but also of expressing and exchanging their views, debating issues, and influencing or contesting public opinion, without the constant need for face-to-face contact. Though people were no longer meeting regularly in the *suq*, greeting each other on the street, or clustering in the *baraha* after work, there was "no shortage of news and views."[77] However, though the public sphere expanded after the arrival of oil, by the early 1960s most of the spaces in which everyday politics played out were shifted outside the city limits and, to some extent, privatized.

In addition to newspapers, other "new mediated forms of social exchange" that emerged in the early oil years were politically oriented civil society organizations.[78] Although technically classified as social or sports clubs, these voluntary associations formed the hub of political activity and challenges to the state in Kuwait during the 1950s. The members and activities of these social clubs led what was known as *al-haraka al-qawmiyya*, or the nationalist movement, of the 1950s. After the advent of oil, social and political opposition in Kuwait increasingly shifted away from the merchant class—who were encouraged to "relinquish political rights in favor of economic privilege"—and toward a rising class of less affluent men educated abroad, epitomized by Ahmad al-Khatib, the leader of the opposition.[79] Al-Khatib grew up in a poor household in Kuwait Town during the economic recession of the 1930s. His father was a member of the town guard who lost his livelihood after being maimed in battle.[80] Believing that education was the best way out of poverty, al-Khatib joined the Mubarakiyya

School, where young Kuwaitis were first exposed to Arab nationalist senti-ments by newly arriving Palestinian teachers.[81] In 1942 al-Khatib earned a state scholarship to finish high school in Lebanon; he then went to medi-cal school at the American University of Beirut. During his time there al-Khatib and his fellow Kuwaiti students became closely involved in the Arab nationalist movement, participating in mass protests such as a student dem-onstration against the Baghdad Pact in 1954.[82]

In 1955 al-Khatib returned to Kuwait a doctor and an Arab nation-alist and became active in newly emerging civil society organizations. Groups like the National Cultural Club, Teachers Club, and Graduates Club attracted wide public participation from a broad spectrum of social groups, including the new middle-class intelligentsia, low-wage govern-ment workers, and non-Kuwaitis. Their members dominated the national press through their own publications, by writing in the country's growing number of daily and weekly newspapers and journals, and by distributing pamphlets around town.[83] These publications gave them a vital conduit for shaping public opinion and communicating their news and views to the public. Throughout the first oil decade, the clubs became the most vocal elements in the Kuwaiti public sphere, from which individuals of their social background had largely been excluded before oil.

Some members of merchant families, such as Yousef al-Qatami, played an active role in the opposition movement of the 1950s. For the most part, however, the merchant class stayed out of nationalist politics. The reduced role of the merchants in sociopolitical commentary and de-bate in Kuwait undermined the *diwaniyya's* position as the principal spa-tial counterpart to the public sphere. Because *diwawin* were attached to family homes, the relocation of the townspeople in new residential areas beyond the Green Belt meant that after 1950 *diwawin* gradually ceased to be a feature of the city center. But their shift away from the urban cen-ter in no way reduced their significance in Kuwaiti social life. Although suburbanized, *diwawin* continued to be important places in which pub-lic opinion was expressed and debated in Kuwait. But as bases of politi-cal participation, organization, and opposition, *diwawin* were somewhat eclipsed in the 1950s by the new social clubs, whose headquarters were located within the city center (specifically in Sharq). The *diwaniyya* was not as entrenched an institution for members of the "young reformist movement" and their followers as it was for the merchants, and Sharq quickly overshadowed Jibla as the political hub of the city.[84]

The nationalist opposition of the 1950s was very much an urban movement. The reformists believed in the power of boycotts, strikes, demonstrations, and taking to the streets to garner public support for their causes. One of the popular sites they used was the new Shuwaikh Secondary School, a boarding school for Kuwaiti and foreign boys established just beyond the western edge of town in 1954. With its state-of-the-art academic and sporting facilities, the school symbolized Kuwait's rapid progress in modern education. The presence of non-Kuwaiti teachers and students, coupled with the school's large stadium, made the Shuwaikh campus a popular place for nationalist rallies, speeches, festivals, and demonstrations. Furthermore, the spatial proximity of social clubs to key urban sites such as the *suq* and the new state-owned al-Hamra and al-Firdous Cinemas in Sharq (which were used for large meetings as well as for the screening of Arab nationalist films)[85] allowed the nationalists to launch in Kuwait a new kind of oppositional politics that used the city as its principal venue. For example, representatives from the different associations often convened at one of the clubs' headquarters and then ventured into the *suq* as a group to collect donations for various causes. In September 1956 the clubs raised $27,370 to support the residents of Gaza.[86] In this respect the nationalists treated the *suq* much as the merchants had before oil.

In many ways, however, the *suq*'s function in giving form to the discursive public sphere altered under the nationalists. In pre-oil Kuwait Town the *suq*, as the place where people went to hear the news, share information, and debate issues, had been the most important spatial counterpart to the urban public sphere. In addition, certain sites within the *suq*, such as the Ahliyya Library and the Mission Bible shop, became spaces where reformists met to discuss politics and organize their activities. But with oil urbanization, the *suq* was no longer the primary site where news and views were exchanged, discussed, and disseminated. On the one hand, the social clubs themselves—along with their discursive counterparts, the newspapers—took over a large part of this function of the old *suq*. On the other hand, more distant homes coupled with new jobs in government ministries or running private businesses meant people did not have as much time to spend in the *suq*. As Lienhardt heard repeatedly during his stay in Kuwait in 1953, "In the old days, when everybody was poor, life was quiet and easy. Now we are rich, we have to work all the time."[87] That is not to say that old social habits died out entirely with the move out of the markets and into new offices. On the basis of his own visits

to various civil service offices, Lienhardt noted that Kuwaiti officials behaved in the workplace much as they once did in the *suq*. Their new office
walls were lined with couches to accommodate the steady stream of visitors
making social and business calls. A lot of information and opinion passed
from one government office to the next in this way.[88] In their reports and
correspondence before oil, British officials in Kuwait always referred to
public opinion as "the bazaar." In 1938, for example, the Political Agent
reported that the bazaar, "where nothing is secret," reacted positively to
news that the British had suggested that the ruler form a council.[89] By the
late 1950s their terminology shifted: news that Abdullah al-Salem had met
with Gamal Abdel Nasser in Damascus in 1958 "won pride of place in the
bazaar and government departments."[90] Though this important aspect of
the *suq*'s traditional sociability survived modernization, it was thus trans-
ferred to a more exclusive realm (accessible mostly to Kuwaiti men of the
bureaucratic class).

Though it lost its role as the primary venue of social and political
debate in Kuwait, the *suq* survived the first decade of oil urbanization as a
secondary site for the physical manifestation of an increasingly vocal and
visible public sphere. Its public nature made the *suq* an important place
for the staging of nationalist demonstrations, strikes, and public speeches,
particularly during the volatile summer and fall of 1956. In response to
Egyptian president Gamal Abdel Nasser's call for a general strike in August 1956 after the nationalization of the Suez Canal, a public demonstration was held at the headquarters of the National Cultural Club in Sharq.
Thousands of supporters showed up to hear pro-Nasser speeches.[91] The
event was suddenly raided without warning by public security forces. Two
days later a large group of protestors were gathered in al-Safat when "a
party of some 20 youths appeared carrying pictures of Nasser." Once again
the security forces intervened and "laid about the crowd indiscriminately
with staves."[92] Two people were allegedly killed and several others were
wounded in the clash. The security forces then proceeded into the *suq* and
smashed the windows of the shops and cafés that were involved in the con-
current strike.[93] The National Cultural Club was closed down for two days.

The events of August 1956 revealed to the government just how politically charged these clubs had become. The Arab nationalist opposition
was garnering tremendous public support on the street from Kuwaitis and
expatriates alike for an ideology that threatened and undermined the very
existence of the ruling family. When the nationalists wanted to hold a

rally to call for a national boycott of Israel, Britain, and France after the tripartite attack on Port Said in November 1956, Abdullah al-Mubarak, Director of Public Security, rejected their request and warned them not to demonstrate. The clubs ignored the warning and went ahead with their plans. However, rather than hold the demonstration in one of the clubs' headquarters, which could be raided, they held their gathering at the *suq* mosque,[94] a public space protected by Islamic law from state intrusion.[95] Government radio broadcasts made every half hour on the day of the protest warned the public not to participate, and army trucks were positioned just outside the entrances to the city.[96] Thousands of protesters convened at the *suq* mosque to hear speeches, and the rally ended peacefully and without incident.[97]

The *suq* was also the principal site of the boycotts and strikes that went along with the nationalist agitation of November 1956. Many businesses cooperated out of genuine solidarity with the cause; others did so through coercion. The nationalists employed female teachers to patrol the *suq* to make sure that all shopkeepers complied with the action.[98] Their ability to compel *suq* proprietors to close whenever Nasser called for a general strike and to adhere to the boycott was indicative of the strong hold they had over both the public and the *suq*. The government responded by taking stronger precautionary measures to prevent the nationalists' public activities. When the clubs distributed a circular in 1957 announcing the creation of a federation of clubs, local hotels were forbidden from renting their premises for club meetings and elections.[99] Security posts were set up at the gates to the Shuwaikh Secondary School that same year, decreasing its public accessibility.[100] When news of the 1958 revolution in Iraq reached Kuwait, Abdullah al-Mubarak put the army, public security, and city police forces at the ready to preempt any civil disobedience or disorder on the streets.[101]

The government's opposition to the nationalists' activities was not motivated solely by ideology. The state's substantial self-appointed task of transforming old Kuwait Town into a rational and modern city hinged on its capacity to manage and control the space it sought to develop. Indeed, the modernist planning principles on which Kuwait's oil urbanization was based had their origins in Baron Haussmann's mid-nineteenth-century redesign of Paris. The ultimate goal of Haussmann's massive public works project was to make the city (and the state) safe from popular insurrections. Control over the city was a precondition to public security (and vice versa).[102] Leaving Kuwait City vulnerable to exploitation by a nationalist politics that indirectly threatened the existence of the ruling family significantly challenged this goal, and tainted the image of Kuwait's state-led urban modernity.

Things took a fatal turn for the opposition in 1959 at a public rally celebrating the one-year anniversary of the United Arab Republic in the Shuwaikh campus stadium. In his speech, Jassim al-Qatami announced that "the Kuwaiti people consented to be ruled from the reign of Sabah I by tribal leadership, and now the time has come for democratic rule by the people."[103] Abdullah al-Salem took these statements as a personal affront against his own rule, particularly given his efforts over the previous nine years to advance Kuwait into the so-called modern era. The ruler turned against the political opposition that, given his own experience as the supporter of the merchant opposition in 1938, he had always tolerated. The next day all clubs and organizations were closed, newspapers and other publications were suspended, and public protests and demonstrations were banned.[104]

Decentering the Public Sphere

Public participation in politics was restored only after independence in 1961, due largely to the mass public support shown for Abdullah al-Salem during Iraqi leader Abd al-Karim Qasim's attempt to annex Kuwait that year.[105] Abdullah established the Constituent Assembly in 1962 (to draft a constitution) and the National Assembly (Parliament) in 1963. However, new approaches were developed to keep both the city and the society under government control. One strategy linked civil society and its channels of opposition intrinsically to the state. Though the new National Assembly gave the public formal access to decision-making, along with an outlet through which to air their grievances, the institution put the opposition out in the open by formally integrating them into the state structure. Press censorship was lifted and voluntary associations were allowed to operate again, but the latter were put under direct government supervision. A new law was passed in 1962 that confined the activities of voluntary associations to "social and welfare purposes." They were banned from engaging in political or religious activity that could endanger the stability of the state.[106] The new Ministry of Social Affairs and Labor had the power to license and terminate all associations; it was also bound to provide them with financial and material assistance (undermining the associations' status as nongovernmental organizations).

One form of assistance was the acquisition of new premises. Some organizations, such as Nouria al-Sadani's Arab Women's Development Society, received from state housing authorities, for a nominal rate, a furnished house in one of the newly developing residential neighborhoods outside the city center. Other organizations, such as the Women's Cultural and Social Society, applied for and received plots of land in the suburbs on which to build their new headquarters with some government assistance.[107] The government's allocation of premises to civil society organizations thus mimicked the distribution of state housing. In addition to minimizing the clubs' potential threat to the stability of the city by suburbanizing them, the government also may not have wanted to give out its high-value urban land to civil society organizations any more than it wanted to build housing on this land. So, all headquarters of voluntary associations and civil society clubs in Kuwait were, like the townspeople themselves, resituated outside the city center in the privatized world of the suburbs. A few of the earliest associations, such as the Graduates Society, the Society of Lawyers, and the Society of Engineers, obtained land on the eastern edge of the Green Belt, just outside the city center. Most clubs, however, became ensconced within the residential areas, sometimes in clusters in particular neighborhoods, such as Qadsiya.

With the suburbanization of the spaces of the public sphere, the city center ceased to be the venue of political debate and contestation in Kuwait. Though the National Assembly was located in the heart of the city, it was increasingly a space in which opposition to the ruling family was replaced with pro-government groups. Furthermore, the Parliament could be dissolved whenever it became too oppositional, as it was between 1976 and 1981 and between 1986 and 1992. Thus it was in the more informal spaces of the public sphere rather than in the formal venue of Parliament that real social and political debate operated, and these spaces were forced to function on the urban periphery. The state was thus able to safeguard its control over the city in the postindependence era. Although organized protests, rallies, and demonstrations were occasionally permitted inside the city center, the old venues that had once given form to the public sphere, such as the *suq* and al-Safat, ceased to be used for social and political purposes. Public demonstrations in the city became restricted to specific areas such as the new Flag Square near the Jahra Gate on the western edge of town. Such events were closely monitored and controlled by the Ministry of Interior and were often organized by the government. During the public celebration of Kuwait's independence from Britain in June 1961, for example, the government bussed school children into the city to take part in parades along Fahad al-Salem Street. Other events, such as a demonstration by LIG housing recipients in 1964, were organized by the public but were usually peaceful.[108] Never again (at least not until 2011) were the police or public security forces deployed within the city center to preempt or curtail mass political protests or disorder as they had been between 1956 and 1959. The places that potentially could promote political activities, such as civil society organizations and *diwawin*, had all been suburbanized. When the state-run Kuwait University was established in 1966, rather than being constructed in the city center as per the 1952 master plan, its campuses were situated in the suburbs of Keifan, Khaldiya, Jabriya, and Adailiya; it also took over the campus of the Shuwaikh Secondary School. Indeed, most volatile demonstrations in the postindependence era (which sometimes included clashes between protestors and the police) took place in spaces outside the city center. One such incident occurred during a demonstration in support of the Intifadah by Kuwaiti and Palestinian students at the university in February 1988, when "several dozen" people were injured.[109]

Political life was thus allocated its own particular space in which to function outside the city, as were all other aspects of people's everyday lives and activities. This move contributed to the fragmentation of a once integrated urban life. In the process, political life, like everyday social life, became less public. The relocation of voluntary associations to the suburbs did not reduce their ability to revitalize the public sphere after independence; in fact the number and variety of clubs and organizations significantly increased over the years.[110] By allowing for the preservation and expansion of the public sphere despite the depoliticization of the city center, both *diwawin* and civil society organizations served in post-1950 Kuwait as a form of "political commons,", which David Harvey describes as "a place for open discussion and debate over what . . . power is doing and how best to oppose its reach."[111] However, with their relocation outside the city center, civil society organizations became similar to *diwawin* in that they straddled the public-private divide.[112]

Both the *diwawin* and civil society organizations were semipublic spaces in the otherwise privatized world of the suburbs. However, the physical location of a particular organization in a particular neighborhood did not mean that the former was integrated into the life of the latter. These were not neighborhood organizations or clubs addressing the specific social or political concerns of the people who lived nearby, nor did their membership consist primarily of local residents. The clubs' spatial proximity to private homes did not, in other words, foster the integration of political, social, and domestic life in the suburbs. Furthermore, though technically open to the public, both civil society organizations and *diwawin* had semiprivate tendencies. Membership in voluntary associations was based on set criteria that divided these organizations along class, occupational, religious, or political lines. *Diwawin* usually attracted visitors who shared the same social circle, economic class, and political interests of the host. Neither was really a site where people of different backgrounds and classes freely interacted and worked toward a common purpose. Political discussion and debate after the advent of oil urbanization lacked a true public commons as existed in the city before oil.

Despite their similarities, after 1962 clubs and *diwawin* differed in one important way. Whereas the clubs came under strict government controls and could be closed down during crackdowns on public freedoms (as when the National Assembly was dissolved in 1976 and 1986), *diwawin* were historically privileged spaces that, because of their location in the inviolable space of the home, were safe from state intrusion.[113] The use of the *diwaniyya* as a forum for political expression and public debate therefore increased whenever the government restricted the press and voluntary associations.[114] Because they could be held without the government permits required for clubs and other meetings, *diwawin* were immune from government bans against public gatherings during these periods.[115] Political activists thus used the *diwaniyya* as an important fallback space during times of political repression.

A vivid example of this use occurred in 1989. For seven weeks, public gatherings were held every Monday night in the private *diwaniyya* of a different member of the dissolved assembly to discuss the restoration of the Kuwaiti Constitution and Parliament. The opposition and their public supporters used their peripheral positioning away from the center of power and in the private space of the suburbs to their advantage. The leaders of the movement—thirty-two members of the defunct Parliament—carefully treated the gatherings, which attracted thousands of citizens each week, as constitutionally sanctioned private meetings to protect themselves from police interference. For instance, they avoided using microphones or amplifiers.[116] But the government did all it could to obstruct the movement. The Ministry of Interior closed down Mishari al-Anjari's *diwaniyya* in Nuzha, the location of the second Monday meeting on December 11. Public security forces were deployed to prevent the crowds from reaching the venue. The public outcry and condemnation of the government's unprecedented actions led Deputy Prime Minister Sabah al-Ahmed to formally apologize to al-Anjari on behalf of the government for the closure. He reassured the public of the sanctity of the *diwaniyya* and guaranteed that the following Monday's gathering would not be disturbed.[117] Only when the movement spilled out of the inner suburbs and into the traditionally pro-government area of Jahra did the government once again disrupt the gatherings by force. The National Guard and police were sent out to prevent people from reaching the venues; they used barbed wire barriers, patrol cars, and swinging batons as obstacles. They were never able, however, to declare any *diwaniyya* officially closed. In addition to exposing the status of the *diwaniyya* as a protected space, the experience of the Monday *diwawin* reveals that the suburbs had replaced the city center as the site of political contestation between state and society.

Saving the City: The 1980s

In 1976 the Kuwait Towers were completed and exposed Kuwaitis to their first complete view of the city they had left for the suburbs over the previous two decades. Other iconic structures completed during this period, such as the Kuwait Airways building, also contained top-floor observation decks that boasted stunning views of the city. It is therefore perhaps not surprising that critiques of the state of the city began to emerge in public and official discourse in the 1980s. As the newspapers lamented the drab and cluttered physical appearance of the city, people also started to notice that the city had become a dead space. According to Suhair al-Mosully, who conducted research on how to revitalize Kuwait's "empty" city center in 1989, "at that time, the people and the government realized that their city was missing something they could not identify, something to do with its traditional spirit."[118] In an attempt to revitalize the downtown area, in 1986 the Municipality commissioned a plan for a mixed-use development in the Sharq al-Seif area. The site (constituting 13 percent of the area inside the Green Belt) would consist of medium-density housing with community facilities, as well as offices for government agencies concerned with art and culture. Al-Mosully believes that "after establishing and reconstituting themselves as a modern society, Kuwaitis regretted the demolition of the traditional city."[119] The idea behind the Sharq al-Seif development was to create a cultural village reminiscent of the historic pre-oil town by using similar architectural motifs and with an emphasis on the "historic context" of the site.[120] This return to the historic city was not unique to Kuwait but was a common response to the decay of once vital and vibrant urban centers in many cities around the world in the late twentieth century. The revitalization of the London Docklands into a new business district (Canary Wharf) beginning in the 1980s is a prime example; the old wharves and warehouses were converted into trendy riverside apartments with restaurants, bars, and shops. However, in London and elsewhere, "the architectural and urbanistic resurgence of the commercial center" sparked by such urban rejuvenation projects produced only "a dull and mutilated version" of the former core of the old city due to the priority given to high-end consumption over noncommercial social uses.[121]

Despite the recourse to community and culture, the Sharq al-Seif project was ultimately a commercial development based on consumption (with retail outlets, restaurants and cafés, and high-rent accommodations). Furthermore, the focus on heritage and "crafts" aimed to make the site a static urban artifact—"an object of cultural consumption for tourists, for aestheticism, avid for spectacles and the picturesque"—rather than a vibrant and lived urban district.[122] Though other heritage projects, such as the renovation of part of the old *suq*, were completed in the late 1980s,[123] the Sharq al-Seif development never actually materialized due to the Iraqi invasion of Kuwait in August 1990. In any case, though it ostensibly endorsed mixed-use development over the strict separation of functions that Kuwait's previous city plans had produced, the project focused more on enhancing the state of the city than on meeting the needs of the city's inhabitants and end users. The sudden emphasis in the 1980s on the need to revitalize the city center—which was also the motivation behind the aforementioned Sawaber Complex—underscored the reality that three decades of oil urbanization had a damaging effect on both the city and everyday urban life in Kuwait. However, the impact of this transformation on urban society and everyday social relations was not yet a subject of discussion. Although the physical problems of the city had become clearly visible by the 1980s, the problems of urban society were less obvious in the early oil decades and therefore went largely unremarked. The improved standard of living enjoyed by the majority of citizens concealed the fact that social relations in Kuwait were actually deteriorating rapidly.

7

The De-Urbanization of Society

The Demographic Upheaval

With the advent of oil-driven modernization and the transformation of the city and the patterns and practices of everyday life, Kuwaiti society went through substantial upheavals. Most significant was the country's dramatic population growth. Exponentially increasing wealth from the launch of the oil industry almost immediately created new demands for, to recall Lienhardt, "all the services that had not been there before—metalled roads, pavements, sewers, piped water, electricity and telephone cables and new buildings—and to produce them all at once."[1] The government's determination to carry out numerous ambitious projects simultaneously and immediately—before most members of the indigenous population had learned the skills necessary to carry out these projects themselves—opened up an enormous and "uniquely attractive" market for foreign labor, both skilled and unskilled.[2] In 1944, two years before the first barrels of oil were exported, Kuwait's population was 70,000. In less than a decade, by 1952, it had more than doubled to 160,000. Five years later, when the first census was taken, the population had reached more than 206,000, and by 1965 it had more than doubled to 467,000.[3] Immigration accounted for the bulk of this growth, but high rates of natural increase among the existing Kuwaiti population due to significantly improved living conditions also played a role. Between 1957 and 1961, the total population of the country grew by 126 percent, while the Kuwaiti population grew by 94 percent.[4]

Immigration to Kuwait began to increase significantly after the discovery of oil in 1938, mainly to meet Kuwait Oil Company needs for manual labor. In the pre-1946 period, Iraq, Iran, Oman, and Saudi Arabia had been the most common sources of in-migration to Kuwait. After the launch of the industry in 1946, Kuwait's maturing economy generated higher demands for literate and technically skilled workers in all sectors, not just in the oil industry. The national composition of migrants changed radically. KOC began recruitment efforts in Beirut and Bombay to attract more skilled labor to Kuwait. At the same time, push factors such as partition in India in 1947 and the *nakba* (catastrophe) in Palestine in 1948 (when more than seven hundred thousand Palestinians fled or were expelled during the war with Israel) caused large-scale movements of people, particularly literate professionals, from those countries to Kuwait. By 1957, new nationalities such as Jordanians, Palestinians, Lebanese, Syrians, Egyptians, Indians, and Pakistanis made up 34 percent of the foreign-born population of Kuwait, while Iraqis and Iranians constituted 49 percent.[5]

By 1964, immigrants provided the bulk of Kuwait's skilled labor and 78 percent of its unskilled labor force; 73 percent were males between the ages of fifteen and fifty. These men were largely transient migrants with no permanent ties to the host country.[6] Even though by the mid-1960s it had become clear that the reliance on foreign labor was not in fact temporary as had been believed in the early 1950s, "the individuals themselves are constantly changing and are regarded by their hosts as changeable."[7] Fakhri Shehab (Abdullah al-Salem's chief economic advisor in the 1960s) provides one of the earliest analyses of this "ephemeral status" of migrant workers in Kuwait and the concomitant deterioration of relations between locals and newcomers. Grim unemployment in neighboring countries drove tens of thousands of manual workers to seek employment in Kuwait's burgeoning economy over the preceding decade. But this seemingly unlimited supply of labor considerably depressed wages. In 1964, an unskilled laborer in Kuwait made between $1.25 to $1.65 a day. Though this amount was higher than average earnings in the region, the high cost of living in Kuwait (where most goods were imported) meant that these workers usually left their families at home. Only well-paid positions awarded to highly educated and technically skilled foreigners provided accommodation that could allow for the migration of whole families. Most laborers therefore remitted their wages back to their home country. This practice created a permanent and substantial drain on the national income (at an approximate loss of $120 million a year at that time, and reaching billions of dollars today). Remittances also meant that the workers' lives within Kuwait were reduced to barely subsistence levels.

Thus the fate of thousands of aliens is to live in squalid hovels, indefinitely separated from their homes and families, desperate for employment; they have exchanged the best of their working years for wages that can just keep them and their dependents alive. Against the background of superabundance and prodigality existing in Kuwait, the wide gulf between the two segments of the population is not only indefensible but is bound to engender social resentment and instability.[8]

The 1957 census revealed that Kuwaitis (that is, individuals whose ancestors had been permanent residents of Kuwait since 1899, as per the 1948 nationality law) made up 55 percent of the total population. By 1961, they reached 50 percent, and by the 1965 census, at 47 percent, they had officially become a minority in the country.[9] The realization that Kuwaitis were rapidly being outnumbered by foreigners who possessed the skills necessary to build and operate their country—skills that the indigenous community still lacked—had significant psychological ramifications. Although Kuwait's pre-oil population had always been culturally diverse, the rapid arrival of so many new people from so many places substantially impacted Kuwaitis' ability and willingness to accommodate, accept, and coexist with strangers.[10] Furthermore, "the turmoil of social change and an unknown future" triggered by this demographic transformation alongside the many other changes that Kuwaitis were witnessing at the time—spatially, socially, and experientially—may have been dislocating for society as a whole.[11] Moments of such dramatic social upheaval often trigger fears of "losing one's identity" through outside threats. Such fears, Richard Sennett argues, create a desire to define an absolute identity, a clear and unambiguous self-image that is coherent, unified, and "filters out threats in social experience" (part of the same enterprise in which modern urban planning is involved).[12] The changes to the Kuwaiti nationality law that were made two years after the 1957 census constituted a significant step toward the creation of this new kind of Kuwaiti collective identity, one increasingly based on consensus (rather than on dissensus, as was the case before oil). As Anh Nga Longva argues, "the presence of the expatriates was a major factor which contributed, if not to making, at least to crystallizing, the Kuwaiti national identity, built on the *community of feeling* [that connected the native population to the Kuwaiti state and the Kuwaiti nation]."[13]

Citizenship and Welfare

The new nationality law promulgated in 1959 extended the required date of settlement from 1899 to 1920, but restricted provisions that allowed for naturalization by virtue of birth or long-term residence. A further amendment to the law in 1960 limited the total number of naturalizations in any given year to a maximum of fifty, "effectively precluding the attainment of Kuwaiti nationality by the majority of the immigrant community."[14] The provision of nationality became a powerful legal instrument deployed by the nascent state to control the country's rapidly growing population, giving the state, rather than other nonstate actors, control over the management of immigration.[15] Before oil, by contrast, newcomers were drawn into existing patronage, community, and *farij* networks, which facilitated their integration into urban society. But, perhaps paradoxically, new residency laws mandated that every foreigner residing in Kuwait had to be sponsored by their employer (known as their *kafil*), effectively making Kuwaiti citizens, rather than the state, legally responsible for the bodies and fates of non-Kuwaitis.[16] The nationality law and other policies that emerged in its wake thus established for the first time political and legal distinctions between nationals and newcomers, officially making the former dominant over the latter.[17] The amendments to the nationality law came at the peak of the conflicts between the government and the Arab nationalist movement discussed in Chapter 6. Egyptian and Palestinian teachers and professionals working in Kuwait were thought to be fueling this ideology among Kuwaitis. The new nationality law can therefore be interpreted as one of several "tactics designed to divide Kuwaitis and expatriates and then coopt the Kuwaitis."[18] The question of citizenship was key to guaranteeing Abdullah al-Salem's nascent state a degree of stability and viability in the face of major economic, political, and social upheaval.[19]

Affluence certainly provided the tools to advance these goals. The state welfare benefits that came with Kuwaiti citizenship made the growing distance between nationals and resident foreigners created by the nationality law most tangible. Before oil, new settlers to Kuwait were absorbed into existing urban networks (such as the *farij* or a *nokhada*'s crew) that ensured their access to moral and material assistance. After oil, newcomers were explicitly restricted from receiving many of the state-provided material benefits (such as free education and housing) that citizens now enjoyed. Citizenship and welfare, as Mai al-Nakib argues, thus "homogenized the heterogeneity of the Kuwaiti population by constructing a common 'outside' all Kuwaitis could identify with."[20] Citizenship also redefined a Kuwaiti national's relationship with the state and with the wider national community. A singular and increasingly exclusive national community was meant to replace and in fact subordinate to the nation-state previous loyalties to place of origin, religious sect, merchant patron, *farij*, family, or tribe, as well as to new ideologies such as Arab nationalism. The strict and narrow definition of Kuwaiti nationality as defined by law—which in 1982 restricted naturalization to Muslims only, alienating Kuwait's Christian community—further homogenized the hybridity of Kuwaiti society by subsuming all other markers of identity to a singular, monovocal national identity. This purification of Kuwaiti communal identity significantly undermined Kuwait's cosmopolitan tradition, and disguised its origins as a society of immigrants.

Insularity and Parochialism

Restrictive access to Kuwaiti nationality made access to the rights and privileges that came with being a citizen extremely exclusive. In addition to welfare benefits and services, other privileges included policies that all imports, retail trades, and contractual business could be transacted only through Kuwaiti agents, that only Kuwaitis had pension rights and permanent tenure in the civil service, and that only Kuwaitis could own land. These privileges were meant to preserve Kuwait's wealth for its citizens in the face of "intruding aliens." By creating clear distinctions between citizens and noncitizens, such policies "permanently estranged and embittered the most efficient and indispensable element in the community—the resident alien. . . . With little or no hope of being permanently integrated into the community, he is left without any sense of allegiance to Kuwait."[21] This situation was in stark contrast to Kuwait's recent pre-oil past, when the town's commercial success hinged on its ability to attract newcomers to permanently settle and integrate into the local community and workforce.

Wealth and privilege, coupled with a growing suspicion and defensiveness toward outsiders, perhaps unsurprisingly created a sense of superiority among Kuwaitis. Their new wealth and power may have enhanced feelings of "solidarity" (a phrase Shehab used) between members of the national population that had first been created by the nationality law (although these feelings did not last).[22] It also widened and sustained the growing gap between nationals and immigrants, and made the former averse to the presence, let alone integration, of the latter. By 1964 Shehab (himself a foreigner in Kuwait, from Iraq) described Kuwaitis as being "instinctively suspicious of strangers and new ideas."[23] Changing patterns of everyday behavior among Kuwaitis revealed this growing sense of superiority and aversion to strangers. In his analysis of his aforementioned 1982 social-residential survey, Abdulrasool al-Moosa noted that, "as part of its system for cultural survival . . . the Kuwaiti section of the population tended to segregate itself in both discreet, though occasionally demonstrative, ways."[24] One defensive measure adopted to distance themselves from the ever-growing "sea of outsiders" was mode of dress, particularly among men.[25] Though in the early oil years young Kuwaiti middle-class men began wearing "Western" clothes (even school uniforms consisted of white shirts and dark trousers), by the late 1950s there was a visible resurgence of the traditional white *dishdasha* (long robe), particularly when young men entered the workforce. Longva argues that this dress code played a major role in "ethnic signalization." There were few visible racial distinctions between Kuwaitis and other Arabs that could set the former apart, and the growing Asian population could not use variations in Arabic accents or names as clues to identify Kuwaitis (and therefore treat them with the deference that nationals were growing to expect from foreigners).[26] Longva gives several anecdotes from her interlocutors that reveal the significance of the *dishdasha* as the most obvious emblem of a purified (male) Kuwaitiness: a young Kuwaiti man dressed in jeans being stopped and checked by police who thought he was a foreigner, a Kuwaiti man in *dishdasha* entering a store and being served by the foreign staff before the waiting non-Kuwaiti customers. As she puts it,

Dressed in European-style clothes, the Kuwaiti could be mistaken for a Western Arab, a Turk, an Iranian, a native of the subcontinent, or a Westerner. Dressed in a dishdasha, his identity was unmistakable. And this identification immediately set in motion a chain of reactions—always the same—among the people he interacted with, especially if they were expatriates. This in turn informed him of, and confirmed, his identity, one that was firmly anchored in social privilege and power.[27]

As part of this process of self-segregation and differentiation, over time citizens found certain public activities socially unacceptable for themselves but suitable for foreigners. Mode of transportation was one example. Kuwaitis became completely reliant on cars, particularly on private transportation. One day during his visit to Kuwait in 1953, Lienhardt spent half an hour with a Kuwaiti friend walking around the city in the heat searching for an acquaintance to give them a ride home. When Lienhardt suggested taking a taxi, his friend refused: "You can take a taxi in Kuwait, but I can't."[28] Whereas in the 1940s it was not uncommon for Kuwaitis to take taxis, by the early 1950s citizens found it socially "demeaning" to use such forms of public transportation, though it was acceptable for foreigners.[29]

Suburbanization also contributed to this practice of self-segregation. As described in Chapter 5, the new suburbs designed for the relocation of the townspeople between the First and Fourth Ring Roads excluded non-Kuwaitis by banning both rentals and multi-occupancy dwellings. Though segregation was initially imposed by the state, over time Kuwaitis in these areas became less amenable to the idea of sharing their space with outsiders. In 1973, the Municipality conducted a housing survey to determine where Kuwaitis who had recently graduated from university would like to live and the sort of housing they would prefer. The survey found that only 3 percent of respondents were willing to open their residential area to non-Kuwaitis. The survey also reveals that, like *dishdashas*, single-family villas had become a symbol of status and distinction for Kuwaitis whereas apartments had became associated with non-Kuwaitis. Ninety-five percent of respondents preferred their neighborhood to be totally devoted to single-family housing, and only 3 percent said they would not mind their area including apartments (the same percentage that was willing to accept non-Kuwaitis as neighbors).[30] Al-Moosa similarly found that his Kuwaiti respondents much preferred to live next to their relatives, coreligionists, and ethnic peers than with strangers and newcomers. They "rejected the suggestion that the state would be best served by mixed residential zones." They were also against having apartments in their area that housed non-Kuwaitis, because they believed that apartments would "[spoil] the aesthetic balance of existing Kuwaitis' residential zones and [offend] local values such as neighbouring houses not overlooking each other and taking away family privacy."[31]

Perhaps unsurprisingly, al-Moosa's non-Kuwaiti respondents were in favor of residential mixing. They believed that mixed areas would enhance social cohesion in Kuwait and allow for the establishment of more constructive social relations between citizens and expatriates. But his Kuwaiti respondents were not interested in establishing social relations with expatriates. They believed that the foreign community was temporary whereas citizens were dedicated to the state for life. The latter therefore "had different, long-term needs that could be satisfied only by separate treatment."[32] So foreigners could live in rented apartments and take taxis because they were not staying permanently (though the reality, of course, was that many stayed for life, and for generations). For citizens, villas and cars emphasized their own rootedness to the place.

Kuwaitis thus increasingly retreated into a more insular and private "national" realm. Some previously public places, such as the *suq*, were made more socially restrictive to keep the newcomers at bay. Insofar as the *suq* was a place for shopping, anyone could use it. As a social space, its shops and offices were an exclusive sphere to which non-Kuwaitis did not have access. "Being a customer was one thing and being invited to sit down was quite another."[33] Kuwaitis also avoided other kinds of public spaces. For example, cafés in post-1950 Kuwait were much more open and accessible to non-Kuwaitis than other spaces in the city. But whereas in the pre-oil period both merchants and nonmerchants socialized in coffee houses, after the influx of foreign immigration Kuwaitis of all classes stopped frequenting the increasing number of cafés in the city, "much as the shaikhs and the important merchants no longer walked along the streets but drove past in their cars." Unlike their shops and offices in the *suq*, which were "places where one could choose one's company . . . cafés were open to anyone who could pay, over-familiar places where the customers mixed together without regard for status and precedence."[34] By the 1950s, status and precedence had become important social aspirations for Kuwaitis of all classes, particularly over non-Kuwaitis. Avoiding public transport and cafés and restricting access to the social side of the *suq* became defensive tactics used by Kuwaitis to distinguish themselves from newcomers.

Affluence and Inertia

The growing desire to define a common "us" in opposition to a common "them," and the changing patterns of behavior this engendered, may have been a defensive response to social upheaval and displacement, a way of protecting Kuwaiti society against unknown future threats or further dislocation. As Sennett argues, "insecurity . . . is at the root of this need for an image of community, of 'us.'"[35] The ever-increasing population of expatriates was kept at a safe distance because mixing could potentially bring in a flood of new influences that might change the nature or character of this new, delicately constructed Kuwaiti collective identity. With the nationality law, Kuwaiti identity became uniform, fixed, and exclusive, whereas before oil it had been hybrid, mutable, and inclusive. This purification of the Kuwaiti community replaced concrete experiences with a "myth of solidarity."[36] That is, by building a consensual image of a unified "us," Kuwaitis no longer had to actually deal with each other to feel a sense of community. This was exacerbated by the fact that the *need* for regular contact and interaction with diverse social groups (not just foreigners but also other Kuwaitis) eroded with affluence. Because of the harsh realities of economic scarcity before oil, people needed to engage in multiple concrete activities and relations with diverse social groups in their everyday lives in order to survive. After the advent of the oil era, that need for cooperation and mutual aid no longer existed. Material abundance thus enhanced the creation of "a community cemented by an act of will rather than by acts of experience."[37]

In 1964, the annual revenue from oil amounted to KD 1,200 per citizen ($3,360). This was money that the government was able to spend on the provision of water, power, education, health care, and housing to its small national population. Kuwait now imported a wide range of luxury goods at an average annual expenditure of nearly $300 million, or about $825 per inhabitant. With guaranteed employment in the public sector, coupled with the "unlimited scope for success" in private business, Kuwaiti families of all classes achieved financial stability and autonomy.[38] Affluence coupled with state welfare removed the need for mutual support and sharing between different individuals and social groups. People could now "withdraw into their self-contained, self-sustaining homes."[39] As Shehab described,

the ease with which wealth has been acquired has . . . inadvertently forced competition out of national life and made Kuwait an insular society . . . As a result, the drive, diligence and risk-taking that characterized the old Kuwaiti are no more. At both ends of the social scale the new citizen is content to enjoy a life of leisure and inertia, and is unwilling that this happy state of affairs should be disturbed. Protected, pampered, lavishly provided for and accountable to no one, he lives in a world of make-believe.[40]

With this isolation and the concomitant flattening of everyday interactions and activities, Kuwaitis now had a much smaller "fund of experiences" on which to base their communal bonds.[41] Rather than feeling related through what they actually did with each other, people began to simply envisage a sense of community on the basis of their sameness as determined by their shared nationality document and the privileges this brought (such as the jealously protected "aesthetic balance" of their shared neighborhoods).[42] In addition to hindering relations between nationals and newcomers, the lavish welfare benefits that Kuwaitis enjoyed "entailed no effort or sacrifice on the part of the public, which sees no need to contribute to a state whose chief problem is what to do with its income." Superaffluence thus removed the need for actual participation in public or community life. As Shehab saw it, "the idea of the state as a communal institution demanding service, sacrifice and devotion" was subordinated to satisfying individual desires.[43] By the early 1960s, easy access to a comfortable and sheltered lifestyle contributed to this valorization of private life over public belonging.

Kuwaitis' social withdrawal came about partly as a result of general lifestyle changes: better communications, improved living standards, the provision of more convenient amenities closer to home in the suburbs, and new employment patterns all contributed to the gradual reduction of public life in Kuwait, as it did in other societies of affluence such as the United States after World War II. The complex interactions and multiple associations that defined everyday life before oil were replaced by simpler points of contact. People's interactions with one another became largely restricted to working and socializing, although even the latter became more limited in its scope. Many of the pragmatic changes in the patterns and practices of everyday life that affluence brought eroded the diversity and multiplicity of city life. The everyday sociability of former public places like the *suq* and *sahel* was significantly reduced in the process. New and improved "means of public engagement" made regular face-to-face interaction between people unnecessary.[44] Better communication services meant that people could now reach each other by telephone, radios allowed Kuwaitis to hear the news of the world directly, and state-controlled radio and television stations, coupled with the launch of the official government gazette *Kuwayt al-Youm* (Kuwait Today) in 1954, gave the government an easy and direct way of communicating with the public. All of these changes eliminated the need to go into the *suq* on a daily basis for noncommercial reasons. The diverse activities that had once drawn people to the *sahel* similarly diminished. Around 97 percent of Kuwaiti households had washing machines by 1969 and women no longer had to go down to the beach to wash their clothes, and government-funded tanks brought water straight from the desalination plants to each family home.[45] Urban Kuwaitis of all classes could now afford to hire domestic help for the daily chores that still required going out; 64 percent of polled residents in Shamiya said they had help in 1969.[46] One day in 1970 Zahra Freeth spotted a woman crossing the Gulf Road carrying a sack of firewood. When she commented that there were still poor people in Kuwait, her mother, Violet Dickson (who lived in Kuwait from 1929 until 1990), responded that the woman must be a foreigner, because by then there were no longer "Kuwaiti citizens so poor that they have to gather firewood like that."[47] As Haya al-Mughni argues, with the material improvements in everyday living, Kuwaiti women in particular "were drawn back into the house."[48]

Indeed, it was the suburbs themselves, and the new kind of domestic-only lifestyle they represented, that most clearly effected a valorization of private life over public belonging in post-1950 Kuwait. Henri Lefebvre argues that suburbs reduce one's everyday experiences from a "right to inhabit"—"to take part in a social life, a community, village or city"—to a more static and simplified notion of habitat: where one physically resides.[49] Historical memory in Kuwait reflects a similar sentiment favoring the community-feeling of the old town to the flatness and isolation of the suburbs. Suburbanization certainly brought material benefits. Houses in the old town were small and cramped whereas houses in the new suburbs were spacious and had central air-conditioning, electricity, running water, and so on. "But in the old town there was cooperation and solidarity between neighbors, and it was better [before oil,] to be honest. Now each person has his own car, house, servants."[50] Such sentiments are pervasive in the personal and collective memories of Kuwaitis who lived through the shift from pre-oil scarcity to oil-funded affluence. Life in the new suburbs was more comfortable and convenient than in the courtyard houses of the old town, but comfort and convenience came at the expense of communal spirit and neighborhood life.

At the time of the initial move, however, most people favored the former over the latter. When the Municipality had tried to acquire people's property to accommodate some rudimentary development projects in the 1940s, many people refused to leave their houses and some were even thrown in jail for obstructing public development. Najat al-Jassim argues that their reluctance to move to a new house (still within the town at that time) was based on their fear of being separated from their neighbors and losing access to their existing social networks in their *farij*.[51] Moving to a new neighborhood would require the establishment of new social ties to gain access to moral and material support. But when new suburbs were produced for the displacement of the townspeople in the 1950s, the state promised to provide modern public services and amenities in the new areas. Through state welfare, people would have access to material assistance no matter who their neighbors were. Extremely higher compensations for the acquisition of their land in the city coupled with the provision of much larger housing options in the suburbs made "the 'emigration' to the outlying areas . . . an almost wholesale exodus."[52]

Nonetheless, there is some truth to present-day nostalgic lamentations for the loss of community spirit that came with the move to the suburbs. In Kuwait's new residential enclaves, "internalization, privacy, and individuality" (to borrow from Teresa Caldeira's analysis of exclusive residential enclaves in São Paolo) were enhanced at the expense of the sociability, public life, and communal experiences that characterized the pre-oil *firjan*.[53] Detached villa living constituted the most immediate and significant social change introduced by the move to the suburbs that enhanced the privacy and isolation that many Kuwaitis began to experience. Plots of land and government houses were allocated to nuclear families only, and communal living was substantially reduced with this new housing standard. By as early as 1965 the idea of living "independently" on one's privately owned property was described in public discourse as part of the Kuwaiti family's "nature" and "tradition," though in truth the courtyard houses clustered tightly together in the old *firjan* hardly represented a tradition of living "independently."[54] The rapid pace of change redefined what Kuwaiti "tradition" actually entailed. When in the late 1970s the government first broached the idea of constructing apartments instead of houses for citizens, Kuwaiti objections expressed similar transformations in housing ideals. Opponents argued that apartment living would cause significant changes in Kuwaiti social and spatial norms. Individual residences in much closer proximity to each other would affect how people behaved within their own homes, because they would have to be careful not to disturb their neighbors.[55] This notion of course sounds very similar to life in the old courtyard houses in the pre-oil period, when houses were separated by only a mud wall and neighbors could hear, smell, and sometimes even see what was happening next door. The characterization of the socio-spatial organization of apartment living as a radical change rather than as a return to the recent past reveals that the lifestyle changes brought about by oil were indeed substantial. Besides, by now apartments were associated with non-Kuwaitis whereas villas were markers of citizens' social prestige. Life in the suburbs thus effected a retreat into privacy and independent living among Kuwait's former townspeople.

However, the spatial organization of these suburbs in contrast to the layout of the pre-oil *firjan* seems to contradict this turn to privacy outside the city. The modern villas were outwardly oriented, with street-facing entrances, low boundary walls, front yards, and large verandahs. This new living standard, coupled with the wide streets and open aspect of the suburbs, created the impression that spatial privacy was not an obstacle preventing neighbors from interacting with one another. However, just as the inward-looking courtyard houses, high walls, narrow streets, and blind alleys of the pre-oil *firjan* paradoxically served as the setting for a much more publicly oriented lifestyle than the urban landscape might suggest, so the exposed villas, front yards, and wide streets of the new suburbs belied the entirely privatized world of these areas. A common complaint among former townspeople, both male and female, when remembering their relocation outside the city is that their relationships with their neighbors completely changed. "In the old town our family knew our neighbors through generations. But in the new suburbs nobody knew each other. We knew who our new neighbors were by name but we never met them face-to-face."[56] The 1969 survey showed that in fact 70 percent of the respondents from Shamiya counted either of their immediate neighbors as close friends. Nonetheless, the common lamentation in *hadar* historical memory on the loss of neighborliness after 1950 suggests that whereas neighbors might have in fact known each other, neighborhood life substantially diminished with the move to the new suburbs.

Lefebvre and others argue that this sense of isolation is characteristic of suburbs and decentralized new towns everywhere. Nonetheless, in Kuwait these changes to residential life can specifically be traced back to the way plots and houses were allocated to the townspeople after 1954, which effected the dispersal of families, *firjan*, and existing community networks. The new spatial distance between members of the formerly close-knit community—who were now scattered in new neighborhoods that were disconnected and separated from one another by main roads and highways—increased the psychological distance between them. People no longer saw their old friends and neighbors as often as they had in the past. As one woman recalled, "I would only ever bump into my old friends by chance," which usually occurred abroad in Beirut or London rather than in Kuwait itself.[57] The dispersal of the townspeople into separate areas also impacted how often relatives visited one another. In 1969, 57 percent of the Shamiya respondents said they visited their relatives only two or three times a month and 21 percent said they visited relatives once a week. Only 15 percent said they visited their relatives three to five times a week.[58] In truth, the suburbs were not that far apart from one another, and cars made the ability to travel from one neighborhood to the next much easier. But people were used to living within walking distance of their closest friends and relatives. Without the (material) need to get to know their new neighbors intimately, people became more socially withdrawn.

Many Kuwaitis of course welcomed the chance to move beyond the scope of neighborhood life and to explore new forms of social interaction emerging in post-1950 Kuwait. Voluntary associations and special-interest clubs flourished throughout the postindependence era, as did private social and beach clubs. But what this meant was that social life occurred elsewhere, away from the realm of one's own private life, fragmenting the daily life of the new suburbanite.[59] In fact, the results of the social-residential survey in 1969 reveal that people in the suburbs simply began to spend more time at home. When asked how they had spent the previous evening, 37.5 percent of Shamiya respondents (the majority) said they had either stayed at home or watched TV (presumably at home). Although around 30 percent had spent the evening in the *diwaniyya*, only five people (half a percent) said they had visited or received friends or family. When asked what they had done the previous weekend, once again 35 percent had either stayed at home or watched television (the next highest activity was "camping in desert—19 percent—followed by "driving car for pleasure"—13.5 percent). Less than one percent spent time with friends or family.[60] Social life was becoming increasingly internalized and private.

In 1963, one decade after the relocation process began, Saba George Shiber noted the following:

Not only has the Kuwaiti changed residential locus but, in addition, he lost the family ties previously engendered by proximity of co-location and he has also changed neighbors. And all this, in relative time, transpired with lightning speed. So far the group, or family, feeling has not yet been re-instated in the new neighborhoods.[61]

When a family moved into a new house in the pre-oil town, social custom dictated that for each day of their first week in the area their neighbors would cook for them to make it easier for the family to settle in. New residents were thus incorporated into existing *farij* networks. After the advent of oil, neighborhoods beyond the Green Belt were constructed and allocated on a mass scale and everyone was therefore new to the area. Not only were existing social networks thus dispersed, but the new suburbanites also had to lay the foundations for new social connections to emerge in their residential areas. By 1982 this had yet to be fully achieved: 56 percent of the Kuwaitis whom al-Moosa interviewed claimed they had no close links with their immediate neighbors.[62] As one woman who had relocated to Bayan admitted, "I was too embarrassed to go introduce myself to my new neighbors because they never showed any interest in wanting to know who we were."[63]

Two factors may have contributed to the lack of reinstatement of the "group feeling" in the new suburbs. First, the new spatial layout of villas and streets was not conducive to the kind of social life that had characterized the pre-oil *firjan*. Though meant to evoke a sense of luxury and extravagance in the suburbs, wide setbacks from the street, large gardens, and boundary walls (even low ones) cut neighbors off from one another.[64] As one woman put it, "We were used to just walking into each other's homes for something as simple as borrowing an onion. We couldn't do that in our new houses."[65] Furthermore, most space between the boundary wall of a villa and the street was used for parking—67 percent of Shamiya residents parked on the street in 1969—and the suburbs (like the city center) therefore lacked sidewalks.[66] When she visited Kuwait in 1970, Freeth saw some older men attempting to hold onto the custom of gathering with neighbors and friends in the evening by bringing chairs outside their gates. They were forced to sit beside "busy highways in all the noise and dust of the evening rush-hour traffic."[67] In 1969 less than a quarter of polled Shamiya residents said they regularly sat outside the gates of their home, and only one of these people said they did so to "feel part of the neighborhood" (the majority claimed they wanted "more open air," perhaps reflecting the confinement of the new suburbs).[68] Even the lives of children were impacted by changes in their surroundings. Before oil, *farij* children spent their days in each other's company, playing on the streets or in the local *baraha*. By 1963, however, it was reported that children in the suburbs were bored. They had too much free time on their hands, and to rectify this problem the government began building recreational facilities and clubs within the new neighborhoods to keep them active, privatizing what was once a very public childhood.[69]

Though the specific context and circumstances of suburbanization were quite different, a comparison can be drawn here with the experiences of Saudi families from the eastern coastal region of al-Qatif who moved into new American-style suburban housing in the oil company town of Aramco in the late 1950s. American company officials were certain that their Home Ownership Loan Program and the modern amenities provided in the new villas (similar to those in subdivision suburbs back home) would be attractive to their Arab employees. However, many Saudi families eventually moved back to their old communities and the program failed. "Social isolation, especially the weakening of extended family ties" was the main factor in this failed attempt at suburbanization, particularly from the perspective of Saudi women. As Nathan Citino argues in his study of this program, "Arab wives rejected the homogenization and anonymity of communities whose geography did not respect their family relationships or reflect the diverse ways in which they actually lived."[70] But whereas these families could opt to move back to their old village communities, in Kuwait the old town had been demolished and no such choice existed. Furthermore, the extreme material wealth that Kuwaitis now enjoyed (in contrast to the less affluent Aramco families) perhaps made the experience more palatable.

A more critical factor that contributed to the lack of interaction and contact between neighbors, and the resultant loss of the "group feeling" in residential areas, was the growth of state services that supplanted community support in the new suburbs. Improvements in state welfare coupled with increased personal wealth meant that "neighborhood responsibilities" were removed.[71] People no longer needed each other to survive. In place of the internal neighborhood networks of the pre-oil period, the suburbs became distribution centers for the most essential state-provided services, such as education, health care, subsidized foodstuffs, cleanliness and hygiene (street cleaning, garbage collection, and so on), and personal and public security. These benefits and services made Kuwaitis externally dependent on the state.[72] But this was not true of the less affluent townspeople, such as Mohammed Ali Abu-Hamad (mentioned earlier), who were still inside the city waiting for their property to be acquired so that they too could move to the new suburbs. In 1964, Abu-Hamad's house had become so run-down that it had been unable to withstand the winter storms that year. It had also became increasingly difficult for Abu-Hamad to provide food for his large family or to repair his dilapidated mudbrick home—two aspects of life in which assistance would have been provided by the *farij* or the broader community before oil.[73] And because the old town was being developed into a bureaucratic and commercial center, no public services like those found in the suburbs were brought into the city. The case of Abu-Hamad and of many others like him who remained inside the Green Belt well into the 1970s reveals how much the residents of the urban community once relied on one another for their own well-being, and shows the impact that the removal of these networks had when they were not replaced by new state services. But for Kuwaitis who had moved to the suburbs, those old mechanisms of moral and material assistance were no longer needed.

Common Bonds Without Common Experiences

In addition to losing participation in community life in the suburbs, people in Kuwait became less accustomed to encountering and confronting difference in their residential areas. As seen in Chapter 5, throughout the early oil decades the state developed separate policies to relocate the townspeople in new suburbs outside the city center, rehouse the former village residents in their same locales, settle the sedentarizing Bedouin in outlying areas, and accommodate the influx of expatriates in separate areas developed by the private sector. These disparate housing schemes separated the population into socially homogenous enclaves in which people's everyday interactions and public encounters with groups outside their own social worlds significantly diminished.[74] With time, Kuwaitis became less amenable to living next to people different from themselves. As already seen, socio-spatial segregation certainly widened the gap between Kuwaitis and non-Kuwaitis. But it also had a significant impact on social relations within the supposedly unified national community. In the aforementioned 1973 graduate housing survey, the vast majority of respondents not only preferred to live next to Kuwaitis, but also wanted their area to be exclusively devoted to other university graduates (so Kuwaitis of a particular socioeconomic class).[75] The long-term outcomes of these state housing policies reveal the inherent volatility of the "national project" of forging a group identity among Kuwaitis on the basis of a myth of solidarity rather than on tangible experiences.[76] Their extreme social segregation impeded the kinds of regular interactions and associations that would allow Kuwaitis of different social classes or backgrounds to relate to one another in concrete ways. Furthermore, unequal housing standards not only segregated but also differentiated between sectors of the national population according to social background (such as *hadar* or *badu*), thereby undermining the image of a unified "us" that citizenship and welfare (including access to housing itself) were meant to engender. As a result, the common bonds meant to hold the national community together through an image of their sameness eventually deteriorated.

The most exclusive residential enclave was the zone of inner suburbs between the First and Fourth Ring Roads, to which the townspeople were relocated. When planning these new neighborhood units beyond the Green Belt, the state had to fulfill its promise of luxury that had coaxed the townspeople out of the city gates. In addition to being socially exclusive (in that both non-Kuwaitis and Bedouin were housed in other areas), these neighborhoods were gratuitously spacious and extravagant. House plots in the inner suburbs, where the average household size was seven people, ranged from 400 to 750 square meters for limited-income group (LIG) housing recipients, and 750 to 1,000 square meters for the recipients of plots only. Most housing plots contained a minimum of 50 percent unbuilt space to be used for gardens, paved areas, parking, and so on.[77] Neighborhood roads were extremely wide and many "large tracts of left-over desert" created by sizeable building setbacks and an abundance of open spaces provided ample room for car parking and tree planting.[78] Shiber and the Buchanan team warned the government against promoting this type of "over-generously planned" residential standard because it was taking up too much space in the built-up areas and was not sustainable in the long term.[79] Nearby areas such as Salmiya and Hawalli, which mainly housed the much larger population of non-Kuwaitis, were already suffering from extremely high density and overcrowding due to limited space.[80] But this policy persisted throughout the neighborhoods within the first four ring roads. Similar to the overabundance of space was the oversupply of amenities. A typical neighborhood unit within the Fourth Ring Road was built to "[provide] its residents with convenience, amenity, safety and interesting visual prospects."[81] In the early 1960s Shiber identified that neighborhood facilities within these areas, such as supermarkets and recreation centers, were often "over-generously built, without the adequate clientele or population to cater to the services they are meant to provide."[82] Large carefully manicured parks were described in 1961 as "the lungs" of al-manatiq al-numuthajiyya, in tune with Garden City terminology.[83]

Residents of a mass government housing estate in the village of Khaitan, by contrast, complained in 1975 that there was no space or garden in their homes or their neighborhood for their children to play in.[84] In the outlying Bedouin areas, the average household consisted of fifteen people, yet houses were built on much smaller plots of 100 to 150 square meters (Figure 20).[85] These Bedouin settlement areas were more spatially in line with American working class subdivision suburbs in that the houses were uniform, simple, and functional, and "incorporated certain assumptions about the social needs of that constituency," as determined by the housing authorities rather than by the residents themselves.[86] In contrast to LIG housing recipients in the inner suburbs (discussed in Chapter 5), residents of outlying areas such as Khaitan and Farwaniya were specifically barred from the provision of "second-story" government loans after their house was paid off. Because most recipients in these areas could not afford to build their own second floor, their homes became overcrowded as their families grew.[87] One resident of Khaitan had waited ten years to get a government house, but by the time he received it his family had grown to nine people. The house had only one bathroom and his application for a loan to build a second bathroom was rejected.[88] The ability to make changes to one's home in the suburbs, for Levittowners and Kuwaiti suburbanites alike, provided visual evidence of "the owners' stake in the society of which they had become an integral part."[89] In Kuwait, such ability gave citizens a stake in the country's oil-era modernization. Without the option to adapt

FIGURE 20. Government-built limited-income group housing for Bedouin in the "outlying areas." *Source: Al-Watan* newspaper.

their homes to suit their own needs, or the right to choose where to live, formerly pastoral Kuwaitis were given less of a stake in their changing society than were *hadar* Kuwaitis.

The standard of houses built for the Bedouin settlement program was permanently below par, and government housing from 1970 onward acquired a negative stigma.[90] Local newspapers regularly published complaints from residents of these areas about their inferior accommodation. In areas like Farwaniya, Khaitan, and Sabahiya, "the houses are filthy, the roads are wrecked and full of potholes, and the walls are crumbling."[91] In Dhaher, rainwater leaked into houses due to poor insulation, improperly fixed limestone on the outer walls, and cheap roofing tiles that broke apart in bad weather.[92] A more dangerous yet frequent occurrence was the explosion of rooftop water tanks that flooded the neighborhood streets, which were much narrower than the gratuitously wide streets of the inner suburbs.[93] The government rarely responded to these issues. In 1964 hundreds of LIG housing recipients in outlying areas held a mass demonstration to complain about the substandard accommodations in which they were living, some of which had even been deemed unlivable by state inspectors. They occupied the office of the Minister of Housing, who never turned up to hear their complaints.[94] The frequent newspaper articles dating from the mid-1960s well into the 1980s exposing the appalling state of the outlying areas reveal that the government rarely rectified these problems. On the other hand, when seven hundred government villas within three inner *hadar* suburbs were declared substandard in 1969, the housing authorities demolished and replaced them with larger, better quality villas.[95]

In 1963, when state housing authorities were focused on relocating the townspeople to the new suburbs, Shiber reported that government policy on LIG housing was commendable for its "debarring of segregation on the grounds of social, ethnic or economic prejudices . . . on the grounds that low- or limited-income housing depresses surrounding property values or [that] the occupants constitute social undesirability."[96] But from the mid-1960s onward, as other groups were brought into state housing schemes, such socio-spatial segregation and differentiation became the norm, fostering deep cleavages within the national population. In al-Moosa's 1982 survey, residents of the inner suburbs were questioned about the desirability of mixing Kuwaiti nationals together in the same residential district regardless of wealth or social origin, which meant bringing together residents of the *hadar* suburbs with those of the outlying villages and Bedouin townships.

One third of respondents expressed a strong resistance to integration, believing it might "[excite] social frictions." Another third remained apprehensive to integration.[97] Those who were vehemently opposed to mixed residential areas believed that "lower-income housing would damage the amenities of the better-class districts by introducing low-grade architecture." Others were more amenable to mixing "provided that suitable styles were adopted for all housing types so that there was no lowering of standards."[98]

By couching their concerns about living alongside Bedouin in material rather than explicitly sectarian terms, these *hadar* respondents echo the sentiments of white American suburbanites who, by the 1950s, expressed similar economic concerns when opposing the sale of homes in their areas to African Americans. Rather than displaying the more explicit racism of the prewar era, white suburbanites claimed that black neighbors would lower their property values. David Freund argues that this new market-driven discourse did not simply disguise an enduring latent racism; rather, the "language and assumptions" of racial thinking had changed in accordance with "the politics of metropolitan change."[99] State-subsidized suburban growth during the postwar era of homeownership encouraged racial exclusion and thus constructed new measures of difference between whites and blacks.[100] In Kuwait, rigid social divisions between townspeople and Bedouin had not been pronounced before oil; many urban families shared lineage with the desert tribes, and tribes regularly settled in the town and became part of the urban population. The "social frictions" between *hadar* and *badu* that were noticeable by the 1980s were arguably generated and sustained by the politics of urban change in Kuwait over the preceding decades.

Al-Moosa concluded that Kuwaitis who lived in the more privileged suburbs considered residents of low-income housing as inferior and treated them accordingly, "a factor that makes integration more difficult."[101] The Bedouin residents of the mass housing projects were well aware of this perception, and of the stark discrepancies between their outlying areas and *al-manatiq al-numuthajiyya*. As one newspaper put it in 1971, "The face of Kuwait is what we witness in the luxurious houses and villas of the [city suburbs] and the streets and buildings of those with envied incomes; its bowels are the houses of those with limited incomes."[102] This sociospatial differentiation was "enough to impose severe social barriers inside the Kuwaiti community."[103] Though housing was an integral part of state welfare schemes that helped construct a consensual image of a Kuwaiti "us," the tangible tensions that disparate state schemes created within the

Kuwaiti national population in the decades after the advent of oil reveal that the feeling of common identity and community that Kuwaitis increasingly embraced was "a counterfeit of experience."[104] Al-Moosa concluded that such extreme social segregation was "dangerous and ominous for the future well-being of the state. Steps must be taken immediately to arrest further deterioration of the value system and social cohesion between groups."[105] However, no tangible steps were taken to alleviate this looming crisis.

The Crisis of the Urban

In 1968, Greek architect Georges Candilis claimed that due to the "brutal dislocations in the condition of life" that the exploitation of oil brought, Kuwait City "lost the qualities of the traditional urbanism of the past" without finding a new urban organization to replace it. The city, he claimed, had lost its "primordial quality of urbanity," once characterized by the integration of habitation, commerce, administration, and worship, and of houses, markets, streets, and squares. The rapid pace of growth after oil "provoked a dissociation of the different functions of [the] city and the break off of relations among the basic elements." As a result, the city was in a state of "urban confusion and disequilibrium."[106] Although Candilis was focusing on the city itself, his critique of Kuwait's oil urbanization echo Lefebvre's criticisms of the effects of modern urban planning on both the city and urban society. Lefebvre argues that suburbanization and functional planning create a dissociated morphology in which the city (a material and architectural fact) becomes paradoxically separated from the urban (the more abstract realm of social relations produced and reproduced in and by the city).[107] On the one hand, the inhabitants and users of the city lose the right to create their surroundings according to their own needs and desires. That right is now in the hands of the state and private enterprises that seize control of the city and appropriate urban functions and jurisdictions. On the other hand, everyday life becomes fragmented as work, private life, leisure, politics, and commerce are separated into discrete spheres. Spontaneity and simultaneity, lived moments, and chance encounters—all key elements of urbanity—are no longer possible because of this socio-spatial segregation.[108] Lefebvre argues that this situation creates a perpetual state of "boredom" in suburbs and new towns across the world, one that is "pregnant with desires, frustrated frenzies, unrealized possibilities."[109] At the same time, whereas urban life once allowed for the encounter and confrontation of difference—between people, ideologies, and ways of living—the maceration of urban life in and by the suburbs brings homogeneity and a growing inability to experience, coexist with, and accept diversity and difference.[110] As Caldeira puts it, residential enclaves thus breed "incivility, intolerance, and discrimination."[111] Lefebvre likens the dissociating process between the city and the urban to a living animal that gradually secretes a seashell, a protective covering that ensures its own survival. The shell represents the premodern city (or "oeuvre") built and modified over time by its inhabitants and users in an effort to stay alive. If you separate the living creature from the seashell it created for itself by the laws of nature—if you separate urban society from the city through suburbanization and modern planning—what remains is "something soft, slimy and shapeless."[112] Alienated from the city, urban society is at risk of becoming ever more frustrated, intolerant, and divisive; that is, its urbanity is at risk of being crushed.

Kuwait witnessed this crisis of the urban after the advent of oil. With modern planning, public participation in urban growth and development all but disappeared. Functional zoning introduced in the 1952 master plan separated previously integrated activities and spheres of behavior. Suburbanization segregated members of society by nationality and social group, and encouraged the valorization of private life over public belonging. With the transformation of the city center into a landscape of wealth and power, the diversity, simultaneity, and spontaneity of urban life deteriorated. By as early as the 1960s, Kuwaiti society became more and more dissociated from the city, and in the process began to lose many of the characteristics that had defined it as an urban society for more than two hundred years. Visitors and travelers to Kuwait in the nineteenth and early twentieth centuries regularly described it as a friendly and accepting place, "attracting Arab and Persian merchants from all quarters by the equity of its rule."[113] But within the first decades of oil urbanization, the hybrid, open, and tolerant cosmopolitanism of the old port society—the worldly outlook and lifestyle that had defined its urbanity and ensured its survival for more than two hundred years before oil—gave way to a highly insular, divided, and increasingly intolerant society. Kuwaiti society, in other words, had lost its own primordial quality of urbanity, just as Candilis believed the city itself had done.

8

The Right to the City

Urban Life and Democracy

The changes to Kuwaiti society discussed in Chapter 7 cannot be attributed solely to wealth and access to state welfare, though of course these factors played a significant role. They are also linked to the dissociation between the city and the urban—or put another way, to society's loss of a right to the city—after the advent of oil. The loss of a right to the city includes not only the spatial loss of access to centrality, but also the loss of people's ability to participate in the production of a city according to their own needs and desires. It also entails the elimination of a right to participate in a vibrant urban life, characterized by "meetings, the confrontation of differences, reciprocal knowledge and acknowledgement (including ideological and political confrontation), ways of living, 'patterns' which coexist in the city."[1] *Urban* life and *urban* society cannot exist without the material base of the city. Without this base, "the urban remains in a state of dispersed and alienated actuality, as kernel and virtuality," and is at risk of disappearing.[2] To return to Lefebvre's aforementioned metaphor, the shell must be put back onto the slimy creature if it is not to be crushed altogether; only with a restored right to the city can the urban be salvaged.

The right to the city is not a simple visiting right, like a daily trip in from the suburbs in the morning and back out at the end of the workday. Lefebvre calls this a pseudo-right.[3] Nor is a right to the city achieved by a restoration of the old city through heritage as the Sharq al-Seif project attempted to do: the city-as-pastiche (or as Saba George Shiber put it in

Kuwait's context, the city dressed "in borrowed theatrical effects") rather than the city-as-oeuvre.[4] The right to the city may be construed as a right to centrality, or a (spatial) right of access to the city and to its various spaces and resources, but not when this centrality is the end in itself—that is, not when centrality is about demarcating turf for a particular group, such as the attempt at renationalizing Kuwait City with the Sawaber Complex in the 1980s. The housing authorities had claimed that Sawaber would allow its residents "to enjoy all the amenities of modern city life while contributing to the larger community of Kuwait Town," suggesting a fluid relationship between residents and city. However, it was simultaneously pitched as "an urban oasis where Kuwaiti families can feel at home," invoking a sense of detachment from its surroundings.[5] Its isolation within the cityscape could hardly provide its residents with "a vibrant, open public forum, full of lived moments and 'enchanting' encounters" in the city.[6] Rather than a reclamation of territory, the restoration of a right to the city is about a "transformed and renewed *right to urban life*," characterized by the simultaneity of everyday functions and activities (private, social, and political), and the spontaneity of chance encounters with the unexpected.[7] This right also includes confrontation and coexistence with diverse people, ideas, and ways of living, and as Eugene McCann puts it, "the right to be free from externally imposed, pre-established classifications of identity" (such as those inflicted by differential housing policies).[8] Finally, the right to the city must include the right to participate in the production of the qualified spaces that make these experiences possible without the ultimate goal of profit.

Claiming a right to the city in this manner is not an end in itself. It is a way station on the road to a bigger goal.[9] For Kuwait, that bigger goal is perhaps best expressed in what Ash Amin and Nigel Thrift call the "democratic city." For them, democracy is not a "romantic vision of agreement and consensus" but rather lies in the "democratization of the terms of engagement." Their form of democracy focuses less on performative display than on civic empowerment and everyday participation.[10] Article 6 of Kuwait's 1962 Constitution claims that the system of government in Kuwait is democratic; article 7 asserts that "justice, liberty, and equality are the pillars of society; cooperation and mutual help are the firmest bonds between citizens."[11] Kuwait's democratic system of government is vividly displayed in its frequent and lively elections, notoriously contentious parliamentary sessions, vocal and active media, and so on. Kuwaitis take pride in the level of political freedom and participation they enjoy, particularly

in comparison with their Gulf neighbors. In fact, democracy is often characterized as inherent to Kuwait's own preindependence past rather than
imported from the West through imperialism. The tradition that the Al
Sabah were chosen by the people in 1752, the pre-oil custom of Kuwait's
rulers to govern through consultation (*shura*) with the town notables, and
the historic institution of the *diwaniyya* are all invoked in present-day discourse as evidence that, from its establishment, Kuwait was ruled more
democratically than autocratically.[12]

However, such performative displays of democracy aside, when it
comes to civic empowerment and participation, Kuwait is a deeply undemocratic place, regardless of its Constitution's claims. Approximately
70 percent of the population (non-nationals) are explicitly excluded from
civic and political participation of any form. For the remaining 30 percent
of the population (nationals), the idea of citizenship is defined primarily by access to state welfare benefits rather than by social democracy or
equality (or by "cooperation and mutual help").[13] Over the decades since
the advent of oil, different groups within the national population (*hadar*,
Sunnis, Muslims, men) have received preferential rights and benefits from
the state over others (*badu*, Shiʻa, non-Muslims, women, respectively). In
1982, Abdulrasool al-Moosa recognized that such differential treatment
was "dangerous and ominous for the future well-being of the state."[14]

From Consensus to Antagonism

The deep social tensions that these discrepancies engendered have
been suppressed by a myth of conflict-free national solidarity. Restrictive
citizenship and immigration policies coupled with Kuwaitis' exclusive access to welfare benefits helped create a vision of a coherent, cohesive, and
consensual national community, but one that detoured around actual social contact and experience.[15] When forging such a myth of community
based on an idea of sameness rather than on what people actually do with
each other, "people draw a picture of who they are that binds them all
together as one being, with a definite set of desires, dislikes, and goals.
The image of the community is purified of all that might convey a feeling of difference, let alone conflict, in who 'we' are."[16] This is a repressive
process, not only because outsiders (such as non-Kuwaitis) are excluded,
but because differences within the community and between its members
must be suppressed in order to maintain a convincing image of sameness.[17]

People are forced to give up their multiple or conflicting loyalties, or else be labeled deviant. Signs of dissonance or conflict between members of the community, and alternative lifestyles or desires, are seen as threatening to the community identity as a whole. Yet without the need, ability, or space to deal concretely and directly with others, existing tensions or conflicts—including those paradoxically created by the very same political project meant to suppress all conflict, such as housing welfare—remain unresolved and potentially become more volatile. Inasmuch as the purification of identity, like orderly planning, is meant to protect the community from unknown, outside, or future threats (in Kuwait's case, maintaining "a system of cultural survival" in the face of an ever growing "sea of outsiders"),[18] the potential for internal violence in this repressive atmosphere grows. The creation of consensual communities often results, in other words, in antagonistic relations and practices.

The long-term effects of this process can be seen in Kuwait's present-day social crises described at the start of this book. Sennett argues that the extent to which people feel urged to keep articulating "who they are" is an index of the level of their own insecurity in that identity, and of people's fear of their inability to survive in social experience with others.[19] More than fifty years since the 1959 nationality law was enacted, such social anxieties are acutely visible in Kuwait today. The recent eruptions of long-standing tensions between *hadar* and *badu* reflect both this insecurity and the dangerous deterioration of social cohesion that al-Moosa predicted in 1982. "Instant repair of the social fabric is not possible," he believed, "but, without an early move to solve the more irritating and divisive problems that were revealed by the [social-residential] field survey, it must be expected that segregation will intensify and dissatisfactions grow."[20] Less than three decades later his predictions proved correct. In 2009, *hadar* politician Mohammed al-Juwaihel stated on his private television station that "true" Kuwaiti citizens consist solely of those families who resided inside the *sur* and in such villages as Jahra and Fahaheel before oil, making the Bedouin sector of society (which today makes up around 65 percent of the national population) not "real" Kuwaitis.[21] Many other urban Kuwaitis certainly harbor similar sentiments about the *badu*, arguably fueled by the fact that *hadar* and *badu* were kept spatially apart for decades.[22] However, rarely had anyone so explicitly and so publicly questioned the consensual idea of "us" that supposedly bound together *hadar* and *badu*, Sunni and Shi'i, rich and poor, and all other Kuwaitis into a single community. By denying the consensus of "who we are," al-Juwaihel was condemned for "fomenting communal and sectarian tensions," and for "[undermining] national unity" and "insulting human dignity."[23] In violation of Kuwait's constitutional protection of the press and free expression, al-Juwaihel's satellite television station on which he made the statements (al-Sur) was shut down, and he was arrested. The Minister of Information urged the Parliament to pass a proposal to monitor online blogs, because comments posted on social media in the wake of the al-Juwaihel incident were seen to be "threatening national cohesion."[24] The government began taking legal action against individuals "who incite divisions in the society," invoking a new "zero-tolerance policy towards anyone seeking to undermine social peace and national cohesion."[25] The extreme measures taken to protect "national unity" reveal that social cohesion and unity are very delicate and tenuous in Kuwait today, with the potential to be unhinged by a single comment made by a single man.

As the myth of Kuwaiti communal solidarity and consensus erodes, the desire to strengthen the image of a common "us" in contradistinction to a common "them" increases. Nearly seventy years since the advent of oil and the influx of foreign immigrants, expatriates are still treated as a threat to Kuwaiti cultural survival. The alienation of foreigners was exacerbated by the Iraqi invasion of Kuwait in 1990. During the occupation, tensions arose between Kuwaitis and Palestinians (the largest and most integrated expatriate community living in Kuwait by 1990)[26] due to myths of Palestinian collaboration with Iraqi soldiers. Though the majority of the community remained loyal to Kuwait throughout the occupation, the unfounded allegations arose due to sightings of Palestinians working with Iraqis at checkpoints and police stations. Shafeeq Ghabra has shown that these were mostly members of the Arab Liberation Front (ALF, an Iraq-sponsored Palestinian organization) sent to Kuwait by the Iraqi administration to intimidate the local Palestinian community.[27] The fact that Kuwaitis were entirely unaware that the Palestinians they saw at checkpoints were from the ALF and not members of the local community—most of whom had been living in Kuwait for decades—reveals the long-term socio-spatial estrangement of citizens and noncitizens. Only in mixed residential areas such as Jabriya did Kuwaitis and Palestinians have the opportunity to work together the way residents of most neighborhoods under occupation did (recalling the way the pre-oil firjan once functioned): sharing food and supplies, hiding out in neighbors' basements, and so on. However, most neighborhoods by 1990 were highly segregated, and Kuwaitis living in their exclusive suburbs were largely unaware of the intimidation and suffering that Palestinians who lived in areas like Hawalli and Nuqra were experiencing at the hands of the occupying forces; nor were they aware that Hawalli residents held a pro-Kuwait demonstration three days after the invasion. The socio-spatial segregation between the two communities, created by decades of state housing and planning policies, thus fueled the misunderstandings that ultimately led to the permanent expulsion of more than three hundred thousand Palestinians from Kuwait in 1991.[28] After the liberation, Kuwaitis became even more insular and distant from the country's majority non-national population, adopting what political scientist Abdul-Reda Assiri calls a "siege mentality": a feeling of being threatened from within and from without.[29]

Today, this siege mentality manifests in policies and laws that target expatriates and reduce the already minimal contact between Kuwaitis and non-Kuwaitis. In 2013, for instance, the Ministry of Health announced plans to segregate public hospital timings, whereby Kuwaitis would be treated in the morning and expatriates in the afternoon. Although the justification was that this would reduce waiting times, in fact it would do so for Kuwaitis and significantly increase waiting times for non-Kuwaitis, who outnumber nationals two to one. This law contradicts the statement made on the website of the forthcoming state-run Al Ahmad Al Jaber Al Sabah Hospital that hospitals are "humanitarian" buildings before they are "patriotic" buildings.[30] In early 2013, the Ministry of Social Affairs and Labor announced plans to cut the number of expatriates residing in Kuwait by one million over the next ten years, vowing to "take decisions and measures" to reduce the population by one hundred thousand annually.[31] That summer, tens of thousands of expatriates were deported for traffic violations, including minor ones for which Kuwaitis only pay fines.[32]

The Agonistic City

Scholar Khaled al-Jenfawi claims that the high levels of intolerance that Kuwaitis today exhibit for people of different religious and cultural backgrounds "goes against our tradition and actually undermines our historical achievements." He believes that the "typical characteristics" of Kuwaiti society include "tolerance, open-mindedness, acceptance of positive social and cultural developments, kind and nice behavior toward those who are different." He laments that many of his fellow citizens view the diverse foreigners residing in the country as threatening rather than as enriching to their own culture and daily experiences.[33] But the cosmopolitanism and cultural hybridization that al-Jenfawi longs for requires meaningful and repeated contact: the slow experience of working, being, living, and playing with others.[34] It is this kind of contact that was removed in post-1950 Kuwait by functional zoning, suburbanization, socio-spatial segregation, and the privatization of public space and public life. These urban policies replaced the tolerance, open-mindedness, and mutuality of the past with the more antagonistic and undemocratic social relations that prevail in Kuwait today. Amin and Thrift argue that in order to encourage democracy as an everyday practice, people need to regularly experience negotiating diversity and difference rather than associate only with people like themselves or people they like.[35] They suggest that the city—with its inherent diversity and multiplicity—is the primary place to experiment with encountering and confronting such difference through everyday participation in agonistic (between friendly enemies, as opposed to both consensual and antagonistic) practices. Agonistic interactions would allow differences and conflicts between individuals or groups to exist in the open, and would force people to deal with their dissimilarities in a shared environment.

The agonistic city that Amin and Thrift suggest mirrors the kind of urban life that Lefebvre describes, characterized by the constant confrontation of different people, ideologies, and ways of living that coexist in the city (unlike the suburbs, which typify sameness). It is also the kind of complex and dissonant everyday life that existed in Kuwait before oil, under the conditions of scarcity. Learning to once again interact and negotiate with different people and ways of life through agonistic rather than antagonistic practices may help quell the present-day violence (the "structural violence" imposed on expatriates, particularly laborers;[36] the physical clashes between *hadar* and *badu;* the mall stabbings described in the Introduction; and so on). Kuwait today does not contain enough spaces or opportunities to mediate hostility, "to force people to look beyond their images of threatening outsiders to the actual outsiders themselves." Sennett suggests that unplanned city spaces that encourage functional diversity and social exploration could be the solution.[37] Yet throughout the past two decades Kuwait has persisted down the path of orderly planning established in the early oil decades, to the continuous detriment of the city, urban life, and everyday social relations and interactions.

Postinvasion Kuwait City

The Iraqi invasion and occupation of 1990–91 marked the first real halt to the process of oil urbanization that began in the 1950s. Kuwait faced a development lull for most of the postoccupation decade, as matters of security, national defense, and postwar reconstruction became top priority. Although after the liberation the government "recognized that future development required a thorough re-appraisal of planning policies and procedures," very little actually changed in the postinvasion period. In 1992, the Municipality commissioned a local firm, Salem al-Marzouk and Sabah Abi-Hanna, to produce a third master plan "to provide a new and comprehensive framework for the future development of the State of Kuwait." The plan was completed in 1997, and though it sought to amend some of the problems of previous plans (for instance, its provisions were properly incorporated into established zoning plans and regulations), as a master plan it was "based on a comprehensive set of objectives derived from the long term development strategy of the State." In determining Kuwait's present and future needs "on a sector by sector basis," the plan represented a continuation of what had come before.[38]

During this same period, however, the state's development strategy of the preinvasion period came under public scrutiny and critique. In 1996, in response to the Municipality's "broken record" message that it would be improving the city once again, the al-Qabas daily newspaper published a multiauthored ten-part article series under the title "The Capital: The Sea's Forgotten Neighbor." The series was based on one overarching question posed in the introduction: "When will the capital return to being a capital?" The articles described Kuwait City as a "ghost town": a city of empty sandlots and cemeteries that was deserted at the end of the workday. They highlighted various reasons for the decline of the city center and suggested possible ways of remedying this "catastrophic reality."[39] In general, most articles in the series pointed to bureaucratic and systemic failures that had prevailed over the four decades of planning before the invasion, and they urged the private sector to play more of a role, alongside the state, in revitalizing the city. They also stressed the need to construct more residential spaces for Kuwaiti citizens inside the city center, as a way of bringing life back to the core after working hours. Much emphasis was placed on land vacancy which, as Suhair al-Mosully also noted in her 1992 city planning master's thesis entitled "Revitalizing Kuwait's Empty City Center," had "adverse economic and aesthetic implications."[40] Neither she nor the *al-Qabas* articles discussed the long-term *social* effects of poor city planning on Kuwait; rather, they focused on the state of the city itself.

The image of emptiness and vacancy—and of the city as a place that had been demolished and neglected—was not entirely inaccurate from a material perspective. Socially, however, the city was not actually vacant. People imagined the city as "isolated" and "empty" because it was almost entirely unused by Kuwaitis, who had grown accustomed to life in the suburbs and in privatized leisure spaces outside the city. But for many people "formally left outside the bounds of citizenship and the possibility of being Kuwaiti," as Reem Alissa puts it, the city center in the 1990s was anything but empty.[41] Not only did thousands of foreign workers live in the city, but on Fridays and Sundays the city buzzed with Arab and Asian workers enjoying their day off (the day of the week depending on their religion). The proximity of the Catholic, Coptic, and Protestant churches, along with a major bus terminal, transformed the open spaces around Fahad al-Salem Street as well as the Sheraton roundabout (a large landscaped traffic circle) into major gathering spaces for service sector employees, manual laborers, and domestic workers (see Figure 13, p. 110). According to Alissa, the roundabout park on Fridays and Sundays was "arguably the only space and time in which Kuwait city experiences the simulteneaity [*sic*] of multiple publics that run the gamut of the social spectrum"—except, of course, suburban Kuwaitis.[42]

The last three articles in the *al-Qabas* series relayed the views of average Kuwaiti citizens on the state of the city. Almost unanimously, the people interviewed expressed contempt for the fact that the city was primarily inhabited by south and southeast Asian workers, who were putting their own "stamp" on the city and changing its traditional character.[43] Those who agreed that the city should include residential areas believed that the foreigners should be moved out and Kuwaitis moved back in. Many suggested that the descendants of the original residents of Sharq, Jibla, and Mirqab should be given priority, and in fact should return to their old *firjan*.[44] Yet most simultaneously agreed that Kuwaitis would refuse to live in apartments (which the limited space inside the city would require) because they had grown accustomed to the "freedom" of their spacious houses in the suburbs and would not use public transportation because they were used to buying groceries in bulk and needed their own cars.[45] In other words, for these citizens a return to the city was a (largely nostalgic) reclamation of turf, not a desire to return to urban living. Only one man suggested that returning to the city might restore eroded Kuwaiti customs of mutual cooperation and support.[46] For the most part, restoring the city was a hypernationalistic goal reflecting the postinvasion siege mentality.

The City Since 2003

Despite all of this discussion on restoring the city, the 1997 plan was, like its predecessors, never implemented. After the U.S.-led invasion of Iraq in 2003, however, a surge in oil prices coupled with the influx of foreign residents and visitors due to the high military, contractor, and business presence across the border triggered a rapid and chaotic building boom that rivaled the construction pace of the 1970s. Kuwait—once the Gulf leader in construction, development, and investment—had been superseded during the hiatus of the late 1980s and 1990s by its regional neighbors, namely Dubai. Catching up required an acceleration in construction projects, and most of those ubiquitous empty spaces that were the cause of such concern in the 1990s rapidly filled up. Once again, this change occurred without a comprehensive plan. In 2009, Kuwait's Parliament approved the country's new 2035 development plan, along with a five-year roadmap to guide development until 2014. Urbanization projects constituted one of its main aspects, with a focus on so-called "mega projects" such as the new city in Subbiya on the northern tip of Kuwait Bay (first proposed by Shankland Cox in 1977), a causeway linking Subbiya with Kuwait City, the Mubarak al-Kabir deepwater port, and the Kuwait Metro plan. Such projects were introduced as grand gestures to counter the perceived lack of development in Kuwait in comparison with its southern Gulf neighbors. However, to date nothing has been implemented. The inability to move forward on the 2035 plan is blamed partially on obstruction tactics by political opposition forces who (rightly) argue that such projects will privilege the elite and foster more government corruption. The successive dissolutions and annulments of Parliament (five since the current ruler came to power in 2005, resulting in six premature elections in eight years) are another factor, because constant changes to the assembly and cabinet have prevented MPs and Ministers from getting things done.

Nonetheless, construction is ongoing. In 2004, in response to private-sector pressure, the Municipality exponentially increased floor-area ratios in commercial areas, allowing buildings to rise up to more than seventy stories depending on plot size. The only attempt to improve the overall infrastructure and capacity of the city to accommodate this added strain was the extension of the First Ring Road to become a full ring. A multilane highway cutting through the city center made many parts of the city less walkable or accessible than ever before. For instance, it killed off access to the Sheraton roundabout, which today is no longer used as a public space by churchgoers and workers on their day off. Also, glass and steel high-rises housing luxury offices rapidly replaced the characteristic low-rise modernist architecture of the 1950s and 1960s. Most notable was the demolition of parts of the old Salmiya shopping district, one of the only early oil developments that combined residential and commercial uses and was fully pedestrianized. Beginning in 2007, the long-term residents of the area were moved out, and half of old Salmiya now consists of indoor shopping complexes, mirroring the newer parts of Salmiya's shopping district developed in the late 1990s. Indeed, shopping malls and luxury hotels and resorts have constituted a major component of the new construction craze. The Avenues is currently Kuwait's largest mall, with a gross area of more than seven hundred thousand square meters by 2015 (and the construction of new sections ongoing). The mall seems to encourage contact with difference, straddling as it does the former no-man's-land between the *hadar* suburbs inside the Fifth Ring Road and the outlying areas beyond the Sixth. Its various shops cater to wealthy Kuwaitis in some parts, and to lower- to middle-income expatriates in others. However, the mall's sheer size (one kilometer in length, and growing) keeps these areas and the people who shop within them highly segregated from one another. Kuwait's current urbanization has thus enhanced the privatization and segregation of everyday urban experience.

The seafront in particular has once again undergone significant economic and cultural privatization. Only the first two phases of Ghazi Sultan's waterfront development project were completed according to plan before the invasion, after which the emphasis on public recreation and culture was abandoned. From the late 1990s onward, malls, private beach clubs, restaurant clusters, and hotels were constructed all along the coast from the city center to Messila. However, the landscaping of the seafront corniche between these developments and the water created a quasi-public area that today attracts a variety of users. Though this space is used mostly for promenading, running, and cycling, many expatriate and lower-income Kuwaiti families also use the few sandy beaches and stretches of grass along the Arabian Gulf Road for picnicking on evenings and weekends, contravening the consumerist focus of the waterfront projects. But in 2012 a law was passed banning barbeques in public places such as beaches and parks. Kuwaitis receive fines for violating the rules, but expatriates are at risk of deportation.[47] The justification for the law was the high volume of trash and burned grass left behind. Such rules contribute to purifying the *sahel* of unplanned activities that do not conform to the area's predetermined uses. They also remove the few options available to the country's majority nonelite population for free, public leisure. As one commentator on a popular local blog that ran the story put it, "There are countless expats here who live in tiny apartments and live on a very limited income. One of their only sources of entertainment is the weekly bbq [barbecue] where they can relax and their kids can run around."[48]

Sahat al-Safat has also been subjected to further privatization. In early 2011, a growing political opposition movement against the prime minister (accused of financial and political corruption) planned to hold demonstrations in al-Safat—the first in decades—after a large political gathering in the suburban *diwaniyya* of an opposition leader was broken up by government special forces in December 2010. The movement climaxed just as thousands of demonstrators were convening on Tahrir Square in Cairo and Pearl Roundabout in Manama. Though some early protests occurred there, the government swiftly cordoned off al-Safat, and the Municipality eventually announced plans for the site's three-million-dinar, two-year renovation. The protestors were forced to restrict their activities to a stretch of grass facing the Parliament building, between the entrance to Qaryat Youm al-Bahhar and its parking lot. This space, which the opposition named Irada (Determination) Square, was first used by women's rights campaigners who gathered there in May 2005, in the days before the parliamentary vote on the women's suffrage bill (which passed). Despite the closure of al-Safat and continuous government efforts to restrict mass rallies and demonstrations in the city, Irada restored a historic function to the city center, public politics, after decades of being relegated to the privatized suburbs.[49] It is perhaps not surprising that when the more historically charged Sahat al-Safat reopened in 2014—with new flooring, lights, and a fountain—it was permanently gated, and locked when not in official use. In February 2015, a host of government ministers kicked off the country's National Day celebrations with a flag-raising ceremony in the middle of the square.

Restoring a Right to the City

Although it clearly echoes historic patterns, the political contestation over al-Safat simultaneously reflects the emergence of something new in Kuwait. The protestors' refusal to hold their demonstrations in the suburbs, despite government attempts to restrict access to the city, reflects their growing demand for a "right to the use of the centre, a privileged space, instead of being dispersed and stuck into ghettos."[50] This is particularly relevant as the vast majority of the 2011 protestors were Bedouin who had been relegated to the outlying areas for decades. But a demand for a right to the center also applies, Lefebvre says, to the privileged. He argues that once cities reach extreme levels of destruction of their former urban realities, a cry and demand for a restored right to the city rises from those who have been most alienated not only from the space of the city but also from the right to participate in urban society and urban life.[51] "The right to the city," David Harvey says, "has to be construed not as a right to that which already exists, but as a right to rebuild and re-create the city . . . in a completely different image."[52] It is not a nostalgic return to the traditional city, as the *al-Qabas* testimonials intimated. Nor can it be restored by the same forces (the government and urban "experts") or the same process (planning from above) that eliminated it.[53] Rather, a right to the city can be achieved only through new approaches, largely through the efforts of new social forces. There are signs that young people in Kuwait today—not only marginalized Bedouin but also middle-class suburbanites—"want actively to bring something new into being . . . something 'richer' in social life than what the suburb offers."[54] Whether consciously or not, various groups are taking advantage of the failed implementation of comprehensive, top-down plans to slowly start re-inhabiting the city, "testing new ground" as they go.[55] Under the guise of stagnation at the top, an urban alternative is slowly emerging from below that has the potential to forge a new spatial and social reality for Kuwait. By reinvigorating the urban experience in diverse ways, these groups have the collective potential to counter the de-urbanizing tendencies of decades of top-down planning. Numerous trends can be identified (from neighborhood improvement groups to food markets), but two in particular reveal a clear demand for a right to the city.

The most telling evidence of this budding desire for a new kind of urban experience is the growing popularity of the city center as a place for small local businesses. The establishment of homegrown cafés, restaurants, shops, and art galleries has been a popular trend among young Kuwaitis since around 2005, challenging Fakhri Shehab's assessment in the 1960s that Kuwaiti entrepreneurs no longer deviated from established patterns. These new business owners came of age in the postinvasion period of hyperconsumerism, when Western franchises dominated the retail and food markets. The growth of local entrepreneurship in these same industries over the past decade is slowly offering residents new alternatives in their consumption patterns. More significantly, it is revitalizing the city center in ways that no previous state-led attempt has been able to achieve. Most of these small businesses are unable to afford the high rents and overhead of shopping malls—and besides, many do not want to be in privatized complexes. The city center has offered a viable, affordable, and experiential alternative on which young entrepreneurs have capitalized.

The trend started in the historic Merchants' Market directly facing the new Seif Palace constructed on the space of the old port, in a 1960s structure built as part of Shiber's central business district. This block originally contained a strip of shops selling fishing and sailing equipment catering to the port and *dhow* harbors. After the port was removed and only one small harbor remained, these shops began to decline. Because the structure was old, *khuluw* ("key money," or an inducement paid to a landlord by someone wishing to rent a commercial space) and rent were much cheaper there than in malls and other new buildings in the city. The shops therefore attracted the attention of young enterprising Kuwaitis looking for locations for their new small businesses. Within a couple of years, most of the shops were sold and the strip became Kuwait City's first example of unplanned urban gentrification. The area's success drew attention to the city center as a potential haven for small business owners, particularly given the presence of old buildings with cheaper rents. Over the ensuing years many local enterprises opened in old and, eventually, new buildings in the city. In the case of the latter, most have tended to go for street-front locations with easy sidewalk access rather than indoor complexes, suggesting a desire to be more connected to the space of the city itself regardless of the actual building location.

The latest area in the city to be revitalized by small local businesses is just south of the historic *suq* area (now known as Mubarakiyya); it is therefore popularly called SoMu. Several alleys between a cluster of buildings within the *suq* meet in a courtyard, and over the past two years this area has been renovated and revamped under the auspices of one young entrepreneur, Ahmed al-Ghanim. According to al-Ghanim, the area was "very much ignored" when he and his business partner, Bader al-Hejailan, began looking for a location for their boutique, Thouq (which sells locally designed clothes and craft items).[56] Many of the shops around the courtyard were abandoned, and the pavement and other public facilities (such as a central gazebo with benches) were completely run-down. Al-Ghanim paid the *khuluw* to buy out most of the shops in the area, which he has since rented out to small local restaurants, cafés, and shops. The Municipality was slow to respond to his requests to have the common areas cleaned up and renovated, so upon his request a local real estate developer, Tamdeen, donated its services by laying down new bricks, fixing the streetlamps, benches, and gazebo, and landscaping the open areas.

The potential effects of such citizen-led urban projects are mixed. Although they are spontaneous rather than planned developments, these gentrified districts are highly commercialized and remain the purview of the social elite. Most of the cafés and restaurants are unaffordable to the majority of expatriates who live and work in the city. Their main clientele are Kuwaitis who work in the central business district during the day and eat there on their lunch breaks. They also attract suburbanites who increasingly come into the city to socialize in the evenings and on weekends. Furthermore, al-Ghanim's ultimate goal is to "[change] the retail scene in the market" by bringing in high-end luxury brands to Mubarakiyya.[57] This would significantly transform the *suq*'s distinctly nonelite, and noncommercialized, character. The *suq* went through its first renovations in the 1980s, and many parts—including the vegetable and fish markets—were refurbished in the late 1990s, bringing shoppers and visitors back to the city's historic commercial district. In 2012, Mubarak's dilapidated *kishk* in the Money Changer's Square was renovated as a historic site, and in 2013 the Mubarakiyya School building was turned into an education museum. Aside from these heritage projects, the renovated *suq* area was not overly gentrified or made into a pastiche tourist district (as in the case of Doha's Suq Waqif or Dubai's Bastakiya Quarter). Over the past few years, the *suq*'s main arteries, particularly the large Suq al-Gharabally street, have been pedestrianized. The *suq*'s *sha'by* ("popular," meaning "informal" and "inexpensive" in local discourse) restaurants and public plazas, frequented mostly by expatriates and lower-income Kuwaitis, are bustling on weekends. Older Kuwaiti men of mixed backgrounds sit in the old-style coffee shops adjacent to lower-income nationals and non-nationals who frequent the surrounding shops (where not a single foreign franchise exists).

SoMu, by contrast, aims at a much more elite customer base, particularly middle- and upper-class Kuwaitis, to lure them away from malls and back to the city. SoMu undoubtedly represents an interesting experiential contrast to the surrounding markets and thus brings the kind of diversity that all cities need. However, according to a local magazine feature on Mubarakiyya for which SoMu's founders were interviewed, the purpose of the project was "to take back the area."[58] As one of the new business owners told me in conversation, before SoMu, so few Kuwaitis came to the area, when it was derelict and full of shops catering to migrant workers (such as Indian takeaways); now that the area is cleaned up it is full of Kuwaitis. The renovated area has a strong nationalist feel to it. A large wall mural and a public art sculpture both declare in bold colors, "I love Kuwait" (in Arabic). Far from embracing the diversity of its surroundings, SoMu puts a distinct Kuwaiti stamp on the area. On the one hand, this attitude may reflect a sense of pride that young Kuwaitis are finally breaking through the "inertia" (to recall Shehab's term) that has plagued society since the advent of oil; on the other hand, it also echoes the sentiments of the 1996 al-Qabas testimonials. Though many of the new entrepreneurs in the city claim they prefer being in a hip urban environment rather than in a shopping mall, the return to the city that some (not all) of these business owners and many of their customers seek appears to be more of an attempt to reclaim turf—to renationalize the city center—than to restore the diversity that city life actually entails. In this context, reclaiming a right to the city is about reclaiming spatial centrality—not (it seems) from the sources of wealth and power who stripped the public of that right after the advent of oil urbanization, but rather from non-nationals who spend much more time inhabiting the city than middle- and upper-class Kuwaitis.

These gentrified areas might therefore be catering to the latest generation of the same capitalist elite whose offices had once been located in Shiber's CBD. Nonetheless, they still hold the potential to restore a lost sense of urbanity. True to their main goal, they are indeed attracting Kuwaitis to the city for reasons other than work for the first time in decades, and in so doing they are bringing them into more regular contact with different kinds of people and ways of living. Though these forays into the city depict what was previously described here as a simple "visiting right," and though SoMu feels rigidly segregated from the surrounding markets, the young Kuwaiti suburbanites who go there now spend their evenings and weekends in much closer proximity to spaces occupied by expatriate laborers and lower-income Kuwaitis. Members of these separate social worlds increasingly penetrate the spaces occupied by the other as they move through the city, particularly because parking is hard to come by and people have to walk through the city to reach their destinations. The gap between Kuwaitis and non-Kuwaitis, the rich and the poor, the bureaucrat and the laborer shrinks tremendously inside the city—much more than in the suburbs or The Avenues—making these businesses important hubs for the growth of a new urbanity.

Arguably the strongest current claim to public rights to the city in Kuwait is located in Salmiya rather than in the city center itself. The Secret Garden—a public community gardening project kick-started in 2014 by Maryam al-Nusif and a small group of friends and family[59]—demonstrates the transformative potential of residents to reshape the urban landscape to satisfy collective social needs. In explaining her own motivations for initiating the project, al-Nusif described everyday life in Kuwait as "superficial" and "not honest." Before the garden, she craved "a real experience"— walking to public places and interacting with strangers—and longed for "spontaneous and serendipitous" occurrences.[60] So, in September 2014, she, her mother, and a small group of friends began cleaning up a run-down garden (known officially as Baghdad Park) close to her family home in Salmiya. The garden has no boundaries and is easily accessible from the street on three sides and bordered by buildings on the fourth. When they started the project, one of the adjacent residential buildings provided them with water and electricity until the government responded to their request to repair the damaged water and electricity mains. The team dug a compost pit in one sector of the park, built picnic tables and benches in another, and planted another large sector with a variety of vegetables, herbs, plants, and flowers. The group meets every Saturday to work on the garden, joined regularly by neighbors and members of the general public (who follow their activities on social media).

Because Salmiya is a commercial district, the majority of its residents are non-Kuwaitis living in rented accommodations, though some parts of the district contain Kuwaiti-owned villas. The garden sits between these two residential worlds. When the volunteers began working, their presence was challenged by the only group in the neighborhood that actually used the space. Because the garden was derelict and surrounded by overgrown trees, local non-Kuwaiti teenagers hung out there at night to smoke and play cards. When the gardening group started fixing up the space, they constantly found things vandalized: new lights and other fixtures broken, trash strewn around, and so on. Al-Nusif was aware that the teenagers resented having a spotlight suddenly put on a space that gave them some freedom. Because the purpose of the garden was to bring the community together, she initially did not want to alienate them by getting angry. But while the younger children of the neighborhood got involved in the gardening project, the older ones continued their challenging behavior, until they were explicitly told to stop their vandalism. They eventually stopped pushing back, and though they still use the garden at night, they have started cleaning up after themselves. The Secret Garden group, meanwhile, leave out tables with rugs on them for the teenagers to play cards on, and they accept that they often have to sweep up mounds of cigarette butts in the morning. This contestation, and eventual conciliation, over rights to the space between its old and new users reflects a completely different approach to urban coexistence than SoMu. The objective for the group who started fixing up the garden (a mix of Kuwaitis and non-Kuwaitis) was not to appropriate the space and completely change its spatial and social identity. They had no desire to push out the garden's existing users, or its existing uses. Nor did they intend to seal themselves off from the surrounding social world by making the space more exclusive. By sharing the space and keeping it public, the makers of the Secret Garden thus created a new kind of public realm in Kuwait.

The experience of the Secret Garden emphasizes the value of demographic and functional diversity in city districts. Although located outside the city center, Salmiya is more urban than suburban in that it contains a mix of uses (residential, commercial, educational, bureaucratic) in a densely built-up area. This diversity has been key to the garden's growth as a community space. Though al-Nusif lives nearby, many members of the core group who started the project do not. Nonetheless, various residents of the neighborhood, from young children to elderly women, soon got involved. A south Asian laborer who lives in the area showed an interest in the group's activities and now turns the compost pits a few times a week for a wage that the volunteers pay him. Brian Collett, an American landscape architect working with the Kuwait Institute for Scientific Research, stumbled on the project while walking home one day and now volunteers regularly, bringing his own technical expertise. Local businesses have been getting involved in the garden as much as the local residents. The restaurants along Baghdad Street, where the garden is located, donate their food scraps for the compost pit. The building next door is occupied by a physical rehabilitation clinic and one day the physiotherapists came down and offered to teach the gardeners stretches and exercises to relax after a hard day's work in the sun. As a community space, the garden is serving as a bridge between Salmiya's Kuwaiti and non-Kuwaiti residents. Al-Nusif lives in the neighborhood with her mother and grandmother, but it was only through the garden that her grandmother became friends with a group of Arab women who live in an older building adjacent to the space and regularly sit outside drinking coffee and talking. The involvement of al-Nusif and other Kuwaiti residents in the project facilitated the government's repair of the badly damaged water and electricity infrastructure in the park, to the benefit of all.

As a result of this initiative, the garden has been completely revived and is used at different times of day by different people: neighborhood children who now play in a cleaner and safer environment, teenagers who smoke and play cards at night, employees of the area who eat on the benches during their lunch break, and so on. The Secret Garden group regularly hosts a small-scale food market (called Shakshooka) in the garden, using the fees the vendors pay to sustain their activities. The vendors are of mixed nationalities and backgrounds, as are the members of the public who attend, many of whom wander in from the neighborhood. The group has met some resistance to this practice by state authorities because they do not have a license to conduct commercial activity on public (state-owned) land. As this book was going to press, a final resolution was yet to be reached. Nonetheless, unlike the dead and gated Sahat al-Safat in the city center, the Secret Garden is a public space in its truest form: "a vibrant, open public forum, full of lived moments and 'enchanting' encounters."[61] In April 2015, for example, a theater troupe held a free public workshop in the garden, which involved building a stage and engaging in two hours of acting exercises. Many random passers-by joined in, and at the end of the night one young neighbor got his guitar and he and his friends led everyone in the garden in a sing-along, a moment that al-Nusif described as "magical."[62] The garden project is perhaps Kuwait's only current example of unplanned, cooperative urbanism; no single group controls the garden, and all have equal rights of access to the space. It is the kind of unplanned and unzoned place that, by encouraging functional diversity and social exploration, could be the antidote to the orderly city planning that eroded Kuwait's primordial quality of urbanity.[63]

Beyond Planning to Public Citizenship

After the advent of oil Kuwait's existing urban conditions were entirely remade for modern, orderly city planning. The pre-oil landscape was
demolished, a central bureaucratic administration in charge of urban planning and development was created, the land acquisition scheme allowed
for the complete reordering of land into real estate, and so on. However,
only the 1952 master plan actually materialized, though the part of the
plan dealing with the city center was never followed due to the complica-
tions discussed in Chapter 4. None of the subsequent plans were ever implemented, "despite following accredited standards." This does not mean
that the plans failed. Rather, it reveals that planning as a method of city
formation itself failed in post-oil Kuwait. "This brings into question the
credibility of such a framework for urban production, as well as a need
to understand the reason for its ineffective implementation."[64] The latter
issue—why Kuwait's modernist project failed to achieve its ultimate goal
of making Kuwait the best planned and most socially progressive state in
the Middle East—has been one of the purposes of this book. The former
issue—the possibility of identifying new frameworks for urban production—is the *raison d'être* of Madeenah: a newly formed group of young
architects and intellectuals who call themselves "a Kuwaiti spatial practice."

In challenging the existing framework for urban production—that
is, state-led urban planning and development that satisfies political goals
at the expense of the everyday needs and practices of multiple users—
Madeenah begins by challenging the framework by which knowledge on
the city is produced. The accumulation of knowledge is always the first
step in the urban development process. Indeed, Kuwait's multiple master plans contain hundreds of pages of statistics and analyses on demo-
graphics, employment figures, residential patterns, land values, and so on.
However, according to Madeenah, such information is not always reliable
given the constant fluctuations in population (which is precisely why Kuwait's master plans consistently underestimated growth figures) and other
unexpected economic and political factors. Yet not only is this research
used to produce a master plan *for* the city, but it also serves as a seemingly
comprehensive body of knowledge *about* the city. Madeenah differenti-
ates between this kind of explicit knowledge, which "can be codified and
therefore easily communicated," and tacit knowledge, which is "embodied
and generated through experiences in a particular context, and is there-

fore harder to communicate and more difficult to transfer."[65] Madeenah is more concerned with the latter; it seeks to create a new kind of knowledge base on the city by aggregating and making accessible the tacit knowledge of diverse city users. It does this by curating public walking tours of different segments of the city that are led by Madeenah's team or by various guides—architects, artists, residents—who share their own understandings and experiences of the spaces traversed and explored on the tour. Some tours, such as one led by Maryam al-Nusif and her grandmother, explore certain neighborhoods. Others take participants into parts of the city that many people do not see from their cars (such as the spaces behind the facades of Fahad al-Salem Street). The tours encourage people to think about the city in new ways (many include time for discussion) and to feel more connected to their physical surroundings.

Through these tours, the city becomes more than a product of urban and architectural plans, more than buildings and empty lots, more than a successful or failed example of urban planning. It becomes a lived space, "haunted" not by all its cemeteries (as the 1996 al-Qabas articles claimed it was) but by the multiple memories, experiences, relationships, and identifications that permeate the spaces of the city.[66] By generating new ways of thinking about and experiencing the urban landscape, and by utilizing crowdsourcing methods in collecting data on the city, Madeenah believes that "difficult urban situations . . . may be resolved using elastic strategies."[67] Armed with this new tacit knowledge of the city (which Madeenah hopes to share through an online archive), local civic and social institutions can start to challenge state development plans by proposing alternative urban solutions that satisfy communal demands. Madeenah's walking tours of the city, beyond just sharing interesting knowledge, thus offer a new framework for urban production, one that mediates between government institutions and other centralized entities on the one hand and the individual city user on the other. In a city where top-down planning has failed as a method of urban production, Madeenah's bottom-up alternative offers Kuwait a new way forward. It replaces the totalizing God's-eye, panoptic view of the urban planner—the view from the top of a skyscraper that, as de Certeau puts it, "makes the complexity of the city readable"— with the everyday practices of walkers whose "bodies follow the thicks and thins of an urban 'text' they write without being able to read it."[68]

Madeenah also therefore challenges modernist planning's privileging of the "prince" and "genius," a paradigm that persists today throughout the

Gulf, where foreign consultants are still considered the best "experts" to guide urban growth and design. In Madeenah's alternative, not only local architects but also regular city users become the "experts" of the city whose everyday experiences and desires create the framework for urban growth and change. This is the essence of what James Scott describes as *mētis*: practical skills and local know-how gained from daily practices and experiences. He contrasts such local knowledge with the abstract and scientific knowledge deployed by the state and its technical experts, whose dismissal of local knowledge as insignificant explains why so many high modernist schemes failed so miserably at creating a successful social order.[69] Scott argues that *mētis* "is most valuable in settings that are mutable, indeterminant (some facts are unknown), and particular," such as cities.[70] Yet from 1950 onward, Kuwait's urbanization was based entirely on foreign technical expertise that made no "adjustments for local conditions."[71] Such *mētis* was precisely what Shiber had noticed was missing from Kuwait's first decade of urban planning, during which "Kuwait and Kuwaiti society—different from all known planning precedents—were overlooked and their problems lightly disposed of by pencil and T-square."[72] Madeenah brings *mētis* back into Kuwait's urbanization.

Conclusion

Initiatives like the Secret Garden and Madeenah make salient Amin and Thrift's belief that "the city is more than a place of common access and encounter. . . . It is a place of becoming, and the fulfilment of social potential, of democratic experimentation through the efforts of citizens themselves."[73] By recognizing the rights of all users, Kuwaitis and non-Kuwaitis alike, to make equal claims on the spaces of the city, the garden and the walking tours broaden the scope of meanings and practices of belonging in Kuwait. The city thus emerges as a strategic site for the reformulation of citizenship that moves beyond legal distinctions between nationals and non-nationals (defined by access to benefits or the right to participate in politics) to include other kinds of civil, socioeconomic, and cultural rights that all people, including non-nationals, possess.[74] To think of citizenship in such substantive terms—which the city permits more so than the suburbs—is not yet common in Kuwait, but it is arguably essential for a country in which formal citizens constitute the minority.

Furthermore, as James Holston describes, cities offer "new possibilities for democracy that transform people *as* citizens."[75] Beyond simply voting, active citizenship requires the "active participation in the business of rule" (as opposed to a passive sense of entitlement to benefits).[76] It was this kind of active citizenship—which as Shehab first noted in 1964 was gradually dismantled in Kuwait after the advent of oil—that was missing the night Jaber Youssef was murdered in The Avenues in 2012. Amin and Thrift argue that public citizenship "has to be practiced and valued if we want to enhance the 'ability of social actors to intervene in public life.'"[77] To experience citizenship as an everyday practice, people need to constantly experience negotiating diversity and difference—among people, ideas, activities, experiences, and lifestyles.[78] For this way of life to work in a city-state like Kuwait, nationals need to be more open to interacting and coexisting with the country's majority non-national population, and to reviving the hybrid cosmopolitanism that defined Kuwaiti urban society for more than two hundred years before oil. The city itself—not the suburbs—is the key site for such hybridization and the strengthening of mutuality, as was the case with Kuwait Town before oil.[79] It is a prime moment in Kuwait to consider the role of the city in rethinking citizenship in these ways, as the concept of national citizenship itself, formally established in 1959, is witnessing a period of uncertainty today. The coherence and cohesion of the national community is eroding, the role and position of the ruling family vis-à-vis the citizenry is coming under greater scrutiny, the exclusionary nature of formal citizenship is constantly challenged (by women, *bidun*, and other marginalized groups), the relevance of cultural identities that national citizenship subordinates (such as tribal affiliation or religious sect) is growing, the primary practice of formal citizenship (namely electoral politics) is deteriorating, and the reality that noncitizens constitute the majority of the country's population shows no sign of changing. Restoring a right to the city—that is, heeding the cries and demands of the various groups that are reinhabiting the city in myriad ways—opens up new opportunities for social becoming and belonging that defy the precepts of orderly planning and transcend the barriers of formal citizenship, and (in so doing) can potentially salvage Kuwait's primordial quality of urbanity.

Reference Matter

Notes

Preface

1. Benjamin, *Selected Writings*, 262.
2. Quoted in Harvey, *Social Justice*, 23.
3. Harvey, *Social Justice*, 24.
4. De Certeau, *Everyday Life*, 108.
5. Benjamin, *Selected Writings*, 262.

Introduction

The epigraph to this chapter is from Case, "Boom Time," 802.

1. Though original reports on the crime stated that at least one of the men (the killer) was *bidun* ("without," meaning without citizenship, or a stateless person), later reports did not specify whether he was a Kuwaiti national or *bidun* but stated only that he was apprehended in a residential camp where *bidun* live.
2. Al-Sultan, "Naher Tabib."
3. *Arab Times*, "Lebanese Doctor."
4. Kuwait News Agency, "Interior Ministry."
5. Nayef, "Mall Stabbing."
6. Gallo, *No One Helped*, 78–79.
7. Gallo, *No One Helped*, 77, 79.
8. Gallo, *No One Helped*, 163–64.
9. *Arab Times*, "Lebanese Doctor."
10. Frieden and Sagalyn, *Downtown, Inc.*, 234.
11. Jacobs, *Death and Life*, 30
12. Jacobs, *Death and Life*, 56.
13. Jacobs, *Death and Life*, 56.
14. Le Renard, *Young Women*, 48–49.
15. Minoprio, Spencely, and Macfarlane, "Town Planning," 272.

16. Holston, *Modernist City*, 31.

17. Holston, *Modernist City*, 3–4.

18. Scott, *Seeing Like a State*, 88, 5.

19. Scott, *Seeing Like a State*, 61.

20. Al-Barges, *Twenty-Five*, 32.

21. Gardiner, *Kuwait*, 21.

22. Holston, *Modernist City*.

23. Quoted in Scott, *Seeing Like a State*, 117.

24. Lienhardt, *Disorientations*, 29.

25. Freeth, *New Look*, 13.

26. Freeth, *New Look*, 17.

27. Gardiner, *Kuwait*, 14.

28. Holston, *Modernist City*, 25, 105, 138–39.

29. Hussain, "al-Nahda al-Murtaqibah," 79.

30. Shehab, "Kuwait."

31. Freeth, *New Look*, 190–91.

32. Freeth, *Kuwait*, 83.

33. Banks, "Notes on a Visit," 50.

34. Holston, *Modernist City*, 23.

35. Shiber, *Kuwait Urbanization*, 75.

36. In English-language sources before oil, the term *Kuwait Town* was commonly used. This term is used throughout the book for the space that was the precursor to *Kuwait City*, a phrase that became more common after 1950.

37. Shiber, *Kuwait Urbanization*, 76.

38. Shiber, *Kuwait Urbanization*, 118.

39. Shiber, *Kuwait Urbanization*, 117.

40. Shehab, "Kuwait."

41. Ffrench and Hill, *Kuwait*, 21.

42. Crystal, *Oil and Politics*, 81.

43. Shehab, "Kuwait."

44. Dowding, *Koweit*, 19.

45. Cornn, "Ma Salaama."

46. Kemball, "Memoranda," 109.

47. Al-Moosa, "Kuwait," 56.

48. Izzak and Sharaa, "Enraged Tribesmen."

49. Calderwood, "Fifty Years."

50. *National*, "Police Clash."

51. *Arab Times*, "Awazem Storm."

52. Toumi, "Minister Seeks."

53. Shehab, "Kuwait."

54. Case, "Boom Time," 786.

55. See Kanna, *Superlative City*.

56. Starling, "World's Most Obese."

57. Toumi, "Kuwait Has World's Highest."

58. Shehab, "Kuwait."

59. Menoret, *Joyriding*, 120.

60. Shehab, "Kuwait."

61. Menoret, *Joyriding*, 105.

62. Lefebvre, *Writings*, 75.

63. Lefebvre, *Writings*, 77–78.

64. Jacobs, *Death and Life*, 140.

65. Sennett, *Uses of Disorder*, 57.

66. Jacobs, *Death and Life*, 143–44.

67. Candilis, "Kuwait," 1–3.

68. Candilis, "Kuwait," 1, 2.

69. Amin and Thrift, *Cities*, 4.

70. Freeth, *New Look*, 93.

71. Amin and Thrift, *Cities*, 32.

72. Sennett, *Uses of Disorder*, 50–51.

73. Holston, *Modernist City*, 57.

74. Holston, *Modernist City*, 9.

75. Sennett, *Uses of Disorder*, 8, 7.

76. Holston, *Modernist City*, 9–10.

77. Al-Barges, *Twenty-Five*, 9.

78. Al-Barges, *Twenty-Five*, 26.

79. Fuccaro, *Histories*, 11.

80. Holston, *Modernist City*, 10.

81. "Resident's Annual Report" (1955), *Persian Gulf Administration Reports*, vol. 11.

82. Gardiner, *Kuwait*, 14.

83. Scott, *Seeing Like a State*, 6, 4.

84. Lefebvre, *Production of Space*, 65–66; Stanek, *Henri Lefebvre*, 159.

85. Lefebvre, *Production of Space*, 65.

86. Lefebvre, *Production of Space*, 66.

87. Fuccaro, *Histories*, 5.

88. Elsheshtawy, "Great Divide," 2.

89. Kanna and Keshavarzian, "UAE's Space Race," 35.

90. Prakash, *Spaces of the Modern City*, 2.

91. Fuccaro, *Histories*, 5.

92. See, for instance, Potter, *Persian Gulf in Modern Times*.

93. Dennis, *Cities*, 1.

Chapter 1

1. Fuccaro, *Histories*, 47.

2. *Bani* means "sons of." A tribal name (such as ʿUtub) can be used with or without *Bani*.

3. Fattah, *Politics of Regional Trade*, 23–25.

4. Pelly, "Remarks," 72–73.

5. Kemball, "Memoranda," 109.

6. Kemball, "Memoranda," 109.

7. Jones, "Extracts," 52; Brucks, "Memoir," 575; Pelly, "Remarks," 73.

8. Lorimer, *Gazetteer*, 1053–58.

9. Al-Rushaid, *Tarikh*, 109; al-Qina'i, *Safhat*, 8.

10. Tétreault, *Stories of Democracy*, 34.

11. Povah, *Gazetteer*, 44.

12. IO/R/15/5/236: Political Agent, Kuwait (hereafter PA) to Political Resident (hereafter PR), Bushehr, November 26, 1912.

13. "Administration Report for the Kuwait Political Agency" (1916), *Persian Gulf Administration Reports*, vol. 7.

14. Kuwait Municipality, *Planning and Urban Development*, 14–15.

15. "Agreement of 23 January 1899 with Ruler of Kuwait," reprinted in Abu-Hakima, *Modern History*, 184–86.

16. Fuccaro, *Histories*, 50.

17. IO/R/15/5/65: Koweit Draft Agreement: Between His Britannic Majesty's Government and the Ottoman Empire, March 26, 1913.

18. IO/R/15/5/65: PA, Kuwait to PR, Bushehr, August 12, 1912.

19. IO/R/15/5/65: Anglo-Turkish Agreement Between His Britannic Majesty's Government and the Ottoman Empire, July 29, 1913.

20. For more details on the conflicts of 1920–21 and their impact on Kuwait's boundaries, see F. al-Nakib, "The Lost 'Two-Thirds.'"

21. IO/R/15/5/99: PA, Kuwait to High Commissioner, Baghdad, May 20, 1920.

22. Stocqueler, *Fifteen Months*, 18.

23. Mylrea, "Kuwait Before Oil," 86–87.

24. IO/R/15/5/100: Copy of the Najd-Kuwait Agreement of 'Uqair Conference, December 22, 1922.

25. Freeth, *Kuwait*, 67; Lorimer, *Gazetteer*, 896.

26. Lorimer, *Gazetteer*, 462.

27. Lorimer, *Gazetteer*, 461.

28. Lindt, "Politics," 625.

29. Lorimer, *Gazetteer*, 1074.

30. Buckingham, *Travels*, 463.

31. IO/G/29/25/233: Samuel Manesty and Harford Jones Brydges, "Report on the British Trade with Persia and Arabia," August 15, 1790.

32. Buckingham, *Travels*, 462–63.

33. Kemball, "Memoranda," 109–10.

34. Villiers, *Sons of Sindbad*, 353; Lorimer, *Gazetteer*, 1006.

35. Kuwait Engineers Office, *Sharq al-Seif*, 1.

36. Kemball, "Memoranda,"109; Kemball, "Statistical," 296; Pelly, "Remarks," 73; Pelly, "Recent Tour," 119.

37. "Administration Report for the Kuwait Political Agency" (1912), *Persian Gulf Administration Reports*, vol. 7.

38. "Administration Report for the Kuwait Political Agency" (1905–1906), *Persian Gulf Administration Reports*, vol. 6.

39. IO/R/15/5/236: PA, Kuwait to PR, Bushehr, November 26, 1912.

40. Marcus, *Middle East*, 65.

41. Lorimer, *Gazetteer*, 1055.

42. Lorimer, *Gazetteer*, 1054.

43. Kemball, "Memoranda," 109; Kemball, "Statistical," 296; Pelly, "Remarks," 74.

44. Rush, *Al-Sabah*, 2.

45. Hennell, "Secret Report," April 24, 1841, quoted in Rush, *Al-Sabah*, 2.

46. Hennell, "Secret Report," quoted in Rush, *Al-Sabah*, 2; Pelly, "Recent Tour," 119.

47. Brydges, *Account of the Transactions*, 12.

48. Pelly, *Report*, 10.

49. Al-Hijji, *Kuwait*, 54.

50. Pelly, *Report*, 10.

51. Dowding, *Koweit*, 18.

52. Al-Qina'i, *Safhat*, 14.

53. Lorimer, *Gazetteer*, 1076–77.

54. "Administration Report for the Kuwait Political Agency" (1907–1908), *Persian Gulf Administration Reports*, vol. 6.

55. "Administration Report for the Kuwait Political Agency" (1910), *Persian Gulf Administration Reports*, vol. 6.

56. IO/R/15/5/179: Notes on Kuwait, prepared by PA, Kuwait, April 27, 1944.

57. Raunkiaer, *Through Wahhabiland*, 33–34.

58. Copies of this and other *waqf* documents are archived online at http://kuwait-history .net.

59. Al-Salamah, *Lamhat min Tarikh*, 37.

60. Al-Shaybani and al-Mutairi, *al-Watha'iq al-Asliyya*, 82.

61. Al-Hijji, *Kuwait*, 108.

62. Abu Abdullah, interviewed by Farah al-Nakib, April 14, 2009, Kuwait.

63. IO/R/15/5/18: Extracts from Kuwait News for week ending August 31, 1910.

64. Al-Hijji, *Kuwait*, 103.

65. IO/R/15/5/236: PA, Kuwait to PR, Bushehr, November 13, 1912.

66. "Administration Report for the Kuwait Political Agency" (1924), *Persian Gulf Administration Reports*, vol. 8.

67. Abdullah, *al-Haraka al-Adabiyya*, 345.

68. Al-Qina'i, *Safhat*, 40–44.

69. Lienhardt, *Disorientations*, 61.

70. Al-Rushaid, *Tarikh*, 122.

71. Mylrea, "Council of War," 5.

72. Al-Hijji, *Kuwait*, 108.

73. Mylrea, "Kuwait Before Oil," 93–96.

74. IO/R/15/5/179: H.R.P. Dickson (PA Kuwait), "Note on Kuwait Principality at the End of the Year (1933)."

75. Abdullah, *al-Haraka al-Adabiyya*, 350.

76. The Kuwait Oil Company was a partnership between the Anglo-Persian Oil Company (later British Petroleum) and the Eastern and General Syndicate (later Gulf Oil, then Chevron).

77. IO/R/15/5/205: PA, Kuwait to PR, Bushehr, March 19, 1938.

78. Al-Hijji, *Kuwait*, 63.

79. Crystal, *Oil and Politics*, 47.

80. "Administration Report for the Kuwait Political Agency" (1930), *Persian Gulf Administration Reports*, vol. 8.

81. "Administration Report for the Kuwait Political Agency" (1932), *Persian Gulf Administration Reports*, vol. 9.

82. IO/R/15/1/505: PA, Kuwait to Secretary to PA, Bushehr, May 25, 1931.

83. "Kuwait Intelligence Summary: April 16–30, 1936," *Political Diaries*, vol. 12.

84. IO/R/15/5/205: Administration of Kuwait, July 8, 1938.

85. IO/R/15/5/205: Administration of Kuwait, July 8, 1938.

86. IO/R/15/5/205: Translation of article on Kuwait in *al-Kifah*, February 12, 1938; PA, Kuwait to PR, Bushehr, March 4, 1938.

87. "Kuwait Intelligence Summary: January 16–31, 1938," *Political Diaries*, vol. 13.

88. Crystal, *Oil and Politics*, 55.

89. IO/R/15/5/205: PA, Kuwait to PR, Bushehr, June 29, 1938.

90. IO/R/15/5/205: "A New Movement in Kuwait," *al-Zaman*, April 3, 1938 (article in Iraqi newspaper translated in PA, Kuwait to PR, Bushehr, June 24, 1938).

91. Crystal, *Oil and Politics*, 45.

92. IO/R/15/5/206: PA, Kuwait to PR, Bushehr, December 22, 1938.

93. IO/R/15/5/205: PR, Bushehr to Secretary of State for India, December 21, 1938.

94. IO/R/15/5/206: PA, Kuwait to PR, Bushehr, January 6, 1939.

95. "Administration Report for the Kuwait Political Agency" (1941), *Persian Gulf Administration Reports*, vol. 10.

96. IO/R/15/1/545: PA, Kuwait to PR, Bushehr, April 18, 1940.

97. IO/R/15/1/545: PR, Bushehr to PA, Kuwait, April 25, 1940.

98. Al-Jassim, *Baladiyyat al-Kuwayt*, 190.

99. Copies of this and other property deeds are archived online at http://kuwait-history.net.

100. Mylrea, "Kuwait Before Oil," 43–44.

101. Mylrea, "Kuwait Before Oil," 46–52.

102. "Administration Report for the Kuwait Political Agency" (1913), *Persian Gulf Administration Reports*, vol. 7.

103. "Administration Report for the Kuwait Political Agency" (1908), *Persian Gulf Administration Reports*, vol. 6.

104. Lorimer, *Gazetteer*, 1049.

105. "Administration Report for the Kuwait Political Agency" (1906–1907), *Persian Gulf Administration Reports*, vol. 6.

106. Mylrea, "Kuwait Before Oil," 59–60.

107. "Administration Report for the Kuwait Political Agency" (1906–1907), *Persian Gulf Administration Reports*, vol. 6.

108. "Administration Report for the Kuwait Political Agency" (1906–1907), *Persian Gulf Administration Reports*, vol. 6.

109. "Kuwait News: July 16–31, 1930," *Political Diaries*, vol. 9; "Kuwait News: June 16–30, 1930," *Political Diaries*, vol. 9.

110. Mylrea, "Kuwait Before Oil," 45.

111. "Kuwait Intelligence Summary: May 16–31, 1938," *Political Diaries*, vol. 13.

112. "Kuwait Intelligence Summary: July 16–31, 1945," *Political Diaries*, vol. 16.

113. IO/R/15/5/205: Captain G. S. de Gaury (PA, Kuwait), "Improvements introduced by Kuwait Council."

114. "Kuwait News: April 16–30, 1930," *Political Diaries*, vol. 9.

115. Al-Jassim, *Baladiyyat al-Kuwayt*, 190.

116. IO/R/15/5/378: "Military Report and Route Book," 60.

117. Al-Jassim, *Baladiyyat al-Kuwayt*, 191.

118. Al-Jassim, *Baladiyyat al-Kuwayt*, 201.

119. Al-Jassim, *Baladiyyat al-Kuwayt*, 196.

120. Al-Jassim, *Baladiyyat al-Kuwayt*, 193.

121. IO/R/5/15/194: PR, Bushehr to Secretary to Government of India, Simla, April 22, 1941.

122. IO/R/15/5/194: PA, Kuwait to PR, Bushehr, March 28, 1941.

123. "Kuwait Intelligence Summary: March 16–31, 1941," *Political Diaries*, vol. 14.

124. Al-Khatib, *al-Kuwayt*, 33.

125. Al-Khatib, *al-Kuwayt*, 34.

126. "Kuwait Intelligence Summary: June 16–30, 1948," *Political Diaries*, vol. 18.

127. IO/R/15/5/205: Improvements introduced by the Kuwait Council.

128. "Administration Report for the Kuwait Political Agency" (1948), *Persian Gulf Administration Reports*, vol. 11; "Administration Report for the Kuwait Political Agency" (1949), *Persian Gulf Administration Reports*, vol. 11.

129. Broeze, "Kuwait Before Oil," 179–80.

Chapter 2

1. For further discussion of Kuwait as a port town, see F. al-Nakib, "Inside a Gulf Port."

2. Stocqueler, *Fifteen Months*, 19; Raunkiaer, *Through Wahhabiland*, 39.

3. Villiers, *Sons of Sindbad*, 308.

4. Lorimer, *Gazetteer*, 1049.

5. Mylrea, "Kuwait Before Oil," 33.

6. Al-Shamlan, *Pearling*, 57.

7. Jamal, *Aswaq*, 28.

8. Villiers, *Sons of Sindbad*, 308.

9. "Administration Report for the Kuwait Political Agency" (1912), *Persian Gulf Administration Reports*, vol. 7.

10. Raunkiaer, *Through Wahhabiland*, 43.

11. Villiers, *Sons of Sindbad*, 308.

12. Villiers, *Sons of Sindbad*, 308.

13. Jamal, *Aswaq*, 7.

14. Lorimer, *Gazetteer*, 1047; "Administration Report for the Kuwait Political Agency" (1905–1906), *Persian Gulf Administration Reports*, vol. 6.

15. "Administration Report for the Persian Gulf Political Residency" (1907–1908), *Persian Gulf Administration Reports*, vol. 6.

16. "Administration Report for the Kuwait Political Agency" (1912), *Persian Gulf Administration Reports*, vol. 7.

17. Freeth, *Kuwait*, 50.

18. Jamal, *Aswaq*, 8.

19. "Administration Report for the Kuwait Political Agency" (1916), *Persian Gulf Administration Reports*, vol. 7.

20. Dowding, *Koweit*, 18.

21. Zwemer, "Koweit Occupied," 7.

22. IO/R/15/5/236: PA, Kuwait to PR, Bushehr, November 26, 1912.

23. Al-Farhan, *Ma'jam al-Mawadi'*, 153–54.

24. Pelly, "Remarks," 73–74; Pelly, "Recent Tour," 120; Zwemer, *Arabia*, 128.

25. Povah, *Gazetteer*, 44.

26. Mylrea, "Kuwait Before Oil," 39.

27. Tonkiss, *Space*, 67.

28. Tonkiss, *Space*, 67.

29. Lewcock and Freeth, *Traditional Architecture*, 7.

30. Dickson, *Forty Years*, 171; "Administration Report for the Kuwait Political Agency" (1944), *Persian Gulf Administration Reports*, vol. 10.

31. "Kuwait Intelligence Summary: April 1–15, 1934," *Political Diaries*, vol. 11.

32. Dickson, *Forty Years*, 139; Calverley, "Trial by Ordeal," 3–4.

33. Mylrea, "Medievalism," 13–14.

34. "Kuwait Intelligence Summary: June 16–30, 1938," *Political Diaries*, vol. 13; "Kuwait Intelligence Summary: July 16–31, 1938," *Political Diaries*, vol. 13.

35. "Kuwait Intelligence Summary: June 16–30, 1938," *Political Diaries*, vol. 13.

36. IO/R/15/5/206: PA, Kuwait to PR, Bushehr, March 12, 1939.

37. "Kuwait Intelligence Summary: September 16–30, 1943," *Political Diaries*, vol. 15.

38. Mylrea, "Lord Hardinge," 11.

39. Al-Hijji, *Kuwait*, 31.

40. Al-Hijji, *Kuwait*, 31.

41. Tonkiss, *Space*, 68.

42. Mr. M. Dashti, interviewed by Farah al-Nakib, April 7, 2009, Kuwait.

43. Tonkiss, *Space*, 68.

44. De Jong, "Gasoline Tin," 10.

45. For images of such scenes, see Facey and Grant, *First Photographers*.

46. Villiers, *Sons of Sindbad*, 321.

47. Jamal, *Aswaq*, 7.

48. Freeth, *Kuwait*, 105.

49. Villiers, *Sons of Sindbad*, 310.

50. Tonkiss, *Space*, 67.

51. Raunkiaer, *Through Wahhabiland*, 53–54.

52. Bennett, "New Beginning," 14.

53. Stark, *Baghdad Sketches*, 192; Freeth, *New Look*, 107.

54. Villiers, *Sons of Sindbad*, 321.

55. Lewcock and Freeth, *Traditional Architecture*, 7.

56. Al-Shamlan, *Pearling*, 92.

57. Mr. M. al-Saddah, interviewed by Farah al-Nakib, April 5, 2009, Kuwait; Abu Abdullah interview (see Chapter 1, note 62).

58. IO/R/15/5/205: PA, Kuwait to PR, Bushehr, June 25, 1938.

59. Villiers, *Sons of Sindbad*, 321.

60. Kuwait Mission, "Annual Report . . . 1930–1931," 12.

61. Habermas, *Structural Transformation*, 27.

62. Tonkiss, *Space*, 68.

63. Crystal, *Oil and Politics*, 59; "Kuwait Intelligence Summary: June 16–30, 1940," *Political Diaries*, vol. 14.

64. Mylrea, "Encouraging Evangelistic Work," 16.

65. Bennett, "New Beginning," 13.

66. Scudder, "May Your Feat," 15.

67. Al-Shamlan, *Pearling*, 93.

68. Al-Khatib, *al-Kuwayt*, 31.

69. Lorimer, *Gazetteer*, 1049–50.

70. Harrison, "Our Medical Work," 10.

71. Khalfallah, "Tatawwur al-Maskan."

72. "Architecture in Gulf Countries," 7–9.

73. Al-Khars and al-Aqruqah, *al-Bayt al-Kuwayty*, 56–58.

74. Al-Farhan, *Tarikh al-Mawaqi'*, 476.

75. Dehrab, "Childhood," 178.

76. Freeth, *Kuwait*, 105.

77. Al-Farhan, *Tarikh al-Mawaqi'*, 476, 479.

78. Facey and Grant, *First Photographers*, 109.

79. Mr. K. al-Saleh, interviewed by Farah al-Nakib, January 29, 2008, Kuwait; Abu Abdullah interview (see Chapter 1, note 62).

80. Abu Abdullah interview (see Chapter 1, note 62).

81. Lorimer, *Gazetteer*, 1058–59.

82. Mylrea, "Kuwait Before Oil," 125–27.

83. Abu Abdullah interview (see Chapter 1, note 62).

84. "Kuwait Intelligence Summary: March 16–31, 1939," *Political Diaries*, vol. 13.

85. IO/R/15/5/188: PA, Kuwait to PR, Bushehr, April 10, 1930.

86. IO/R/15/5/94: PA, Kuwait to Civil Commissioner, Baghdad, August 28, 1920.

87. Al-Khatib, *al-Kuwayt*, 30.

88. Mr. A. al-Ghunaim, interviewed by Farah al-Nakib, April 2, 2009, Kuwait.

89. Al-Khatib, *al-Kuwayt*, 30.

90. Mylrea, "Working for Kuwait's Women," 11.

91. Niebuhr, *Travels*, 248; Pelly, "Remarks," 75; Pelly, "Recent Tour," 121; Zwemer, *Arabia*, 128; Dowding, *Koweit*, 18.

92. Dehrab, "Childhood," 179.

93. Calverley, "Education in Kuwait," 12.

94. IO/R/15/5/19: PA, Kuwait to High Commissioner, Baghdad, February 15, 1917; IO/R/15/5/19: "Extracts from Kuwait News for week ending February 19, 1917."

95. "Administration Report for the Kuwait Political Agency" (1930), *Persian Gulf Administration Reports*, vol. 8.

96. Kuwait Mission, "Annual Report . . . 1932," 14.

97. "Kuwait Intelligence Summary: March 16–31, 1939," *Political Diaries*, vol. 13.

98. Al-Jassim, *Baladiyyat al-Kuwayt*, 197.

99. Abu-Lughod, "Islamic City," 167–69.

100. Al-Mughni, *Women*, 45.

101. Lewcock and Freeth, *Traditional Architecture*, 2.

102. Lewcock and Freeth, *Traditional Architecture*, 15, 2.

103. Abu-Lughod, "Islamic City," 167.

104. Mylrea, "Working for Kuwait's Women," 12.

105. See, for instance, al-Mughni, *Women*, chapter 2.

106. Al-Mughni, *Women*, 45.

107. Mylrea, "Picnics in Koweit," 6.

108. Mylrea, "Working for Kuwait's Women," 12.

109. Stark, *Baghdad Sketches*, 222.

110. Mylrea, "Kuwait Before Oil," 108.

111. Mylrea, "Kuwait Before Oil," 125.

112. Calverley, *My Arabian Days*, 75.

113. Longva, *Walls Built on Sand*, 192.

114. Kuwait Engineer's Office, *Sharq al-Seif*, 1.

115. Abu-Lughod, "Islamic City," 162.

116. Lewcock and Freeth, *Traditional Architecture*, 3.

117. Khalfallah, "Tatawwur al-Maskan."

118. Khattab, "Socio-Spatial Analysis," 141.

119. Dickson, *Forty Years*, 81–82.

120. Al-Saddah interview (see note 57).

121. Abu-Lughod, "Islamic City," 168.

122. Abu-Lughod, "Islamic City," 168.

123. Abu-Lughod. "Islamic City," 176.

124. Umm Talal, interviewed by Farah al-Nakib, April 4, 2009, Kuwait.

125. Stark, *Baghdad Sketches*, 224–25.

126. Al-Ghunaim interview (see note 88).

127. The man in this anecdote wished to remain anonymous.

128. "Administration Report for the Kuwait Political Agency" (1923), *Persian Gulf Administration Reports*, vol. 8.

Chapter 3

1. Sennett, *Uses of Disorder*, 57.
2. Sennett, *Uses of Disorder*, 57.
3. Sennett, *Uses of Disorder*, 40.
4. Murphey, "Evolution of the Port City," 225.
5. Villiers, *Sons of Sindbad*, 321.
6. Pelly, *Report*, 11.
7. Pelly, *Report*, 10.
8. Dowding, *Koweit*, 19.
9. Pelly, *Report*, 11.
10. IO/R/15/5/105: "The Ikhwan Attack on Jahrah," from PA, Kuwait to Deputy PR, Bushire, October 19, 1920; al-Rushaid, *Tarikh*, 344.
11. Rihani, *Muluk al-'Arab*, 590–91.
12. Mylrea, "Kuwait Before Oil," 62.
13. Kuwait Mission, "Annual Report" (1927), 4–5.
14. Calverley, *My Arabian Days*, 71–72.
15. Mylrea, "Kuwait Before Oil," 140–45.
16. Lorimer, *Gazetteer*, 1051–52.
17. Olayan and al-Bi'aini, *Yahud al-Kuwayt*, 10; Scudder, *Arabian Mission's Story*, 220, 240 (note 75).
18. IO/R/15/5/102: PA, Kuwait to Civil Commissioner, Baghdad, September 19, 1918.
19. Calverley, "Education in Kuwait," 14.
20. Lorimer, *Gazetteer*, 1051–52.
21. Crystal, *Oil and Politics*, 40.
22. Fuccaro, "Pearl Towns," 107.
23. Young, "Postcolonial Remains," 34.
24. Young, "Postcolonial Remains," 35.
25. Kemball, "Memoranda," 109.
26. Al-Khatib, *al-Kuwayt*, 27.
27. Lorimer, *Gazetteer*, 1053.
28. Mr. M. H. Dashti, interviewed by Farah al-Nakib, April 6, 2009, Kuwait.
29. Al-Hijji, *Kuwait*, 27.
30. Lorimer, *Gazetteer*, 1051–52.
31. IO/R/15/5/236: PA, Kuwait to PR, Bushehr, November 26, 1912; Mylrea, "Kuwait Before Oil," 111.
32. "Administration Report for the Kuwait Political Agency" (1918), *Persian Gulf Administration Reports*, vol. 7.
33. IO/R/15/5/102: PA, Kuwait to Civil Commissioner, Baghdad, September 19, 1918.
34. IO/R/15/5/205: PR at Kuwait to India Office, London, October 19, 1938.
35. Simon, "Imposition of Nationalism," 100.

36. IO/R/15/5/205: PR at Kuwait to India Office, London, October 19, 1938.

37. Pelly, "Remarks," 76.

38. Dickson, *Forty Years*, 106.

39. Lienhardt, *Disorientations*, 92.

40. Al-Hijji, *Kuwait*, 44.

41. Al-Hijji, *Kuwait*, 45.

42. Al-Hijji, *Kuwait*, 45.

43. IO/R/15/5/18: Extracts from Kuwait News for week ending August 31, 1910.

44. Villiers, *Sons of Sindbad*, 322.

45. Fuccaro, *Histories*, 100.

46. Villiers, *Sons of Sindbad*, 322.

47. Jamal, *al-Hiraf*, 153.

48. Kuwait Mission, "Annual Report . . . 1938," 11.

49. M. H. Dashti interview (see note 28).

50. Kapenga, "Shop on Main Street," 14.

51. Umm Talal interview (see Chapter 2, note 124); Mr. A. al-Bashir, interviewed by Farah al-Nakib, April 15, 2009, Kuwait.

52. Sennett, *Uses of Disorder*, 48.

53. M. H. Dashti interview (see note 28).

54. Dehrab, "Childhood," 184

55. Al-Saddah interview (see Chapter 2, note 57).

56. Al-Khars and al-Aqruqah, *al-Bayt al-Kuwayty*, 14.

57. Al-Khars and al-Aqruqah, *al-Bayt al-Kuwayty*, 14.

58. Abu-Lughod, "Islamic City," 168.

59. Abu Abdullah interview (see Chapter 1, note 62).

60. Lorimer, *Gazetteer*, 1051.

61. Dehrab, "Childhood," 178.

62. Fuccaro, "Pearl Towns," 106

63. M. H. Dashti interview (see note 28).

64. Lewcock and Freeth, *Traditional Architecture*, 10.

65. Umm Talal interview (see Chapter 2, note 124).

66. Umm Ayyam, interviewed by Farah al-Nakib, April 13, 2009, Kuwait.

67. Al-Saddah interview (see Chapter 2, note 57).

68. Abu Abdullah interview (see Chapter 1, note 62).

69. Limbert, *Time of Oil*, 56.

70. Mr. F. al-Farhan, interviewed by Farah al-Nakib, March 30, 2009, Kuwait.

71. Mr. A. al-Moosa, interviewed by Farah al-Nakib, July 27, 2008, Kuwait.

72. Lewcock and Freeth, *Traditional Architecture*, 6.

73. Dehrab, "Childhood," 180.

74. Mylrea, "Annual Report," 13.

75. Scudder, "May Your Feat," 15.

76. Al-Saddah interview (see Chapter 2, note 57).

77. Al-Saddah interview (see Chapter 2, note 57).

78. Al-Saleh interview (see Chapter 2, note 79).

79. Sennett, *Uses of Disorder*, 155.

80. Al-Mughni, *Women*, 49.

81. Calverley, "Progress," 7–8.

82. Kuwait Mission, "Annual Report . . . 1932," 14.

83. Kuwait Mission, "Annual Report . . . 1937," 11.

84. Calverley, *My Arabian Days*, 22.

85. Mylrea, "Kuwait Before Oil," 107–8.

86. Limbert, *Time of Oil*, 37.

87. Dehrab, "Childhood," 181; al-Bashir interview (see Chapter 3, note 51); Mr. T. Rajab, interviewed by Farah al-Nakib, April 14, 2009, Kuwait.

88. Dehrab, "Childhood," 181.

89. Tonkiss, *Space*, 67–68.

90. Stark, *Baghdad Sketches*, 222.

91. Stark, *Baghdad Sketches*, 208.

92. Lewcock and Freeth, *Traditional Architecture*, 6.

93. Tonkiss, *Space*, 5.

94. Dennis, *Cities*, 154–55.

95. Lienhardt, *Shaikhdoms*, 54.

96. Sennett, *Uses of Disorder*, 49.

Chapter 4

1. "Administration Report for the Kuwait Political Agency" (1951), *Persian Gulf Administration Reports*, vol. 11.

2. International Bank for Reconstruction and Development, *Economic Development*, 23.

3. "Resident's Annual Report" (1954), *Persian Gulf Administration Reports*, vol. 11.

4. Shiber, *Kuwait Urbanization*, 151.

5. "Administration Report for the Kuwait Political Agency" (1950), *Persian Gulf Administration Reports*, vol. 11.

6. "Political Resident's Annual Review" (1950), *Persian Gulf Administration Reports*, vol. 11.

7. Minoprio, Spencely, and Macfarlane, "Town Planning," 272.

8. Shiber, *Kuwait Urbanization*, 78–79.

9. IO/R/15/5/205: "A New Movement in Kuwait," *al-Zaman*, April 3, 1938 (article in Iraqi newspaper translated in PA, Kuwait to PR, Bushehr, June 24, 1938).

10. Case, "Boom Time," 777.

11. "Persian Gulf Annual Review" (1956), *Persian Gulf Administration Reports*, vol. 11.

12. Rupert Hay, *The Persian Gulf States* (Washington: Middle East Institute, 1959), quoted in Crystal, *Oil and Politics*, 69.

13. Crystal, *Oil and Politics*, 57.

14. Case, "Boom Time," 777.

15. Lienhardt, *Disorientations*, 91.

16. "Kuwait Diary: February 22–March 25, 1954," *Political Diaries*, vol. 19.

17. "Residency Summary: August 12, 1954," *Political Diaries*, vol. 19.

18. "Residency Summary: November 14, 1955," *Political Diaries*, vol. 20; "Residency Summary: January 19, 1956," *Political Diaries*, vol. 20.

19. FO/371/132757: Managing Director, KOC, to Foreign Office (with notes of January 20, 1958 regarding Kuwait Situation), February 12, 1958.

20. "Administration Report for the Kuwait Political Agency" (1954), *Persian Gulf Administration Reports*, vol. 11.

21. Lienhardt, *Disorientations*, 35.

22. Lienhardt, *Disorientations*, 50.

23. FO 371/98444: Decree of Law No. 2 Regarding Kuwait Nationality, December 15, 1948.

24. In 1957 the total population was 206,473, consisting of 113,622 Kuwaitis and 92,851 non-Kuwaitis. By 1961 the total population was 321,621, with 161,909 Kuwaitis and 159,712 non-Kuwaitis. Kuwait Ministry of Planning, *Annual Statistical Abstract*, 27.

25. Kuwait Amiri Decree No. 15 of 1959, Kuwait Nationality Law, Article 1.

26. Longva, *Walls Built on Sand*, 48.

27. Crystal, *Oil and Politics*, 88.

28. Each of these three categories (citizens by origin, naturalized citizens, and *bidun*) constituted about one third of the total "native" population at the time. Abu-Hamad, "Bedoons of Kuwait."

29. Al-Mughni, *Women*, 59–60.

30. Al-Hijji, *Kuwait*, 132.

31. Lienhardt, *Disorientations*, 35.

32. Minoprio, Spencely, and Macfarlane, "Planning Problems," 104.

33. Gardiner, *Kuwait*, 21.

34. Minoprio, Spencely, and Macfarlane, "Plan," 1.

35. Harvey, *Condition of Postmodernity*, 16.

36. Dennis, *Cities*, 35.

37. Al-Barges, *Twenty-Five*, 32.

38. Holston, *Modernist City*, 5.

39. M. Dashti interview (see Chapter 2, note 42).

40. Alissa, "Oil Town of Ahmadi," 53.

41. Abu Abdullah interview (see Chapter 1, note 62).

42. Freeth, *Kuwait*, 83.

43. Colin Buchanan and Partners, *Studies, Second Report*, vol. 3, 13.

44. Gardiner, *Kuwait*, 64.

45. Minoprio, Spencely, and Macfarlane, "Town Planning," 272.

46. Colin Buchanan and Partners, "Kuwait," 1131.

47. Jacobs, *Death and Life*, 14.

48. Lienhardt, *Disorientations*, 35.

49. Minoprio, Spencely, and Macfarlane, "Plan," 2.

50. Jamal, "Kuwait," 1453.

51. Minoprio, Spencely, and Macfarlane, "Town Planning," 273.

52. Gardiner, *Kuwait*, 34.

53. Minoprio, Spencely, and Macfarlane, "Plan," 2.

54. Minoprio's plan for the reconstruction of Chelmsford, not technically a new town, used features such as the neighborhood unit that were part of postwar new town planning orthodoxy. Fuller and Home, "Chelmsford," 17.

55. Meller, *Towns*, 37–38.

56. Meller, *Towns*, 72.

57. Gardiner, *Kuwait*, 24.

58. Fuller and Home, "Chelmsford," 12.

59. Gardiner, *Kuwait*, 26.

60. Gardiner, *Kuwait*, 26; Fuller and Home, "Chelmsford," 17.

61. The KOC town of Ahmadi had also been designed using Garden City principles, predating the Minoprio, Spencely, and Macfarlane plan by about five years. See Alissa, "Oil Town of Ahmadi," 46.

62. Jacobs, *Death and Life*, 18, quoting Nathan Glazer.

63. Gardiner, *Kuwait*, 35.

64. Grindrod, "Model City," 377.

65. Colin, Buchanan and Partners, *Studies, Second Report*, vol. 3, 14.

66. Scott, *Seeing Like a State*, 57.

67. Minoprio, Spencely, and Macfarlane, "Plan," 11.

68. Minoprio, Spencely, and Macfarlane, "Plan," 13.

69. Minoprio, Spencely, and Macfarlane, "Plan," 16.

70. Ffrench and Hill, *Kuwait*, 35; Kuwai Municipality, "Reactions," 7.

71. Al-Najjar, "Decision-Making Process," 1.

72. Central Bank of Kuwait, *Kuwaiti Economy*, 59.

73. Al-Najjar, "Decision-Making Process," 134.

74. "Residency Summary: November 1951," *Political Diaries*, vol. 19; Al-Najjar, "Decision-Making Process," 140–41.

75. Al-Najjar, "Decision-Making Process," 123–24.

76. Al-Najjar, "Decision-Making Process," 213.

77. Al-Najjar, "Decision-Making Process," 278–79.

78. Ffrench and Hill, *Kuwait*, 35. Kuwait switched from using the Indian rupee to using its own currency after independence in 1961.

79. Central Bank of Kuwait, *Kuwaiti Economy*, 58.

80. For more on how Abdullah al-Salem balanced between placating his family and the merchants, see Crystal, *Oil and Politics*, 64–70, 73–76.

81. Abu Abdullah interview (see Chapter 1, note 62).

82. "Kuwait Diary: February 25–March 24, 1958," *Political Diaries*, vol. 20.

83. "Kuwait Diary: June 29–July 20, 1954," *Political Diaries*, vol. 19.

84. Al-Najjar, "Decision-Making Process," 98.

85. Shankland Cox Partnership, *Master Plan*, 78.

86. Ffrench and Hill, *Kuwait*, 36.

87. Hay, "Impact," 366; Shiber, *Kuwait Urbanization*, 117.

88. Crystal, *Oil and Politics*, 67.

89. "Administration Report for the Kuwait Political Agency" (1950), *Persian Gulf Administration Reports*, vol. II.

90. Shiber, *Kuwait Urbanization*, 28.

91. Crystal, *Oil and Politics*, 68.

92. "Resident's Monthly Summaries: May 1952," *Persian Gulf Administration Reports*, vol. II.

93. "Resident's Monthly Summaries: May 1952," *Persian Gulf Administration Reports*, vol. II.

94. "Resident's Annual Report" (1953), *Persian Gulf Administration Reports*, vol. II; al-Najjar, "Decision-Making Process," 154.

95. "Resident's Annual Report" (1955), *Persian Gulf Administration Reports*, vol. II.

96. Al-Najjar, "Decision-Making Process," 116.

97. Ffrench and Hill, *Kuwait*, 36.

98. Ffrench and Hill, *Kuwait*, 36.

99. Shankland Cox Partnership, *Master Plan*, 78.

100. Shiber, *Kuwait Urbanization*, 117.

101. "Resident's Monthly Summaries: November 1952," *Persian Gulf Administration Reports*, vol. II.

102. Shehab, "Kuwait."

103. Shehab, "Kuwait."

104. Shiber, *Kuwait Urbanization*, 116.

105. Shiber, *Kuwait Urbanization*, 117.

106. Shiber, *Kuwait Urbanization*, 401.

107. *Al-'Araby*, "Mawlid Shari'," 83.

108. Shiber, *Kuwait Urbanization*, 399.

109. *Al-'Araby*, "Mawlid Shari'," 85.

110. *Al-'Araby*, "Mawlid Shari'," 80–81.

111. *Al-'Araby*, "Mawlid Shari'," 81.

112. Shiber, *Kuwait Urbanization*, 165; *Al-'Araby*, "Mawlid Shari'," 81–83.

113. Shiber, *Kuwait Urbanization*, 400.

114. Shuaib, "Urban Development," 4.

115. Shiber, *Kuwait Urbanization*, 120–21.

116. Shiber, *Kuwait Urbanization*, 161.

117. Shiber, *Kuwait Urbanization*, 158.

118. Shiber, *Kuwait Urbanization*, 166.

119. Shiber, *Kuwait Urbanization*, 159.

120. Jamal, "Kuwait," 1454.

121. Colin Buchanan and Partners, *Studies, Final Draft Interim Report*, 2.

122. "Proposals for Restructuring Kuwait," 179.

123. Sultan, "Kuwait," 793.

124. Sultan, "Kuwait," 793.

125. Sultan, "Notes."

126. Sultan, "Notes."

127. Sultan, "Notes."

128. Sultan, "Kuwait," 793.

129. Grill, *Urbanisation*, 6.

130. Shankland Cox Partnership, *Master Plan*, 78.

131. Shankland Cox Partnership, *Master Plan*, 78.

132. Ahmad, "Migrant Domestic," 27.

133. SSH, *New Master Plan*, 2.

134. SSH, *New Master Plan*, 2.

135. Vale, *Architecture*, 15.

136. Crystal, *Oil and Politics*, 94–96.

137. Parkyn, "Kuwait Revisited," 40.

138. Holod and Rastorfer, "Water Towers," 178.

139. Holod and Rastorfer, "Water Towers," 179.

140. Holod and Rastorfer, "Water Towers," 181.

141. Vale, *Architecture*, 3.

142. Colin Buchanan and Partners, *Studies, Second Report*, vol. 3, 16.

143. Colin Buchanan and Partners, *Studies, Technical Paper 32*, 3.

144. Colin Buchanan and Partners, *Studies, Second Report*, vol. 3, 16.

145. Colin Buchanan and Partners, *Studies, Second Report*, vol. 3, 60.

146. Connah, "Seif Palace Extension."

147. Mahgoub, "Globalization," 166.

148. The completion of this extension was delayed due to the Iraqi invasion of 1990 and was not finished until 1999.

149. Crystal, *Oil and Politics*, 97.

150. Gardiner, *Kuwait*, 59.

151. Parkyn, "Kuwait Revisited," 40.

152. Vale, *Architecture*, 220.

153. Parkyn, "Kuwait Revisited," 42.

Chapter 5

1. Shiber, *Kuwait Urbanization*, 93.

2. See Cullen, *American Dream*, chapter 3.

3. Meller, *Towns*, 37.

4. Kelly, *Expanding the American Dream*, 165.

5. Al-Mosully, "Revitalizing," 93.

6. Colin Buchanan and Partners, *Studies, First Report*, 4.

7. Minoprio, Spencely, and Macfarlane, "Plan," 16.

8. Colin Buchanan and Partners, *Studies, Technical Note OA. 24*, 7.

9. Colin Buchanan and Partners, *Studies, Technical Paper 18*, 10–11, 24; and *Technical Note OA. 24*, 8.

10. Colin Buchanan and Partners, *Studies, Technical Paper 18*, 11.

11. Colin Buchanan and Partners, *Studies, Technical Paper 18*, 40.

12. Al-Moosa, "Kuwait," 50.

13. Colin Buchanan and Partners, *Studies, First Report*, 4.

14. Shihab, "al-Haraka al-Ta'awuniyya"; Za'balawy, "al-Jam'iyyat."

15. Za'balawy, "al-Jam'iyyat," 128.

16. Al-Moosa, "Kuwait," 50.

17. Shihab, "al-Haraka al-Ta'awuniyya," 127.

18. Shihab, "al-Haraka al-Ta'awuniyya," 130.

19. Colin Buchanan and Partners, *Studies, Technical Paper 18*, 24–25.

20. Al-Moosa, "Kuwait," 49.

21. Kuwait Municipality, "Social-Residential Survey."

22. Al-Moosa, "Kuwait," 49.

23. Al-Moosa, "Kuwait," 49.

24. Al-Najjar, "Decision-Making Process," 188–89.

25. *Majallat Souwt al-Khalij*, "Al-Asil wa-l-Sura."

26. Colin Buchanan and Partners, *Studies, Technical Note OA. 24*, 7–8.

27. Colin Buchanan and Partners, *Studies, Technical Paper 18*, 7.

28. Colin Buchanan and Partners, *Studies, Technical Paper 18*, 22.

29. Shiber, *Kuwait Urbanization*, 94.

30. Alissa, "Oil Town of Ahmadi," 53.

31. Al-Bahar, "Contemporary," 63.

32. Al-Bahar, "Contemporary," 64–65.

33. Al-Bahar, "Contemporary," 64–65.

34. Freeth, *New Look*, 51.

35. Al-Bahar, "Contemporary," 65.

36. Dennis, *Cities*, 223.

37. Freeth, *New Look*, 17.

38. Kelly, *Expanding the American Dream*, 55.

39. Kelly, *Expanding the American Dream*, 60.

40. Shiber, *Kuwait Urbanization*, 227.

41. Shiber, *Kuwait Urbanization*, 224.

42. *Al-Talee'a*, "Buyut Dhuwy al-Dakhal al-Mahdud."

43. *Al-Rai al-'Aam*, "Lajnat al-'Ara'idh."

44. Kelly, *Expanding the American Dream*, 17.

45. Al-Bahar, "Contemporary," 63.

46. Al-Bahar, "Contemporary," 63.

47. Dennis, *Cities*, 205.

48. Freeth, *New Look*, 53.

49. Freeth, *New Look*, 51.

50. Mahgoub, "Kuwait," 163.

51. Al-Mughni, *Women*, 54.

52. Freeth, *New Look*, 35.

53. Al-Mughni, *Women*, 59.

54. Freeth, *New Look*, 37.

55. Sultan, "Designing for New Needs," 94.

56. Sultan, "Criteria for Design," 165.

57. Sultan, "Criteria for Design," 167.

58. Al-Mohameed, "al-Quyud wa-l-Azma."

59. Colin Buchanan and Partners, *Studies, Technical Paper 18*, 40.

60. Tétreault, *Stories of Democracy*, 118–22.

61. All Kuwaiti election results from 1962 onward are available on the Kuwait Politics Database prepared by Michael Herb, Georgia State University: http://www.kuwaitpolitics.org.

62. As a non-Kuwaiti, this official preferred not to be named. Interviewed by Farah al-Nakib, July 7, 2008, Kuwait.

63. Crystal, *Oil and Politics*, 83.

64. Lienhardt, *Disorientations*, 38.

65. Al-Moosa, "Kuwait," 48.

66. Alissa, "Oil Town of Ahmadi," 45.

67. Alissa, "Oil Town of Ahmadi," 48.

68. Colin Buchanan and Partners, *Studies, Technical Paper 18*, 5.

69. Colin Buchanan and Partners, *Studies, Technical Note OA. 24*, 12.

70. Colin Buchanan and Partners, *Studies, Technical Note OA. 24*, 5.

71. Colin Buchanan and Partners, *Studies, Technical Paper 18*, 5. The 19 percent of Salmiya, Hawalli, and Kuwait City residents who were Kuwaitis are explained by the fact that some state-built limited-income housing had been distributed in these areas in the 1950s. The 28 percent non-Kuwaiti composition of the inner neighborhoods consisted mainly of expatriate domestic workers and noncitizen family members living within Kuwaiti households. Ffrench and Hill, *Kuwait*, 48.

72. Colin Buchanan and Partners, *Studies, Second Report*, vol. 3, 4.29.

73. Colin Buchanan and Partners, *Studies, Technical Paper 18*, 6–7.

74. See note 71.

75. Colin Buchanan and Partners, *Studies, Technical Paper 18*, 25.

76. Minoprio, Spencely, and Macfarlane, "Planning Problems," 104.

77. Shiber, *Kuwait Urbanization*, 227.

78. Colin Buchanan and Partners, Technical *Studies, Note OA. 18*, 4.

79. Cartwright, "Kuwait Creates a Suburbia," 47–49.

80. Jensen, "Competition for Township," 18–19.

81. *Ajyal*, "'Asr al-'Ishish."

82. Crystal, *Oil and Politics*, 81.

83. Colin Buchanan and Partners, *Studies, Technical Note OA. 24*, 12.

84. Colin Buchanan and Partners, *Studies, Technical Note OA. 24*, 7.

85. Musa'ed, "Ma Huwa al-Sir."

86. Musa'ed, "Ma Huwa al-Sir."

87. *Al-Siyasa*, "Ma'a Qarar al-Majlis al-Balady."

88. Sadik, "Nation-Building," 232.

89. Kuwait Municipality, "Social-Residential Survey."

90. Colin Buchanan and Partners, *Studies, Technical Note OA. 18*, 4.

91. Colin Buchanan and Partners, *Studies, Technical Note OA. 18*, 11.

92. *Al-Talee'a*, "Buyut Dhuwy al-Dakhal al-Mahdud."

93. *Al-Talee'a*, "Buyut Dhuwy al-Dakhal al-Mahdud."

94. Crystal, *Oil and Politics*, 88–89.

95. Crystal, *Oil and Politics*, 88.

96. Al-Mubaraki, *Hin Isti'ad al-Sha'b*, 89.

97. Al-Mubaraki, *Hin Isti'ad al-Sha'b*, 93.

98. For election results, see the Kuwait Politics Database: http://www.kuwaitpolitics.org.

99. Sadik, "Nation-Building," 262–63.

100. For the long-term effects of these housing policies on *hadar/badu* relations in Kuwait, see F. al-Nakib, "Revisiting Hadar and Badu."

101. Gardiner, *Kuwait*, 26–27.

102. Colin Buchanan and Partners, *Master Plan*, 86.

103. Jacobs, *Death and Life*, 133–34.

104. Gardiner, *Kuwait*, 69.

105. Colin Buchanan and Partners, *Studies, Technical Note KT. 21.*

106. *Al-Nahda*, "Shiqaq Sakaniyya."

107. Shankland Cox Partnership, *Master Plan*, 78.

108. Sadik, "Nation-Building," 256.

109. *Al-Nahda*, "Shiqaq Sakaniyya."

110. Arthur Erickson Architects, *Sawaber*, 1.

111. Arthur Erickson Architects, *Sawaber*, 2.

112. Arthur Erickson Architects, *Sawaber*, 1.

113. Arthur Erickson Architects, *Sawaber*, 2.

114. Gardiner, *Kuwait*, 46.

115. Sadik, "Nation-Building," 257.

116. Lefebvre, *Writings*, 77.

Chapter 6

1. Gardiner, *Kuwait*, 46.

2. Al-Mutawa, *Parks*, 78.

3. Al-Mutawa, *Parks*, 94.

4. Al-Mutawa, *Parks*, 45.

5. Al-Mutawa, *Parks*, 88.

6. Al-Mutawa, *Parks*, 80.

7. "Kuwait Annual Report" (1949), *Persian Gulf Administration Reports*, vol. 11.

8. Jamal, *Aswaq*, 29.

9. Executions were held in the palace yard until 1985, and resumed again in 2002.

10. Al-Hijji, *Kuwait*, 132–33.

11. Freeth, *New Look*, 95.

12. Freeth, *New Look*, 101.

13. Freeth, *New Look*, 96.

14. Shiber, *Kuwait Urbanization*, 204.

15. Colin Buchanan and Partners, *Studies, Technical Paper 37*, 14; Freeth, *New Look*, 88–89.

16. Naseef, "Shawati' al-Kuwayt," 88.
17. *Al-'Araby*, "Aswaq al-Kuwayt," 46.
18. *Al-'Araby*, "Aswaq al-Kuwayt," 52.
19. Freeth, *New Look*, 104–5.
20. Lienhardt, *Disorientations*, 42.
21. Freeth, *New Look*, 104.
22. Minoprio, Spencely, and Macfarlane, "Plan," 4.
23. Menoret, *Joyriding*, 98.
24. Shiber, *Kuwait Urbanization*, 75.
25. Shiber, *Kuwait Urbanization*, 391.
26. Freeth, *New Look*, 93.
27. Umm Ahmed, interviewed by Farah al-Nakib, June 25, 2008, Kuwait.
28. Al-Fahad, "Tajmil al-Manatiq."
29. Shiber, *Kuwait Urbanization*, 391.
30. Al-Mutawa, *Parks*, 86.
31. Tonkiss, *Space*, 68.
32. Lienhardt, *Disorientations*, 38.
33. Lienhardt, *Disorientations*, 38.
34. Devecon, *Safat Square*.
35. Taylor, "Waterfront," 14.
36. Cohen, "Modernity," 55.
37. Freeth, *New Look*, 83.
38. "Proposals for Restructuring," 179.
39. Devecon, *Safat Square*.
40. Devecon, *Safat Square*.
41. *Al-Qabas*, "Iftitah Mashru' Sahat al-Safat."
42. Devecon, *Safat Square*.
43. Devecon, *Safat Square*.
44. Sennett, *Fall of Public Man*, 12.
45. *Al-Yaqaza*, Untitled.
46. *Al-Watan*, "al-Qu'ood."
47. *Al-Qabas*, "al-Safat."
48. Colin Buchanan and Partners, *Studies, Technical Paper 37*, 16, 22.
49. Davis, *City of Quartz*, 226
50. Freeth, *New Look*, 55.
51. Colin Buchanan and Partners, *Studies, Technical Paper 37*, 19.
52. Naseef, "Shawati' al-Kuwayt," 88.
53. Al-Mutawa, *Parks*, 89.
54. *Al-Rai al-'Aam*, "al-Majlis al-Balady."
55. Taylor, "Waterfront," 14.
56. Konvitz, *Cities and the Sea*, 37.
57. Taylor, "Waterfront," 16.
58. Taylor, "Waterfront," 16.

59. Colin Buchanan and Partners, *Studies, Technical Paper 37*, 13–14.

60. Quoted in Alissa, "Oil Town of Ahmadi," 52.

61. Khalaf, "Nationalisation," 46.

62. Khalaf, "Nationalisation," 48.

63. Khalaf, "Nationalisation," 46.

64. Dennis, *Cities*, 1, 4, 6.

65. Al-Fahad, "Tajmil al-Manatiq"; al-Qabas, "Limatha la Takun al-Kuwayt"; al-Mutairi, "Min Yiwaqif al-'Udwan."

66. *Al-Qabas*, "Lawhat Jidariyya."

67. *Al-Qabas*, "al-Qabas Tansher."

68. Khaz'al, "al-Houti."

69. *Al-Qabas*, "al-Qabas Tansher."

70. Al-Saeed, "Matlub Waqfa."

71. Jacobs, *Death and Life*, 144.

72. Tonkiss, *Space*, 67–68.

73. *Al-Salmiya*, "al-Salmiya Bayn al-Madhi wa-l-Hader."

74. Kuwait Municipality, "Social-Residential Survey."

75. Lefebvre, *Writings*, 143.

76. Amin and Thrift, *Cities*, 135–37.

77. Amin and Thrift, *Cities*, 147.

78. Tonkiss, *Space*, 67.

79. Crystal, *Oil and Politics*, 82.

80. Al-Khatib, *al-Kuwayt*, 24–25.

81. Al-Khatib, *al-Kuwayt*, 38.

82. Al-Khatib, *al-Kuwayt*, 82.

83. "Kuwait Annual Report" (1956), *Persian Gulf Administration Reports*, vol. 11.

84. "Kuwait Annual Report" (1956), *Persian Gulf Administration Reports*, vol. 11.

85. "Kuwait Diary: November 29–December 23, 1956," *Political Diaries*, vol. 20.

86. Al-Khatib, *al-Kuwayt*, 126–28.

87. Lienhardt, *Disorientations*, 42.

88. Lienhardt, *Disorientations*, 58.

89. IO/R/15/5/205: PA, Kuwait to PR, Bushehr, June 25, 1938.

90. "Kuwait Diary: June 20–July 28, 1958," *Political Diaries*, vol. 20.

91. Al-Khatib, *al-Kuwayt*, 133; Crystal, *Oil and Politics*, 81.

92. "Kuwait Diary: July 31–August 26, 1956," *Political Diaries*, vol. 20.

93. Letter from the Council of Clubs to Shaikh Abdullah al-Salem, quoted in al-Khatib, *al-Kuwayt*, 134–36; FO/371/120570: Translation of petition addressed to His Highness the Ruler of Kuwait by the Club's Union, August 14, 1956.

94. FO/371/120557: Translation of an appeal to the people of Kuwait, November 3, 1956.

95. Tétreault, "Civil Society," 278.

96. Al-Khatib, *al-Kuwayt*, 146.

97. Al-Khatib, *al-Kuwayt*, 147.

98. FO/371/120558: Report on situation in Kuwait probably by KOC staff (unsigned), November 13–20, 1956.

99. "Kuwait Annual Report" (1957), *Persian Gulf Administration Reports*, vol. 11.

100. "Kuwait Diary: November 21–December 23, 1957," *Political Diaries*, vol. 20.

101. "Persian Gulf Monthly Report: July 3–August 6, 1958," *Political Diaries*, vol. 20.

102. Scott, *Seeing Like a State*, 61.

103. Quoted in al-Khatib, *al-Kuwayt*, 188–89.

104. Al-Khatib, *al-Kuwayt*, 190.

105. For more on the link between the Iraqi threat and Kuwait's advancement of democracy, see Herb, *Wages of Oil*, chapter 3.

106. Al-Mughni, *Women*, 37.

107. Al-Mughni, *Women*, 70–71.

108. *Majallat Souwt al-Khalij*, "al-Ma'sat Allaty Ya'eeshaha."

109. "Chronology," 469.

110. Ghabra, "Voluntary Associations," 200, 202.

111. Harvey, *Rebel Cities*, 161.

112. Tétreault, "Civil Society," 279.

113. Tétreault, "Civil Society," 277.

114. Ghabra, "Voluntary Associations," 205.

115. Tétreault, "Civil Society," 279.

116. Al-Mubaraki, *Hin Isti'ad al-Sha'b*, 39.

117. Al-Mubaraki, *Hin Isti'ad al-Sha'b*, 60.

118. Al-Mosully, "Revitalizing," 119.

119. Al-Mosully, "Revitalizing," 119.

120. Kuwait Engineers Office, *Sharq al-Seif*, 8–9.

121. Lefebvre, *Writings*, 73.

122. Lefebvre, *Writings*, 148.

123. For more on this phenomenon, see F. al-Nakib, "Kuwait's Modern Spectacle," 21–24.

Chapter 7

1. Lienhardt, *Disorientations*, 35.

2. Shehab, "Kuwait."

3. Ffrench and Hill, *Kuwait*, 20.

4. Ffrench and Hill, *Kuwait*, 20.

5. Ffrench and Hill, *Kuwait*, 22.

6. Shehab, "Kuwait."

7. Shehab, "Kuwait."

8. Shehab, "Kuwait."

9. Shehab, "Kuwait."

10. Shiber, *Kuwait Urbanization*, 117.

11. Sennett, *Uses of Disorder*, 9.

12. Sennett, *Uses of Disorder*, 9.

13. Longva, *Walls Built on Sand*, 189 (emphasis added).

14. Ffrench and Hill, *Kuwait*, 21.

15. Fuccaro, "Pearl Towns," 111.

16. For more on the *kafala* system, see Longva, *Walls Built on Sand*, chapter 4.

17. Fuccaro, "Pearl Towns," 111.

18. Crystal, *Oil and Politics*, 81.

19. Longva, *Walls Built on Sand*, 50.

20. M. al-Nakib, "Outside in the Nation Machine," 204.

21. Shehab, "Kuwait."

22. Shehab, "Kuwait."

23. Shehab, "Kuwait."

24. Al-Moosa, "Kuwait," 45.

25. Al-Moosa, "Kuwait," 53.

26. Longva, *Walls Built on Sand*, 116.

27. Longva, *Walls Built on Sand*, 120–21.

28. Lienhardt, *Disorientations*, 38.

29. Being in a taxi was not considered demeaning, however, for Bedouin Kuwaitis, who often *were* taxi drivers. Lienhardt, *Disorientations*, 37.

30. Al-Essa, Haddad, and Sultan, "Graduate Housing," 14.

31. Al-Moosa, "Kuwait," 51.

32. Al-Moosa, "Kuwait," 51.

33. Lienhardt, *Disorientations*, 42.

34. Lienhardt, *Disorientations*, 43.

35. Sennett, *Uses of Disorder*, 34.

36. Sennett, *Uses of Disorder*, 57.

37. Sennett, *Uses of Disorder*, 33.

38. Shehab, "Kuwait."

39. Sennett, *Uses of Disorder*, 48.

40. Shehab, "Kuwait."

41. Sennett, *Uses of Disorder*, 18.

42. Al-Moosa, "Kuwait," 51.

43. Shehab, "Kuwait."

44. Amin and Thrift, *Cities*, 147.

45. Kuwait Municipality, "Social-Residential Survey."

46. Kuwait Municipality, "Social-Residential Survey."

47. Freeth, *New Look*, 86.

48. Al-Mughni, *Women*, 62.

49. Lefebvre, *Writings*, 76.

50. Abu Abdullah interview (see Chapter 1, note 62).

51. Al-Jassim, *Baladiyyat al-Kuwayt*, 199.

52. Shiber, *Kuwait Urbanization*, 93.

53. Caldeira, *City of Walls*, 308.

54. *Al-'Araby*, "Al-Kuwayt Tu'ammin al-Sakan," 123.

55. *Al-Nahda*, "Shiqaq Sakaniyya."

56. Al-Saddah interview (see Chapter 2, note 57).
57. Umm Ayyam interview (see Chapter 3, note 66).
58. Kuwait Municipality, "Social-Residential Survey."
59. Lefebvre, *Writings*, 143.
60. Kuwait Municipality, "Social-Residential Survey."
61. Shiber, *Kuwait Urbanization*, 223.
62. Al-Moosa, "Kuwait," 48.
63. Umm Ayyam interview (see Chapter 3, note 66).
64. Freeth, *New Look*, 91.
65. Umm Ayyam interview (see Chapter 3, note 66).
66. Kuwait Municipality, "Social-Residential Survey."
67. Freeth, *New Look*, 91.
68. Kuwait Municipality, "Social-Residential Survey."
69. *Al-Hadaf*, "Bayt li-Kul Muwatin."
70. Citino, "Suburbia and Modernization," 17–18.
71. Al-Moosa, "Kuwait," 49.
72. Al-Moosa, "Kuwait," 55.
73. *Majallat Souwt al-Khalij*, "Al-Asil wa-l-Sura."
74. Caldeira, *City of Walls*, 309.
75. Al-Essa, Haddad, and Sultan, "Graduate Housing," 13–14.
76. Longva, *Walls Built on Sand*, 187.
77. Colin Buchanan and Partners, *Studies, Technical Note OA. 24*, 7.
78. Colin Buchanan and Partners, *Studies, Technical Paper 18*, 7.
79. Shiber, *Kuwait Urbanization*, 226.
80. Shiber, *Kuwait Urbanization*, 222.
81. Shiber, *Kuwait Urbanization*, 221.
82. Shiber, *Kuwait Urbanization*, 225.
83. *Al-'Araby*, "Al-Kuwayt Tu'ammin al-Sakan," 126.
84. Al-Mohameed, "al-Quyud wa-l-Azma."
85. Colin Buchanan and Partners, *Studies, Technical Paper 18*, 15.
86. Kelly, *Expanding the American Dream*, 46.
87. Al-Mohameed, "al-Quyud wa-l-Azma."
88. Al-Mohameed, "al-Quyud wa-l-Azma."
89. Kelly, *Expanding the American Dream*, 111.
90. Al-Rashed, "al-Masakin al-Sha'biyya."
91. *Al-Talee'a*, "Buyut Dhuwy al-Dakhal al-Mahdud."
92. Al-Ajmy, "Nitarna 10 Sanawat."
93. Al-Rashed, "al-Masakin al-Sha'biyya."
94. *Majallat Souwt al-Khalij*, "al-Ma'sat Allaty Ya'eeshaha."
95. Colin Buchanan and Partners, *Studies, Technical Paper 18*, 13.
96. Shiber, *Kuwait Urbanization*, 224.
97. Al-Moosa, "Kuwait," 51.
98. Al-Moosa, "Kuwait," 51.

99. Freund, *Colored Property*, 12–13.

100. Freund, *Colored Property*, 12.

101. Al-Moosa, "Kuwait," 52.

102. *Al-Talee'a*, "Buyut Dhuwy al-Dakhal al-Mahdud."

103. Al-Moosa, "Kuwait," 56.

104. Sennett, *Uses of Disorder*, 36.

105. Al-Moosa, "Kuwait," 56.

106. Candilis, "Kuwait," 1–3.

107. Lefebvre, *Writings*, 80–81, 103.

108. Merrifield, *Henri Lefebvre*, 71.

109. Lefebvre, *Introduction to Modernity*, 124.

110. Lefebvre, *Introduction to Modernity*, 122.

111. Caldeira, *City of Walls*, 309.

112. Lefebvre, *Introduction to Modernity*, 116.

113. Pelly, *Remarks*, 73.

Chapter 8

1. Lefebvre, *Writings*, 75.

2. Lefebvre, *Writings*, 103, 148.

3. Lefebvre, *Writings*, 158.

4. Shiber, *Kuwait Urbanization*, 159.

5. Arthur Erickson Architects, *Sawaber*, 1.

6. Merrifield, *Henri Lefebvre*, 71.

7. Lefebvre, *Writings*, 158 (emphasis in original).

8. McCann, "Race, Protest, and Public Space," 181.

9. Harvey, *Rebel Cities*, xviii.

10. Amin and Thrift, *Cities*, 131.

11. Kuwait Constitution, articles 6 and 7.

12. Tétreault, *Stories of Democracy*, 34.

13. Longva, *Walls Built on Sand*, 48.

14. Al-Moosa, "Kuwait," 56.

15. Sennett, *Uses of Disorder*, 36.

16. Sennett, *Uses of Disorder*, 36.

17. For more on the role of education and the national curriculum in building this national consensus, see R. al-Nakib, "Education and Democratic Development."

18. Al-Moosa, "Kuwait," 45, 53.

19. Sennett, *Uses of Disorder*, 10.

20. Al-Moosa, "Kuwait," 56.

21. Calderwood, "Fifty Years."

22. See F. al-Nakib, "Revisiting Hadar and Badu."

23. Kuwait News Agency, "Kuwait Speaker."

24. Toumi, "Minister Seeks."

25. Toumi, "Minister Seeks."

26. Palestinians began immigrating to Kuwait after the *nakba* of 1948. Unlike most other expatriate populations, they came to Kuwait with the intention of settling long-term, due to their inability to return to their homeland. The Palestinian community, composed largely of doctors, engineers, teachers, professors, and other high-level professionals, settled in Kuwait with their families and played an indispensable role in modernizing Kuwait throughout the first four decades of oil.

27. Ghabra, "Iraqi Occupation," 122–23.

28. For a full analysis of the effects of this loss, see M. al-Nakib, "'The People Are Missing.'"

29. Assiri, *Kuwait's Foreign Policy*, 145.

30. http://www.jaberalahmadhospital.com/en/faqs.php.

31. Harper, "Kuwait to Push Out."

32. *Telegraph*, "Speeding?"

33. Al-Jenfawi, "Kuwait Constitution."

34. Amin and Thrift, *Cities*, 137.

35. Amin and Thrift, *Cities*, 150.

36. Gardner, *City of Strangers*, 2.

37. Sennett, *Uses of Disorder*, 142.

38. SSH, *Third Kuwait Master Plan*, 1.

39. *Al-Qabas*, "al-'Asimah." Quotes from part 1.

40. Al-Mosully, "Revitalizing," 13.

41. Alissa, "Modernizing Kuwait," 89.

42. Alissa, "Modernizing Kuwait," 89.

43. *Al-Qabas*, "al-'Asimah," parts 8, 9, and 10 (quote from part 10).

44. *Al-Qabas*, "al-'Asimah," parts 8 and 10.

45. *Al-Qabas*, "al-'Asimah," part 9.

46. *Al-Qabas*, "al-'Asimah," part 10.

47. Toumi, "Kuwait to Deport."

48. http://248am.com/mark/kuwait/seafront-bbqs-now-illegal.

49. For more on the protests and Irada, see F. al-Nakib, "Urban Alternative" and "Public Space."

50. Lefebvre, "Les illusions de la modernité," cited in Kofman and Lebas, "Lost in Transposition," 34.

51. Lefebvre, *Writings*, 158, 79–80.

52. Harvey, *Rebel Cities*, 138.

53. Lefebvre, *Writings*, 178.

54. Sennett, *Uses of Disorder*, 185.

55. Amin and Thrift, *Cities*, 156.

56. *Bazaar*, "Mubarakiya."

57. *Bazaar*, "Mubarakiya."

58. *Bazaar*, "Mubarakiya."

59. The core members of the group include Waleed al-Nasrallah, Alaa al-Mashaan, Yusra Ahmad, Lubna Saif Abbas, Brian Collett, Dina Kadry, and Bassam (a nine-year-old neighbor).

60. Maryam al-Nusif, interviewed by Farah al-Nakib, April 1, 2015, Kuwait (follow-up May 10, 2015).

61. Merrifield, *Henri Lefebvre*, 71.

62. Al-Nusif interview (see note 60).

63. Sennett, *Uses of Disorder*, 142.

64. Al-Zouman, al-Fraih, and al-Ghunaim, "Local Knowledge."

65. Al-Zouman, al-Fraih, and al-Ghunaim, "Local Knowledge."

66. De Certeau, *Everyday Life*, 108.

67. Al-Zouman, al-Fraih, and al-Ghunaim, "Local Knowledge."

68. De Certeau, *Everyday Life*, 92–93.

69. Scott, *Seeing Like a State*, 310–11.

70. Scott, *Seeing Like a State*, 316.

71. Scott, *Seeing Like a State*, 317.

72. Shiber, *Kuwait Urbanization*, 120–21.

73. Amin and Thrift, *Cities*, 150.

74. Holston, *Cities and Citizenship*, vii; Holston and Appadurai, "Cities and Citizenship," 4.

75. Holston, *Cities and Citizenship*, viii (emphasis added).

76. Holston and Appadurai, "Cities and Citizenship," 5.

77. Amin and Thrift, *Cities*, 146, quoting Alain Touraine.

78. Amin and Thrift, *Cities*, 150.

79. Amin and Thrift, *Cities*, 143.

Glossary of Key Terms

'abat (plural *'ibiy*)   Black robe worn by Kuwaiti women.

al-manatiq al-numuthajiyya   "Model areas," referring to the neighborhoods developed by the state within the first four ring roads.

al-manatiq al-kharijiyya   "Outlying areas," referring to the townships developed by the state as part of the Bedouin settlement program.

'amara (plural *'amayer*)   Warehouse or storage space.

'arda   Bedouin war dance.

badu (singular *badawi*)   Bedouin in Kuwaiti dialect.

baraha   Small open space where several streets converge.

datcha   Coral and mud bench built out from the front wall of a house.

dhow   Wooden Arabian sailing vessel.

diwaniyya (plural *diwawin*)   Nightly gathering of male guests; also, the section of a house where the gathering is held.

farij (plural *firjan*)   Neighborhood.

firya   Small opening or door connecting two courtyard houses.

fedawiyya   The ruler's personal armed guard.

furda   Town port.

hadar   Townspeople or sedentary urbanites.

kishk   Kiosk; the ruler's office in the *suq*.

majlis   Public audience; also, council or assembly.

nokhada (plural *nowakhada*)   Ship captain.

nig'a (plural *inga'*)   Tidal jetty.

Political Agent   The main British India Office (Foreign Office after 1957) official stationed in Kuwait, who served as the Persian Gulf Political Resident's representative.

Political Resident   The principal British India Office (Foreign Office after 1957)
  official in the Persian Gulf, stationed in Bushehr, Iran, from 1763 to 1946, then in
  Bahrain in 1971.

sahel   Seafront or coastline.

sikka (pl. *sikik*)   Small inner street.

suq (pl. *aswaq*)   Town market.

sur   Town wall.

tathmin al-arady   Land acquisition scheme.

waqf (pl. *awqaf*)   Islamic endowment.

zakat   Islamic alms.

Bibliography

Archival Sources and Collections

British India Office and Foreign Office Record Files

IO/R/15/1: Bushehr Political Residency, 1763–1947.

IO/R/15/5: Kuwait Political Agency, 1904–49.

IO/G/29: East India Company Factory, Persia and Persian Gulf, c. 1620–1833.

FO/371: Political Departments: General Correspondence, 1906–66.

Collections of Documents

Persian Gulf Administration Reports 1873–1957, 11 vols. Cambridge, UK: Archive Editions, 1989. Includes the following:

Administration Reports for the Kuwait Political Agency

Administration Reports for the Persian Gulf Political Residency

Kuwait Annual Reports

Resident's Annual Reports

Political Resident's Annual Reviews

Persian Gulf Annual Reviews

Resident's Monthly Summaries

Political Diaries of the Arab World: Persian Gulf 1904–1965, edited by R. Jarman, 24 vols. Cambridge, UK: Archive Editions: 1990/1998. Includes the following:

Kuwait News

Kuwait Intelligence Summaries

Kuwait Diaries

Residency Summaries

Persian Gulf Monthly Reports

The Arabian Mission: Field Reports, Quarterly Letters, Neglected Arabia, Arabia Calling, 8 vols. Gerrards Cross, UK: Archive Editions, 1993. Includes all *Neglected Arabia* articles listed in this Bibliography.

Authored Works

Abdullah, Mohammed Hassan. *Al-Haraka al-Adabiyya wa-l-Fikriyya fi-l-Kuwayt*. Kuwait: Rabtat al-Adaba' fi-l-Kuwait, 1973.

Abu-Hakima, Ahmad Mustafa. *The Modern History of Kuwait, 1750–1965*. London: Luzac, 1983.

Abu-Hamad, Aziz. *The Bedoons of Kuwait: "Citizens Without Citizenship."* New York: Human Rights Watch, August 1995. http://www.hrw.org/legacy/reports/1995/Kuwait.htm.

Abu-Lughod, Janet. "The Islamic City—Historic Myth, Islamic Essence, and Contemporary Relevance." *International Journal of Middle East Studies* 19, no. 2 (May 1987): 155–76.

Ahmad, Attiya. "Migrant Domestic Workers in Kuwait: The Role of State Institutions." *Middle East Institute Viewpoints: Migration and the Gulf*, February 2010, 27–29.

Ajyal. "'Asr al-'Ishish Yihal 'ala al-Taqa'ud." March 25, 1979.*

Al-Ajmy, Fahad Musa'ed. "Nitarna 10 Sanawat li-l-Husul 'Alayha wa ba'ad 10 Sanawat Satasqut 'Alayna." *Al-Watan*, May 4, 1987.*

Al-'Araby. "Mawlid Shari' fi al-Kuwayt." August 1960.

———. "Al-Kuwayt Tu'ammin al-Sakan li-Dhuwy al-Dakhal al-Mahdud min Abna'iha." August 1961.

———. "Aswaq al-Kuwayt Bayn al-Ams wa-l-Youm." December 1969.

Al-Bahar, Huda. "Contemporary Kuwaiti Houses." *MIMAR* 15 (January/March 1985): 63–72.

Al-Barges, Barges Hamoud. *A Twenty-Five Year Era of Kuwait's Modern Advancement: On the Occasion of the Silver Jubilee of the National Day on February 25, 1986*. Kuwait: Kuwait News Agency Information and Research Department, 1986.

Al-Essa, Abdulaziz, Charles Haddad, and Ghazi Sultan. "Graduate Housing Survey for the State of Kuwait." 1973.

Al-Fahad, Nasser Abdulaziz. "Tajmil al-Manatiq Qabl al-Qimma." *Al-Rai al-'Aam*, December 19, 1986.*

Al-Farhan, Farhan. *Tarikh al-Mawaqi' wa-l-Amkena fi Dawlat al-Kuwayt*. Kuwait: Al-Risala Press, n.d.

———. *Ma'jam al-Mawadi' wa-l-Mawaqi' wa-l-Amkena fi-l-Kuwayt*. Kuwait: al-Jam'iyya al-Kuwatiyya li-l-Dirasat wa-l-Buhuth al-Takhassusiyya, 1999.

Al-Hadaf. "Bayt li-Kul Muwatin Khilal Hatha al-'Aam." September 18, 1963.*

Al-Hijji, Yacoub Yusuf. *Kuwait and the Sea: A Brief Economic History*. London: Arabian, 2010.

Alissa, Reem. "Modernizing Kuwait: Nation-Building and Unplanned Spatial Practices." *Berkeley Planning Journal* 22, no. 1 (2009): 85–91.

———. "The Oil Town of Ahmadi since 1946: From Colonial Town to Nostalgic City." *Comparative Studies of South Asia, Africa and the Middle East* 33, no. 1 (2013): 41–58.

Al-Jassim, Najat. *Baladiyyat al-Kuwayt fi Khamsin 'Aamman*. Kuwait: Kuwait Municipality, 1993.

---

* These articles are filed at the newspaper archive of the Center for Gulf and Arabian Peninsula Studies at Kuwait University (Shuwaikh Campus).

Al-Jenfawi, Khaled. "Kuwait Constitution Protects Freedom of Religion." *Arab Times*, April 12, 2012.

Al-Khars, Mohammed, and Mariam al-Aqruqah. *Al-Bayt al-Kuwayty al-Qadim*. Kuwait: Centre for Research and Studies on Kuwait, 2003.

Al-Khatib, Ahmed. *Al-Kuwayt: Min al-Imara ila al-Dawla: Dhikrayat al-'Amal al-Watany wa-l-Qawmy*. Beirut: Al-Markaz al-Thaqafy al-'Araby, 2007.

Al-Mohameed, Bassam. "Al-Quyud wa-l-Azma fi Buyut Dhuwy al-Dakhal al-Mahdud." *Al-Risala*, May 18, 1975.*

Al-Moosa, Abdulrasool. "Kuwait: Changing Environment in a Geographical Perspective." *British Society for Middle Eastern Studies Bulletin* 11, no. 1 (1984): 45–57.

Al-Mosully, Suhair. "Revitalizing Kuwait's Empty City Center." MSc thesis, Massachusetts Institute of Technology, 1992.

Al-Mubaraki, Yousef Mubarak. *Hin Isti'ad al-Sha'b al-Kuwayty Dusturahu: Waqa'i' wa Watha'iq Diwawin al-Ithnayn 1990–1986*. Kuwait: Kuwait National Bookshop, 2008.

Al-Mughni, Haya. *Women in Kuwait: The Politics of Gender*. London: Saqi Books, 2001.

Al-Mutairi, Mousa. "Min Yiwaqif al-'Udwan 'ala Jamal al-Madina?" *Al-Nahda*, December 23, 1989.*

Al-Mutawa, Subhi Abdullah. *Kuwait City Parks: A Critical Review of their Design Facilities Programs and Management*. London: Kegan Paul International, 1985.

Al-Nahda. "Shiqaq Sakaniyya li-Dhuwy al-Dakhal al-Mahdud!" May 30, 1980.*

Al-Najjar, Ghanim. "Decision-Making Process in Kuwait: The Land Acquisition Policy as a Case Study." PhD thesis, University of Exeter, 1984.

Al-Nakib, Farah. "The Lost 'Two-Thirds': Kuwait's Territorial Decline Between 1913 and 1922." *Journal of Arabian Studies* 2, no. 1 (June 2012): 19–37.

———. "Kuwait's Modern Spectacle: Oil Wealth and the Making of a New Capital City, 1950–90." *Comparative Studies of South Asia, Africa and the Middle East* 33, no. 1 (2013): 7–25.

———. "Revisiting Hadar and Badu in Kuwait: Citizenship, Housing, and the Construction of a Dichotomy." *International Journal of Middle East Studies* 46, no. 1 (2014): 5–30.

———. "Towards an Urban Alternative for Kuwait: Protests and Public Participation." *Built Environment* 40, no. 1 (2014): 101–17.

———. "Public Space and Public Protest in Kuwait, 1938–2012." *City* 18, no. 6 (2014): 723–34.

———. "Inside a Gulf Port: The Dynamics of Urban Life in Pre-Oil Kuwait." In *The Persian Gulf in Modern Times: People, Ports, and History*, edited by Lawrence Potter, 199–229. New York: Palgrave Macmillan, 2014.

Al-Nakib, Mai. "Outside in the National Machine: The Case of Kuwait." *Strategies* 13, no. 2 (2000): 201–20.

———. "'The People Are Missing': Palestinians in Kuwait." *Deleuze Studies* 8, no. 1 (2014): 23–44.

Al-Nakib, Rania. "Education and Democratic Development in Kuwait: Citizens in Waiting." Chatham House Research Paper: Future Trends in the GCC, April 2015.

Al-Qabas. "Lawhat Jidariyya 'ala al-Jusur Bi'aydin Fanniya Kuwaytiyya." December 20, 1986.*

———. "Al-Qabas Tansher Tajmil Muthalath al-Hilali—Fahad al-Salem—Abdullah al-Salem." December 27, 1986.*

———. "Limatha la Takun al-Kuwayt Jamila Aydan?" May 18, 1987.*

———. "Iftitah Mashru' Sahat al-Safat 20 al-Jary." February 17, 1988.*

———. "Sahat al-Safat: Tarikh al-Ajyal." November 5, 1993.*

———. "Al-Safat: Awwal wa Ashhur al-Sahat fi al-Kuwayt." March 16, 1995.*

———. "Al-'Asimah: Jarrat al-Bahar al-Mansiya." 10 parts. Part 1: Bara Antoon, November 29, 1996; part 2: Mohammed Zakariya, November 30, 1996; part 3: Mohammed Zakariya, December 2, 1996; part 4: Mohammed Zakariya and Zainab Abdelhadi, December 3, 1996; part 5: Adnan Makawi and Ahmed al-Failakawi, December 4, 1996; part 6: Bara Antoon, December 5, 1996; part 7: Bara Antoon, December 6, 1996; part 8: Faleh al-Fadli and Ahmed al-Failakawi, December 7, 1996; part 9: Ahmed al-Failakawi and Mubarak Abdelhadi, December 8, 1996; part 10: Mubarak Abdelhadi, December 9, 1996.*

Al-Qina'i, Yousef bin Issa. *Safhat min Tarikh al-Kuwayt.* Cairo: Dar Sa'ad Misr, 1946.

Al-Rai al-'Aam. "Lajnat al-'Ara'idh wa-l-Shakawy Tuwasy Biziyadat Qurudh Dhuwy al-Dakhal al-Mahdud ila 'Ashrat Alaf Dinar." August 6, 1976.*

———. "Al-Majlis al-Balady: Iqtirahan min al-Zamel wa-l-'Obayd li-l-'Inayah bi-l-'Asima wa-l-Sawahel." July 16, 1986.*

Al-Rashed, Sa'ud. "Al-Masakin al-Sha'biyya." *Al-Talee'a,* June 12, 1985.*

Al-Rushaid, Abdulaziz. *Tarikh al-Kuwayt.* Kuwait: Qurtas, 1999. Originally published 1929.

Al-Saeed, Mustafa. "Matlub Waqfa li-Muwajahat al-Khatar al-Jadid al-Lathy Yushawwih Jamal al-Kuwayt." *Al-Nahda,* December 23, 1989.*

Al-Salamah, Jasim Mohammed. *Lamhat min Tarikh 'Ashirat al-Bin'ali al-'Utbiyya wa Ba'dh al-Usar al-Kuwaytiyya al-Qadimah al-Muntasiba Laha.* Kuwait: privately published, 2004.

Al-Salmiya. "Al-Salmiya Bayn al-Madhi wa-l-Hader." February 1981.*

Al-Shamlan, Saif. *Pearling in the Arabian Gulf: A Personal Memoir.* London: The London Centre of Arab Studies, 2001. Originally published in Arabic in 1975.

Al-Shaybani, Mohammed and Barrak al-Mutairi, eds. *Al-Watha'iq al-Asliyya.* Kuwait: Markaz al-Makhtutat wa-l-Turath wa-l-Watha'iq, 1994.

Al-Siyasa. "Ma'a Qarar al-Majlis al-Balady bi-Ikhla' al-Dawr fi al-Manatiq al-Namouthaji-yya." May 26, 1973.*

Al-Sultan, Mansour. "Naher Tabib Amam Ruwwad Mujama' al-Avenues." *Annahar,* December 23, 2012.

Al-Talee'a. "Buyut Dhuwy al-Dakhal al-Mahdud." March 6, 1971.*

Al-Watan. "Al-Qu'ood: Istighlal Mamarrat Sahat al-Safat li-'Ardh Muntajat al-Masane'." January 16, 1990.*

Al-Yaqaza. Untitled. June 21, 1990.*

Al-Zouman, Sarah, Sarah al-Fraih, and Deema al-Ghunaim. "Local Knowledge: An Empirical Approach to Practice." Paper presented at the 2nd Gulf Studies Symposium, "Knowledge-Based Development in the Gulf," American University of Kuwait, March 2015.

Amin, Ash, and Nigel Thrift. *Cities: Reimagining the Urban*. Malden, UK: Blackwell, 2007.

Arab Times. "Awazem Storm Scope TV Over Interview with Qallaf." March 19, 2012.

———. "Lebanese Doctor Stabbed to Death at Avenues." December 22, 2012.

"Architecture in Gulf Countries: Kuwait." *Albenaa* 8, no. 47 (April/May 1989): 6–11, 14–47.

Arthur Erickson Architects. *The Sawaber Project Development Study*. Kuwait: National Housing Authority, 1977.

Assiri, Abdul-Reda. *Kuwait's Foreign Policy: City-State in World Politics*. Boulder, CO: Westview Press, 1990.

Banks, R. L. "Notes on a Visit to Kuwait." *Town Planning Review* 26, no. 1 (April 1955), 48–50.

Bazaar. "Mubarakiya: The Old and the New." February 2015.

Benjamin, Walter. *Selected Writings*. Volume 2, Part 1, *1927–1930*, edited by Michael W. Jennings, Howard Eiland, and Gary Smith. Cambridge, MA: Belknap Press, 2005.

Bennett, Arthur K. "A New Beginning at Kuweit." *Neglected Arabia*, no. 73 (1910): 12–15 (vol. 2).

Broeze, Frank. "Kuwait Before Oil: The Dynamics and Morphology of an Arab Port City." In *Gateways of Asia: Port Cities of Asia in the 13th–20th Centuries*, edited by Frank Broeze, 149–90. London: Kegan Paul International, 1997.

Brucks, George Barnes. "Memoir, Description of the Navigation of the Gulf of Persia, with Brief Notices of the Manners, Customs, Religion, Commerce, and Resources of the People Inhabiting Its Shores and Islands." Reprinted in *Arabian Gulf Intelligence: Selection from the Records of the Bombay Government*, New Series, No. XXIV, 1856, edited by R. Hughes Thomas. Cambridge, UK: Oleander Press, 1986.

Brydges, Harford Jones. *An Account of the Transactions of His Majesty's Mission to the Court of Persia in the Years 1807–1811, to Which is Appended "A Brief History of the Wahauby."* London: James Bohnm, 1834.

Buckingham, J. S. *Travels in Assyria, Media, and Persia, Including a Journey from Bagdad by Mount Zagros, to Hamadan, the Ancient Ecbatana, Researches in Ispahan and the Ruins of Persepolis, and Journey from Thence by Shiraz and Shapoor to the Sea-Shore. Description of Bussorah, Bushire, Bahrein, Ormuz, and Muscat, Narrative of an Expedition Against the Pirates of the Persian Gulf, with Illustrations of the Voyage of Nearchus, and Passage by the Arabian Sea to Bombay*. London: Henry Colburn and Richard Bentley, 1829.

Caldeira, Teresa. *City of Walls: Crime, Segregation, and Citizenship in São Paulo*. Berkeley: University of California Press, 2000.

Calderwood, James. "Fifty Years on from Kuwait's Birth, Arguments Still Rage Over Who Is Kuwaiti." *National*, February 23, 2011.

Calverley, Edwin. "The Trial by Ordeal in Arabia." *Neglected Arabia*, no. 107 (1918): 3–8 (vol. 4).

———. "Education in Kuwait." *Neglected Arabia*, no. 142 (1927): 12–15 (vol. 5).

Calverley, Eleanor. "Progress." *Neglected Arabia*, no. 103 (1917): 6–8 (vol. 3).

———. *My Arabian Days and Nights*. New York: Thomas Y. Cromwell, 1958.

Candilis, Georges. "Kuwait." No date (c. 1971).

Cartwright, Alan. "Kuwait Creates a Suburbia." *Middle East Construction* 5, no. 12 (December 1980): 47–49.

Case, Paul Edward. "Boom Time in Kuwait." *National Geographic Magazine*, December 1952.

Citino, Nathan. "Suburbia and Modernization: Community Building and America's Post-World War II Encounter with the Arab Middle East." *Arab Studies Journal* 13/14, no. 2/1 (2005/2006): 39–64.

Central Bank of Kuwait. *The Kuwaiti Economy in Ten Years: Economic Report for the Period 1969–1979*. Kuwait: Central Bank, 1979.

"Chronology: January 16, 1988–April15, 1988." *Middle East Journal* 42, no. 3 (1988): 447–78.

Cohen, Margaret. "Modernity on the Waterfront: The Case of Haussman's Paris." In *Urban Imaginaries: Locating the Modern City*, edited by Alev Çinar and Thomas Bender, 55–75. London: University of Minnesota Press, 2007.

Colin Buchanan and Partners. *Studies for a National Physical Plan for the State of Kuwait and Master Plan for the Urban Areas*. Kuwait: Kuwait Municipality, 1968–1971. Includes the following reports:

Final Draft Interim Report (March 1970).

First Report: The Long Term Strategy (March 1970).

Second Report: The Short Term Plan. Volume 1, *Introduction and the National Physical Plan* (December 1971).

Second Report: The Short Term Plan. Volume 2, *Structure Plan for the Urban Areas* (December 1971).

Second Report: The Short Term Plan. Volume 3, *Kuwait Town Plan and Plan Implementation* (December 1971).

Technical Paper 18: Housing in Kuwait (October 1969).

Technical Paper 32: Government Accommodation (May 1970).

Technical Paper 37: Landscape (prepared by G. P. Youngman, August 1970).

Technical Note OA. 18: New Housing: The Bedouin Sector (August 1970).

Technical Note OA. 24: Housing: The Non-Bedouin Sector (September 1970).

Technical Note KT. 21: Housing in Kuwait Town (September 1970).

———. "Kuwait." *Architects' Journal* 159, no. 21 (May 1974): 1131–32.

———. *Master Plan for Kuwait: Second Review*. Volume 1, *Planning and Policy*. Kuwait: Kuwait Municipality, 1983.

Connah, Roger. "The Seif Palace Extension." *Living Architecture* 5 (1986): 128–31.

Cornn, Michael. "Ma Salaama, Part 2: Looking Back." Kuwait: Michal Cornn's Travels and Trials in Kuwait (blog), August 5, 2005. http://expat.typepad.com/kuwait/2005/08/ma_salaama_part_1.html.

Cullen, Jim. *The American Dream: A Short History of an Idea That Shaped a Nation*. Oxford, UK: Oxford University Press, 2003.

Crystal, Jill. *Oil and Politics in the Gulf: Rulers and Merchants in Kuwait and Qatar*. Cambridge, UK: Cambridge University Press, 1995.

Dalley, Ken. "Kuwait: Into its Second Building Boom." *RIBA Journal* 85, no. 11 (November 1978): 459–80.

Davis, Mike. *City of Quartz: Excavating the Future in Los Angeles.* New York: Vintage Books, 1992.

De Certeau, Michel. *The Practice of Everyday Life,* translated by Steven Rendall. Berkeley: University of California Press, 1988.

De Jong, Everdene (Mrs. Garrett). "The Ubiquitous Gasoline Tin." *Neglected Arabia,* no. 153 (1930): 10–11 (vol. 5).

Dehrab, Saif Abbas. "Childhood in the Sand." In *Remembering Childhood in the Middle East: Memoirs from a Century of Change,* edited by Elizabeth Warnock Fernea, 177–95. Austin: University of Texas Press, 2002.

Dennis, Richard. *Cities in Modernity: Representations and Productions of Metropolitan Space, 1840–1930.* Cambridge, UK: Cambridge University Press, 2008.

Devecon. *Safat Square: Preliminary Design Report.* Kuwait: Kuwait Municipality, 1982.

Dickson, Violet. *Forty Years in Kuwait.* London: George Allen & Unwin, 1971.

Dowding, H. H. *Koweit: A Report.* Simla: Government of India, 1903.

Elsheshtawy, Yasser. "The Great Divide: Struggling and Emerging Cities in the Arab World." In *The Evolving Arab City: Tradition, Modernity and Urban Development,* edited by Yasser Elsheshtawy, 1–26. London: Routledge, 2008.

Facey, William, and Gillian Grant. *Kuwait by the First Photographers.* London: I. B. Tauris, 1998.

Fattah, Hala. *The Politics of Regional Trade in Iraq, Arabia, and the Gulf, 1745–1900.* Albany: State University of New York Press, 1997.

Ffrench, Geoffrey E., and Allan G. Hill. *Kuwait Urban and Medical Ecology: A Geomedical Study.* Berlin: Springer-Verlag, 1971.

Freeth, Zahra. *A New Look at Kuwait.* London: George Allen & Unwin, 1972.

———. *Kuwait Was My Home.* London: George Allen & Unwin, 1956.

Freund, David M. *Colored Property: State Policy and White Racial Politics in Suburban America.* Chicago: University of Chicago Press, 2007.

Fuccaro, Nelida. *Histories of City and State in the Persian Gulf: Manama Since 1800.* Cambridge, UK: Cambridge University Press, 2009.

———. "Pearl Towns and Early Oil Cities: Migration and Integration in the Arab Coast of the Persian Gulf." In *The City in the Ottoman Empire: Migration and the Making of Urban Modernity,* edited by Ulrike Freitag, Malte Fuhrmann, Nora Lafi, and Florian Riedler, 99–116. London: Routledge, 2011.

Fuller, Ana Lescenko, and Robert Home. "On the Planning History of Chelmsford." Papers in Land Management No. 9. Chelmsford: Anglia Ruskin University, 2007.

Gallo, Marcia M. *No One Helped: Kitty Genovese, New York City, and the Myth of Urban Apathy.* Ithaca, NY: Cornell University Press, 2015.

Gardiner, Stephen. *Kuwait: The Making of a City.* Essex, UK: Longman Group Ltd., 1983.

Gardner, Andrew. *City of Strangers: Gulf Migration and the Indian Community in Bahrain.* Ithaca, NY: Cornell University Press, 2010.

Ghabra, Shafeeq. "The Iraqi Occupation of Kuwait: An Eyewitness Account." *Journal of Palestine Studies* 20, no. 2 (1991): 112–25.

———. "Voluntary Associations in Kuwait: The Foundation of a New System?" *Middle East Journal* 45, no. 2 (Spring 1991): 199–215.

Grill, N. C. *Urbanisation in the Arabian Peninsula.* Occasional Papers Series 25. Durham, NC: Centre for Middle Eastern and Islamic Studies, 1984.

Grindrod, John. "Model City Planned for Kuwait." *Official Architecture and Planning* 16, no. 8 (August 1953): 374–78.

Habermas, Jürgen. *The Structural Transformation of the Public Sphere: An Inquiry into a Category of Bourgeois Society*, translated by Thomas Burger and Frederick Lawrence. Cambridge, MA: MIT Press, 1989.

Harper, Justin. "Kuwait to Push Out 1 Million Expats in Next 10 Years." *Telegraph*, March 26, 2013.

Harrison, W. "Our Medical Work." *Neglected Arabia*, no. 88 (1914): 10–13 (vol. 3).

Harvey, David. *The Condition of Postmodernity.* Oxford, UK: Blackwell, 1990.

———. *Social Justice and the City.* Athens: University of Georgia Press, 2009.

———. *Rebel Cities: From the Right to the City to the Urban Revolution.* London: Verso, 2012.

Hay, Rupert. "The Impact of the Oil Industry on the Persian Gulf Shaykhdoms." *Middle East Journal* 9, no. 4 (1955): 361–72.

Herb, Michael. *The Wages of Oil: Parliaments and Economic Development in Kuwait and the UAE.* Ithaca, NY: Cornell University Press, 2014.

Holod, Renata, and Darl Rastorfer. "Water Towers." In *Architecture and Community*, edited by Renata Holod and Darl Rastorfer, 173–80. New York: Aperture, 1983.

Holston, James. *The Modernist City: An Anthropological Critique of Brasilia.* Chicago: University of Chicago Press, 1989.

———, ed. *Cities and Citizenship.* Durham, NC: Duke University Press, 1999.

Holston, James, and Arjun Appadurai. "Introduction: Cities and Citizenship." In Holston, *Cities and Citizenship*, 1–18.

Hussain, Abdulaziz. "Al-Nahda al-Murtaqibah." *Al-Bi'tha*, March 1950.

International Bank for Reconstruction and Development. *The Economic Development of Kuwait.* Baltimore: Johns Hopkins University Press, 1965.

Izzak, B., and Abdellatif Sharaa. "Enraged Tribesmen Torch Juwaihel's Election Tent." *Kuwait Times*, January 31, 2012.

Frieden, Bernard J., and Lynne Sagalyn. *Downtown, Inc.: How America Rebuilds Cities.* Boston: MIT Press, 1991.

Jacobs, Jane. *The Death and Life of Great American Cities.* New York: Modern Library, 1993.

Jamal, Karim. "Kuwait: A Salutary Tale." *Architects' Journal* 158, no. 50 (December 1973): 1452–57.

Jamal, Mohammed Abdulhadi. *Al-Hiraf wa-l-Mihan wa-l-Anshita al-Tijariyya al-Qadima fi al-Kuwayt.* Kuwait: Centre for Research and Studies on Kuwait, 2003.

———. *Aswaq al-Kuwayt al-Qadimah.* Kuwait: Centre for Research and Studies on Kuwait, 2004.

Jensen, Svend. "Competition for Township at Sulaibikhat, Kuwait." *ARUP Journal* 12, no. 3 (September 1977): 16–20.

Jones, Felix. "Extracts from a Report on the Harbour of Grane (or Koweit) and the Island of Pheleechi, in the Persian Gulf (1839)." Reprinted in *Arabian Gulf Intelligence: Selection from the Records of the Bombay Government*, New Series, No. XXIV, 1856, edited by R. Hughes Thomas. Cambridge, UK: Oleander Press, 1986.

Kanna, Ahmed. *Dubai: The City as Corporation.* Minneapolis: University of Minnesota Press, 2011.

———, ed. *The Superlative City: Dubai and the Urban Condition in the Early Twenty-First Century.* Boston: Harvard Graduate School of Design, 2013.

Kanna, Ahmed, and Arang Keshavarzian. "The UAE's Space Race: Sheikhs and Starchitects Envision the Future." *Middle East Report* 248 (2008): 34–39.

Kapenga, Jay. "A Shop on Main Street." *Neglected Arabia*, no. 211 (1947): 12–14 (vol. 7).

Kelly, Barbara. *Expanding the American Dream: Building and Rebuilding Levittown.* New York: SUNY Press, 1993.

Kemball, A. B. "Memoranda on the Resources, Localities, and Relations of the Tribes Inhabiting the Arabian Shores of the Persian Gulf (1845)." Reprinted in *Arabian Gulf Intelligence: Selection from the Records of the Bombay Government*, New Series, No. XXIV, 1856, edited by R. Hughes Thomas. Cambridge, UK: Oleander Press, 1986.

———. "Statistical and Miscellaneous Information Connected with the Possessions, Revenues, Families, &c. of His Highness the Imaum of Muskat; of the Ruler of Bahrain; and of the Chiefs of the Maritime Arab States in the Persian Gulf (1854)." Reprinted in *Arabian Gulf Intelligence: Selection from the Records of the Bombay Government*, New Series, No. XXIV, 1856, edited by R. Hughes Thomas. Cambridge, UK: Oleander Press, 1986.

Khalaf, Sulayman. "The Nationalisation of Culture: Kuwait's Invention of a Pearl-Diving Heritage." In *Popular Culture and Political Identity in the Arab Gulf States*, edited by Alanoud Alsharekh and Robert Springborg, 40–70. London: Saqi, 2008.

Khalfallah, Junaidy. "Tatawwur al-Maskan al-Kuwayty." *Majallat al-Kuwayt* 16 (September 1969).*

Khattab, Omar. "Socio-Spatial Analysis of Traditional Kuwaiti Houses." In *Methodologies in Housing Research*, edited by D. U. Vestbro, Y. Hurol, and N. Wilkinson, 141–58. Tyne and Wear, UK: Urban International Press, 2005.

Khaz'al, Mohammed. "Al-Houti: 8 Malayin Dinar li-Tajmil al-Arsifah." *Al-Watan*, October 14, 1987.*

Kofman, Eleonore, and Elizabeth Lebas. "Lost in Transposition—Time, Space, and the City." In *Writings on Cities*, by Henri Lefebvre, translated by Eleonore Kofman and Elizabeth Lebas, 3–60. Oxford, UK: Blackwell, 1996.

Konvitz, Josef. *Cities and the Sea: Port City Planning in Early Modern Europe.* Baltimore: Johns Hopkins University Press, 1978.

Kuwait Engineers Office. *Sharq al-Seif Area Planning and Schematic Design, Phase I.* Kuwait: Kuwait Municipality, July 1986; revised February 1987.

Kuwait Ministry of Planning. *Annual Statistical Abstract.* 1966.

Kuwait Mission. "The Annual Report of the Arabian Mission." *Neglected Arabia*, no. 140 (1927) (vol. 5).

————. "Annual Report of the Arabian Mission for the Year 1930–1931." *Neglected Arabia*, no. 161 (1932) (vol. 6).

————. "Annual Report of the Arabian Mission for the Year 1932." *Neglected Arabia*, no. 164 (1933) (vol. 6).

————. "Annual Report of the Arabian Mission for the Year 1937." *Neglected Arabia*, no. 181 (1938) (vol. 6).

————. "Annual Report of the Arabian Mission for the Year 1938." *Neglected Arabia*, no. 185 (1939) (vol. 6).

Kuwait Municipality. *Planning and Urban Development in Kuwait*. Kuwait: Kuwait Municipality, 1980.

Kuwait Municipality, Department of Master Planning. "Social-Residential Survey for the State of Kuwait." "Technical Paper Two: Pilot Survey Direct Tabulations." July 1971.

Kuwait Municipality, Master Planning Committee and Advisory Group. "Reactions to the C.B.P. Draft Report on the Short Term Plan of Kuwait." March 1971.

Kuwait News Agency. "Kuwait Speaker Defends Juwaihel Arrest Remarks." December 27, 2009.

————. "Interior Ministry to Adopt New System to Protect Shopping Malls." September 29, 2013.

Lefebvre, Henri. *The Production of Space*, translated by Donald Nicholson-Smith. Oxford, UK: Blackwell, 1991.

————. *Introduction to Modernity*, translated by John Moore. London: Verso, 1995.

————. *Writings on Cities*, translated by Eleonore Kofman and Elizabeth Lebas. Oxford, UK: Blackwell, 1996.

Le Renard, Amélie. *A Society of Young Women: Opportunities of Place, Power, and Reform in Saudi Arabia*. Stanford, CA: Stanford University Press, 2014.

Lewcock, Ronald, and Zahra Freeth. *Traditional Architecture in Kuwait and the Northern Gulf*. London: Archaeology Research Papers, 1978.

Lienhardt, Peter. *Disorientations: A Society in Flux, Kuwait in the 1950s*, edited by Ahmed al-Shahi. Reading, UK: Ithaca Press, 1993.

————. *Shaikhdoms of Eastern Arabia*, edited by Ahmed al-Shahi. Basingstoke, UK: Palgrave, 2001.

Limbert, Mandana. *In the Time of Oil: Piety, Memory, and Social Life in an Omani Town*. Stanford, CA: Stanford University Press, 2010.

Lindt, A. R. "Politics in the Persian Gulf." *Royal Central Asian Journal* 26 (1939): 619–33.

Longva, Anh Nga. *Walls Built on Sand: Migration, Exclusion, and Society in Kuwait*. Boulder, CO: Westview Press, 1997.

Lorimer, John G. *The Gazetteer of the Persian Gulf, Oman and Central Arabia*. Volume 2, *Geographical and Statistical*. Calcutta: Office of the Superintendent Government Printing, 1908. Reprinted by Gerrards Cross, UK: Archive Editions, 1986.

Mahgoub, Yasser. "Globalization and the Built Environment in Kuwait." *Habitat International* 28 (2004): 505–19.

————. "Kuwait: Learning from a Globalized City." In *The Evolving Arab City: Tradi-

tion, Modernity and Urban Development, edited by Yasser Elsheshtawy, 152–83. London: Routledge, 2008.

Majallat Souwt al-Khalij. "Al-Ma'sat Allaty Ya'eeshaha Dhuw al-Dakhal al-Mahdud." January 9, 1964.*

———. "Al-Asil wa-l-Sura fi-l-Kuwayt." January 20, 1964.*

Marcus, Abraham. *The Middle East on the Eve of Modernity: Aleppo in the Eighteenth Century.* New York: Columbia University Press, 1989.

McCann, Eugene. "Race, Protest, and Public Space: Contextualizing Lefebvre in the U.S. City." *Antipode* 32, no. 1 (1999): 163–84.

Meller, Helen. *Towns, Plans and Society in Modern Britain.* Cambridge, UK: Cambridge University Press, 1997.

Menoret, Pascal. *Joyriding in Riyadh: Oil, Urbanism, and Road Revolt.* Cambridge, UK: Cambridge University Press, 2014.

Merrifield, Andy. *Henri Lefebvre: A Critical Introduction.* New York: Routledge, 2006.

Minoprio, Anthony, Hugh Spencely, and P. W. Macfarlane. "Plan for the Town of Kuwait: Report to His Highness Shaikh Abdullah Assalim Assubah, C.I.E., the Amir of Kuwait." November 1951.

———. "Planning Problems of Kuwait." *Architect and Building News*, July 26, 1951, 104.

———. "Town Planning in Kuwait." *Architectural Design*, October 1953, 272–81.

Murphey, Rhoads. "On the Evolution of the Port City." In *Brides of the Sea: Port Cities of Asia from the 16th to 20th Centuries*, edited by Frank Broeze, 223–45. Kensington: New South Wales University Press, 1989.

Musa'ed, Mutlaq. "Ma Huwa al-Sir Wara' Ta'jir al-Buyut al-Hukumiyya wa Fillat wa Malahiq Ashab al-Qasa'im?" *Al-Siyasa*, January 20, 1974.*

Mylrea, Bessie A. "Working for Kuwait's Women." *Neglected Arabia*, no. 92 (1915): 10–12 (vol. 3).

———. "Picnics in Koweit," *Neglected Arabia*, no. 99 (1916): 5–7 (vol. 3).

Mylrea, C. Stanley G. "A Council of War." *Neglected Arabia*, no. 88 (1914): 3–6 (vol. 3).

———. "Lord Hardinge, the Viceroy of India, Comes to Kuwait." *Neglected Arabia*, no. 94 (1915): 11–14 (vol. 3).

———. "Annual Report of Men's Medical Department, Kuweit." *Neglected Arabia*, no. 96 (1916): 12–16 (vol. 3).

———. "Encouraging Evangelistic Work at Kuwait." *Neglected Arabia*, no. 100 (1917): 15–18 (vol. 3)

———. "Medievalism in Arabia." *Neglected Arabia*, no. 158 (1931): 13–15 (vol. 6).

———. "Kuwait Before Oil." Unpublished memoirs, 1945–1951. Middle East Centre Archives, St. Antony's College, University of Oxford (GB165–0214).

Naseef, Munir. "Shawati' al-Kuwayt." *Al-'Araby*, August 1974.

National. "Police Clash with Kuwaiti Tribesmen Who Storm TV Station." February 1, 2012.

Nayef, Munaif. "Mall Stabbing Kills Teenager." *Arab Times*, August 15, 2015.

Niebuhr, Carsten. *Travels Through Arabia and Other Countries in the East*, translated by Robert Heron. Edinburgh: R. Morison, 1792. Originally published 1776–1780 in Dutch.

Olayan, Hamza Salman, and Asem al-Bi'aini. *Yahud al-Kuwayt Waqa'i' wa Ahdath: Dirasa Hawla Hijrat Yahud al-'Aalam al-'Araby.* Kuwait: That al-Salasil, 2012.

Parkyn, Neil. "Kuwait Revisited: Showplace for the World's Architectural Prima Donnas." *Middle East Construction* 8, no. 9 (September 1983): 39–42.

Pelly, Lewis. "Recent Tour Round the Northern Portion of the Persian Gulf." In *Transactions of the Bombay Geographical Society.* Volume 17, *January 1863–December 1864.* Bombay: Education Society's Press, 1865.

———. "Remarks on the Tribes, Trade and Resources Around the Shore Line of the Persian Gulf." In *Transactions of the Bombay Geographical Society.* Volume 17, *January 1863–December 1864.* Bombay: Education Society's Press, 1865.

———. *Report on a Journey to Riyadh in Central Arabia.* Cambridge, UK: Oldeander, 1865.

Povah, J. R. *Gazetteer of Arabia.* Calcutta: Government of India, 1887.

Potter, Lawrence, ed. *The Persian Gulf in Modern Times: People, Ports, and History.* New York: Palgrave Macmillan, 2014.

Prakash, Gyan. "Introduction." In *The Spaces of the Modern City: Imaginaries, Politics, and Everyday Life,* edited by Gyan Prakash and Kevin M. Kruse, 1–18. Princeton, NJ: Princeton University Press, 2008.

"Proposals for Restructuring Kuwait." *Architectural Review* 156, no. 931 (September 1974): 178–190.

Raunkiaer, Barclay. *Through Wahhabiland on Camelback.* London: Routledge & Kegan Paul, 1969. Originally published in Danish in 1913.

Rihani, Amin. *Muluk al-'Arab.* Beirut: Scientific Printing Press, 1990.

Rush, Alan. *Al-Sabah: History and Genealogy of Kuwait's Ruling Family, 1752–1987.* London: Ithaca Press, 1987.

Sadik, Rula Muhammad. "Nation-Building and Housing Policy: A Comparative Analysis of Urban Housing Development in Kuwait, Jordan, and Lebanon." PhD diss., University of California, Berkeley, 1996.

Scott, James. *Seeing Like a State: How Certain Schemes to Improve the Human Condition Have Failed.* New Haven, CT: Yale University Press, 1998.

Scudder, Lewis. "May Your Feat Be Blessed." *Neglected Arabia,* no. 194 (1941): 14–15 (vol. 7).

Scudder, Lewis III. *The Arabian Mission's Story: In Search of Abraham's Other Son.* Grand Rapids, MI: Eerdmans, 1998.

Sennett, Richard. *The Fall of Public Man.* London: Penguin Books, 2002.

———. *The Uses of Disorder: Personal Identity and City Life.* New Haven: Yale University Press, 2008.

Shankland Cox Partnership. *Master Plan for Kuwait: First Review.* Volume 1, *Planning and Policy.* Kuwait: Kuwait Municipality, 1977.

Shehab, Fakhri. "Kuwait: A Super-Affluent Society." *Foreign Affairs,* April 1964. https://www.foreignaffairs.com/articles/kuwait/1964-04-01/kuwait-super-affluent-society.

Shiber, Saba George. *The Kuwait Urbanization: Being an Urbanistic Case-Study of a Developing Country—Documentation, Analysis, Critique.* Kuwait: Kuwait Government Printing Press, 1964.

Shihab, Yousef. "Al-Haraka al-Ta'awuniyya fi-l-Kuwayt." *Al-'Araby,* January 1983.

Shuaib, Hamid. "Urban Development of Kuwait." *Alam Albena* 98 (1989): 4–5.

Simon, Reeva. "The Imposition of Nationalism on a Non-Nation State: The Case of Iraq During the Interwar Period, 1921–1941." In *Rethinking Nationalism in the Arab Middle East*, edited by James Jankowski and Israel Gershoni, 87–104. New York: Columbia University Press, 1997.

SSH (Salem al-Marzouk and Sabah Abi-Hanna). *Third Kuwait Master Plan. Summary: The Framework for Kuwait's Development*. Kuwait: Kuwait Municipality, June 1997.

Stanek, Łukasz. *Henri Lefebvre on Space: Architecture, Urban Research, and the Production of Theory*. Minneapolis: University of Minnesota Press, 2011.

Stark, Freya. *Baghdad Sketches*. London: John Murray, 1947.

Starling, Shane. "World's Most Obese Nation? Kuwait (and the Next Four Are Middle Eastern)." Nutraingredients.com, November 3, 2014. http://www.nutraingredients.com/Suppliers2/World-s-most-obese-nation-Kuwait-and-the-next-four-are-Middle-Eastern.

Stocqueler, J. H. *Fifteen Months Pilgrimage Through Untrodden Tracts of Khuzistan and Persia, in a Journey from India to England Through Parts of Turksih Arabia, Russia, and Germany Performed in the Years 1831 and 1832*. London: Saunders and Otley, 1832.

Sultan, Ghazi. "Notes from the and on the Municipality of Kuwait." Unpublished writings from October 1968 to October 1971 (Sultan family archive).

———. "Kuwait." *Architects' Journal* 160, no. 40 (October 1974): 792–94.

———. "Designing for New Needs in Kuwait." In *Toward an Architecture in the Spirit of Islam*, edited by Renata Holod, 94. Philadelphia: The Aga Khan Award for Architecture, 1978.

———. "Criteria for Design in the Arabian Gulf Region." *Arabian Journal for Science and Engineering* 7, no. 2 (1982): 165–71.

Taylor, Brian Brace. "Kuwait City Waterfront Development." *MIMAR* 34 (January 1990): 13–20.

Telegraph. "Speeding? That's Deportation for You . . . Kuwait Targets Its Expat Population." May 19, 2013.

Tétreault, Mary Ann. "Civil Society in Kuwait: Protected Spaces and Women's Rights." *Middle East Journal* 47, no. 2 (Spring 1993): 275–91.

———. *Stories of Democracy: Politics and Society in Contemporary Kuwait*. New York: Columbia University Press, 2000.

Tonkiss, Fran. *Space, the City and Social Theory: Social Relations and Urban Forms*. Cambridge, UK: Polity Press, 2005.

Toumi, Habib. "Minister Seeks Kuwait House Approval to Monitor Blogs." *Gulf News*, December 23, 2009.

———. "Kuwait Has World's Highest Water Consumption." *Gulf News*, April 25, 2011.

———. "Kuwait to Deport Expats Over Illegal Barbecuing." *Gulf News*, December 28, 2014.

Vale, Lawrence. *Architecture, Power, and National Identity*. New Haven, CT: Yale University Press, 1992.

Villiers, Alan. *Sons of Sindbad*. London: Arabian, 2006. Originally published 1940.

Vora, Neha. *Impossible Subjects: Dubai's Indian Diaspora*. Durham, NC: Duke University Press, 2013.

Warden, Francis. "Historical Sketch of the Uttoobee Tribe of Arabs (Bahrein); from the Year 1716 to the Year 1817." Reprinted in *Arabian Gulf Intelligence:Selection from the Records of the Bombay Government*, New Series, No. XXIV, 1856, edited by R. Hughes Thomas. Cambridge, UK: Oleander Press, 1986.

Young, Robert J. C. "Postcolonial Remains." *New Literary History* 43, no. 1 (2012): 19–42.

Za'balawy, Yousef. "Al-Jam'iyyat Alta'awuniyya bi-l-Kuwayt: al-Ta'awun Nitham Shi'araho al-Fard li-l-Mujtama' wa-l-Mujtama' li-l-Fard." *Al-'Araby*, February 1968.

Zwemer, Samuel M. *Arabia: The Cradle of Islam*. New York: Fleming H. Revell, 1900.

———. "Koweit Occupied." *Neglected Arabia*, no. 49 (1904): 5–8 (vol. 2).

Index

CPSIA information can be obtained
at www.ICGtesting.com
Printed in the USA
FFOW03n2202011017
40514FF